The Secret History of Manchester

Alex Baxendale

Northern Gothic Books

All rights reserved. No part of this publication may be reproduced, stored in a retrival system, or transmitted without permission in writing from Northern Gothic books.

Printed and typeset by Pendulum

CONTENTS

Introduction
5

The Labyrinth
9

Sects and the City
37

The Machinations of John Byrom
49

A Mancunian Messiah
75

The Occult History of the Peterloo Massacre
87

The Battle of the Mesmerists
113

Ghosts in the Machines
137

The Occultist of Burton Road, and other True Tales
207

The Mysterious Masters
233

The Wicca Man and the Witch Queen
259

Conclusion
299

To Gertrude

Introduction

Victorian Manchester was a city of strange and esoteric delights. It was home to psychic healers who claimed to read a person's 'aura'; to psychometric mediums who boasted that an object's past was revealed to them if they touched it; and to projects such as the Manchester Progressive Discussion Class, which was made up of 'truthseekers' who pondered the mysteries of existence.

Most of all, though, Manchester was home to many who attempted to communicate with the dead. From the 1850s onwards, séances were held in darkened drawing rooms by numerous groups of spiritualists. The most renowned was the Angelic Order of Light, which has been likened to a secret society. It contacted both dead earthlings and cosmic entities - such as 'Orissa', and another called 'Cenes', who was from a planet of the same name.

The scene created by the likes of the Angelic Order was so vibrant that Manchester attracted mediums from far and wide. W. J. Colville, for instance, moved from the south coast to the Strangeways district, where he channelled the spirit of an ancient Egyptian who passed on information about the pyramids. Other mediums came from further afield: Louise Firman relocated from the United States and worked with members of the Angelic Order, and another who crossed the Atlantic was a grande dame of the spiritualist movement called Emma Hardinge Britten. Whilst in Manchester, she established the *Two Worlds*, which was a newspaper dedicated to spiritualism; and after she died a 'School for Prophets' was founded in her honour. The school, which was on Bridge Street, aimed to train psychics and mediums who would serve England as the 'mystics of antiquity' had served their civilisations.

An integral part of late Victorian Manchester's occult scene was the Theosophical Society. This organisation, which was founded in 1870s New York by Madame Blavatsky, with the help of Emma Hardinge Britten, was said to have received arcane and mystical knowledge from a group of semi-divine beings known as the 'Masters' or 'Mahatmas'. Several Manchester characters, who became leading figures in the movement, claimed they were visited by the Masters; and during the first decade of the twentieth century, a Masonic-style secret society was formed which promised its members that these supernatural entities would appear before them and give them powers.

Also part of the scene were several prominent Freemasons and occultists who studied various types of magic, including the Egyptian Abramelin method, and John Dee's Enochian system. The most enigmatic was John Thomas, who was also known as 'Charubel'. From a house in Longsight, he ran the Celestial Brotherhood and also the British Society of Occultists. His reputation as a mystic was such that admirers from afar made their way through the tight web of streets between Hyde Road and Stockport Road to visit him.

John Yarker, who was known as Arokiel in the Celestial Brotherhood, was another prominent operator. From his family house on Burton Road, he created an occult network that reached into Europe and the United States. It included renowned figures such as Madame Blavatsky, Aleister Crowley, Gustav Meyrink and Rudolph Steiner; and it involved a bewildering array of arcane societies - such as the Royal Oriental Order of Sikha, and the Sat B'hai.

Other occultists connected with the city included a Crowley protégé called Norman Mudd, and Annie Horniman, who owned Manchester's Gaiety Theatre and was a member of the Hermetic Order of the Golden Dawn.

Historians often claim that orders such as the Golden Dawn, and the Theosophical and spiritualist movements, were part of an occult revival. According to the Reverend Charles Maurice Davis, an early 20th-century writer on the occult, it all amounted to a 'tidal wave of supernaturalism'. However, the wave did not appear spontaneously, for Manchester had long produced characters who were obsessed with the supernatural and the occult.

The Secret History of Manchester is their history. It is a history of those figures - known variously as wise-men, cunning-folk, or even witches and wizards - who were present in the area for centuries. It recounts the tale of Edmund Hartley, who cast his spells in the 1590s, and came up against a superior wise-man in the form of John Dee; and it reveals that over two hundred years later there was such a subculture of these characters that they formed a kind of secret society, which was led by a renowned operator known as 'Old Rollinson', and which held meetings in a Manchester tavern's private room.

This book is also an account of the town's prophets: such as Elias Hall, who claimed to have been taken from earth and given a tour of heaven and hell in the 1540s; three-year-old Charles Bennett, who prophesied during the 1670s and was reputed to speak spontaneously in Latin and Greek; Ann Lee, who was lauded as a female Christ in the 1770s; and James Johnston, who believed the Peterloo Massacre was mirrored by a battle in the spirit world, where the forces of light fought the forces of darkness known as the 'Dragonists'.

This work is also a chronicle, albeit an incomplete one, of the town's sects. It reveals that Manchester produced so many of them that Charles Wesley, during the 1750s, feared that his congregation would 'run into a thousand sects' after he left the town. As well as being fractious and schismatic, the sects were often given to outlandish behaviour: for example, the French Prophets, who gained a foothold in the town around 1710, caused a furore in the south by predicting that one of their deceased leaders would rise from the grave; and members of the Shakers, who were led by Ann Lee, had visions, spoke in tongues, and often kept their neighbourhoods awake as they worked themselves into states of ecstasy during night-long meetings.

Also described is the New Church - one of England's first Swedenborgian sects - which the prophet James Johnston belonged to for a time. This group, which was founded by the Reverend John Clowes after he experienced a holy visitation in the 1780s, believed that communication with the dead was possible. James Johnston certainly believed this and claimed the spirits talked to him every day.

The Secret History of Manchester illustrates how sects such as the New Church, and the prophets and preachers who preceded them, provided the fuel for the occult revival of the last decades of the 19th century. The book also reveals that spiritualism and the occult remained influential during the 20th century, as the city continued to attract a plethora of mystics. One such character, who embraced all kinds of esoteric pursuits, was Alex Sanders. His detractors, of which there were many, labelled him a charlatan, but his followers fully subscribed to his 'Alexandrian' school of magic and helped make Manchester a centre of the modern witchcraft movement during the 1960s.

For a time, Sanders and his 'High Priestess' wife Maxine were nationally famous and often appeared in cinema documentaries, on television shows, and in the tabloids. Today, though, they are largely forgotten outside of the Wicca movement. Similarly, Manchester's prophets, astrologers, magicians, wise-men, cunning-folk, mesmerists, clairvoyants, occultists, theosophists, healers, mystics, fortune tellers, palmists, messiahs, alchemists, and mediums, are unknown and uncelebrated. There are no blue plaques or street names to evoke their spirits. Even Ann Lee, the 'female Christ' who gathered thousands of followers after she emigrated to the United States, is not recognised by any official agency. This book, though, resurrects these characters and reveals a secret history of Manchester that spans five centuries.

CHAPTER ONE

The Labyrinth

At no period in the History of Manchester was there a greater disposition to believe in witchcraft, demonical possession, and the occult sciences, than at the close of the sixteenth century. *Edward Baines*

In 1595, two men from Manchester's hinterlands, Nicholas Starkie and Edmund Hartley, stood in a quiet wood forty-odd miles north of the town. Hartley marked a circle in the earth, embellished it with 'crosses and partitions', and ordered Starkie to walk around its circumference. The rules of magic, he explained, forbade him from doing it himself.

There were many, even in those superstitious times, who scoffed at the notion that simple shapes marked in the earth, which took no more than a few minutes to create, could be powerful. But in the case of Hartley's circle, they were wrong, for the effects of it would be considerable. Two years later, when Hartley stood trial for bewitching seven members of Starkie's family and household staff, the fact that he made the circle was the clinching evidence which led to his execution. News of the 'Seven in Lancashire' then spread throughout England, inspiring Ben Jonson to mention them in his play, *The Devil is an Ass*; and in 1612, a relation of the Starkies, the magistrate Roger Nowell, may have been influenced by the Hartley affair when he persecuted the Pendle witches.

The affair began in February 1594, when the inhabitants of Cleworth Hall, which stood in Tyldesley, suffered from strange bouts of hysteria. Ann Starkie, who was nine years old, had a fit that was said to have lasted nine weeks, and which infected her brother, John, and several adult inhabitants of the hall. They crawled on their knees for hours at a time, called their neighbours 'devils with horns', ran wildly through the house, and were struck dumb.

The obvious conclusion was that they were possessed, but Nicholas Starkie initially resisted this notion and sought medical advice. After spending a large sum on tests and consultations, and after seeking the advice of a local churchman, who proved to be useless, he turned to Edmund Hartley.

Hartley has been remembered as a wise or cunning-man who knew of spells, charms, and potions, and has been compared with figures who were devoted to alchemy and the cabala, such as Edward Kelley. He has also been seen as an opportunist and a conman: for he secured lodgings and a pension of £2 a year from Starkie and pushed for much more. Yet he wasn't merely a conman, because he managed to calm the children and staff, and when young John suffered from a nosebleed which seemed interminable only Hartley could stem the flow.

The calm at Cleworth Hall, which lasted for approximately 18 months, ended after Starkie refused Hartley's demands for a house and grounds. The wise-man was so upset that he 'sent a loud whupping noise in his anger', and the chaos began again. Margaret Byrom, a thirty-year-old relative of the Starkies from Salford, was violently thrown around the kitchen by an unseen force and complained that her stomach felt as if it contained a 'rolled-up calf'. After falling ill, she left for Salford, where she 'disgusted her friends and family' by either fasting or 'sloshing up her meat like some greedy dog or hog'. Another woman, a thirty-year-old maid called Jane Ashton, suffered from stabbing pains in her throat and began to howl. Furthermore, the girls made 'filthy and unsavoury' comments about furry devils entering little holes, which got them banned from church.

Once again, Starkie asked Hartley to help. It was at this point, after the two men travelled north to visit Starkie's father, that the wise-man traced the circle in the earth. Creating such circles had long been seen as a way of summoning spirits, who were obliged to do the bidding of those who invoked them. Natural philosophers performed the ritual when attempting to gain knowledge of the universe; treasure hunters performed it to ask the spirits where to look, and cunning folk drew the circles for many other reasons.

Hartley may have drawn his circle to intimidate Starkie. The crosses and partitions, which hinted at the sacred geometry of cabalists, may have been his way of demonstrating that he was indeed a wise-man; that he was privy to hermetic and esoteric knowledge; and that it would be prudent if Starkie retained his services.

But Starkie was not impressed. When Hartley ordered him to 'tread out' the circumference of the circle, he refused; and a short time later, he made a trip to Manchester to get advice on how to handle the wise-man and the situation at Cleworth Hall. Hartley, had he known about the trip, would have had good reason to worry: for Starkie intended to seek out Dr John Dee, who was a natural philosopher of European renown, and who, in the magical stakes, made Hartley look like a bumbling village tyro.

Enter Dr Dee

Dee, who was born in London in 1527, struggled to shrug off a dismal reputation for most of his adult life. He was commonly viewed, as one historian noted, 'as a sorcerer and a necromancer, and a black magician left over from a medieval past'. Dee argued that he gained this image at Cambridge after his skills with cogs and gears made an actor appear to be flying during a production of Aristophanes' *Pax*. Several historians believed this, but it was an attempt by Dee to play down his dark image by attributing it to trivial causes. The real cause of his dark reputation was the trouble he found in 1555, during the reign of Mary I. Her authorities considered the astrological charts which he produced for Princess Elizabeth to be evidence of conjuring and arrested him.

John Booker

During the 16th and 17th centuries, astrology was thought to have something of the night about it. The Bishop of Worcester, in the mid-1500s, went as far as to claim that 'calculation by astrology' was the 'greatest and abominable evil'. Despite such strong condemnation, the country was, as Daniel Defoe noted, addicted to astrology; and some, such as the Mancunian John Booker, made a good living from it. Booker's interest in charts and almanacks developed whilst he attended Manchester Grammar School, and he won fame in 1613 by predicting a solar eclipse. After moving to London, he got through 1000 cases a year and was patronised by Lords and Ladies, businessmen, gamblers, intellectuals, artists, alchemists seeking the philosopher's stone, and by those tracking down missing people or goods. He was also used by the authorities when a prisoner escaped from the Tower of London; and by Mr William Godfrey, who thought he had been 'bewitched by some evil body' and hoped to identify the culprit.

Astrology, though, was not as kind to Dee as it would be to Booker: for the chart that he drew for Princess Elizabeth led to the confiscation of his books; to his house being sealed up because of the 'suspicion of magic'; and to the accusation that he indulged in 'lewd vayne practices of calculating and conjuring'. His situation grew worse after his arrest as rumours of his witchcraft spread through London. The French ambassador heard that he possessed pierced wax images of the Queen, and Dee was also said to have gained magical revenge after a man who accused him of dabbling in darkness saw one of his children die and another go blind.

It was a dangerous time to fall foul of the authorities: for the Queen was busy earning her 'Bloody Mary' sobriquet by making martyrs out of those who refused to convert to Catholicism. The Blackley-born John Bradford, and George Marsh - a Bolton man who preached in Eccles - were also arrested in 1555. Bradford was accused of 'trying to stir up a mob' and was burnt at the stake in Newgate Prison. Marsh met the same fate in Chester.

Dee had more luck than Bradford and Marsh and spent only three months in jail. Three years later, after Elizabeth's coronation, he gained some influence in official circles - which led to him being portrayed as the Merlin figure in the Queen's court. But whereas the magician from the Arthurian legends was central to Camelot, Dee's position was precarious, and he was by no means the only wise-man to advise the monarch on occult matters. It is easy to see, though, why the comparisons were made: for members of the court consulted Dee to ensure that Elizabeth's coronation was held on an astrologically propitious date; they asked him to nullify the power of an effigy of the Queen which was found at Lincoln Inn's Fields, with a pin struck through its heart; and when a comet appeared over London and caused panic, they turned to him for reassurance. He was also roped in when other wise-men made attacks on the Queen. He countered, for instance, the predictions of Elizabeth's death made by an alchemist and occultist called John Prestall; and when the French claimed that Nostradamus foresaw a catastrophe which would consume the monarch, he was prevailed upon to reassure the court that it was nonsense.

Edward Kelley

But as noted, Dee was never secure, and despite enjoying royal patronage he still suffered attacks on his character. In *Actes and Monuments*, which was a 1563 account of Protestant and Puritan martyrs such as John Bradford, John Foxe described him as a 'great conjurer'. Dee argued that this 'damnable skalaunder' had stigmatised him as a 'Caller of Divels', and managed to get the description removed from a later edition. The damage, though, was done - for every cathedral and most ordinary parish churches possessed the first edition of the book.

During the early 1580s, Dee created more controversy when he began communicating with angels. It was a way, he claimed, of becoming closer to God, but his critics believed he was conjuring. And by using Edward Kelley as a skryer, or medium, Dee did nothing to allay their fears - for Kelley was a known conman. He was found guilty of counterfeiting coins in Lancaster and had his ears clipped in punishment. (Later, Kelley revealed his suspect side to Dee when he claimed that the spirits had commanded they swap wives.)

He was, though, no ordinary conman. He was Oxford-educated and had gained esoteric knowledge when working with Thomas Allen, who was a renowned natural philosopher, astrologer, and mathematician; and rather than being content as a mere 'coiner', Kelley dreamt of perfecting alchemy. Armed with an esoteric text called *The Book of Dunstan,* and a vial of red powder, which he claimed a 'spiritual creature' alerted him to, he set about transmuting base metal to gold.

Sigillium Dei

It was his skills as a skryer, though, that attracted Dee. Several of the magus's early skryers peered into the crystal ball and did not see enough, but Kelley was a different prospect. He gazed into the ball and saw things such as the Sigillum Dei, known as the seal or symbol of God, which, like the magic circle that Edmund Hartley made, supposedly gave the initiated power over certain entities.

Kelly, though, did not merely see symbols. He looked into the crystal and saw a whole world; a world which was the domain not only of the standard Christian Trinity, but also of a fourth supreme entity known as 'Galvah', and a host of angels. Dee noted that the world consisted of four 'watchtowers', which corresponded to the elements of earth, air, fire, and water, and which were ruled by the angels. Most of the angels - such as Faax, Lmmag, Navaa, and Oodpz - were classed as 'minor', but others were highlighted for their special talents: Amox, for instance, was said to be skilled at locating precious metals and stones. Others, such as Gabriel and Uriel, were of biblical fame.

The realm also consisted of 30 'Aires' or Aethyrs', which were similar to the heavens. Adepts were said to be able to access the Aires by using a system of 'calls' or 'keys' - which the spirits gave Kelley in a strange language that Dee called 'Enochian', after the Old Testament character who conversed with God.

Those who believe that Kelley was more than a conman argued that it would have been hard for him to fabricate such a wealth of material. They also noted that he relayed predictions from Uriel which came true. For instance, in 1583, the angel told Kelley of Mary Queen of Scots' forthcoming execution and warned him that a foreign power would attempt to invade England.

Yet these predictions were fairly safe - for Mary had long been leading a perilous existence, and fears of a Spanish invasion and a Catholic uprising were commonplace. Furthermore, Kelley's Enochian language was not completely original - with some of the terms coming from Agrippa and other Hermetic philosophers.

Kelley's detractors, therefore, claim that Dee should have clipped him round his already clipped ears and bade him farewell. But Dee believed in the skryer and took him on a long trek around Europe. After six turbulent years, which saw the pair excommunicated by the Vatican, Dee returned home and eventually ended up in Manchester. Kelley, though, never returned. For a time he prospered under the aegis of Rudolf II in Prague and received a knighthood. In a letter, which Dee received whilst in Manchester, Kelley invited him back to serve the Emperor. Dee, though, declined the offer, which was the right decision, for Kelley was soon imprisoned in a castle in Most, probably to stop him taking his alchemical knowledge out of the country; and just a few months after penning the letter, he fell from one of the castle's turrets and died.

If Dr Dee was such an eminent figure, who was familiar with the English monarch and the Holy Roman Emperor, then why did he end up in Manchester? The answer, for most historians, was that he was in exile. They claim that after he returned from Prague he lost favour with the court, which decided to dispatch him to some distant realm; and Lancashire - that 'dark corner of the land' - was considered distant enough. Elizabeth, who never ventured further than Nottingham, certainly considered the county to be distant. Others thought it was crime-ridden and generally immoral, and even Ferdinando Stanley, who was one of the aristocratic rulers of Lancashire, claimed it was 'backward'. As for Manchester - the Bishop of Chester claimed it was unreachable because of 'impassable swamps' on the southern and westerly sides.

Over the years, such tales became the accepted truth. Dee was repeatedly cast as a washed-up and weary old wizard, who was shooed off to a backwater. Yet he did not completely fall out of favour with the court - for he retained the Queen's affection and almost landed a plum position at St. Paul's before arriving in Manchester. It was only the opposition of Archbishop Whitgift, who considered him to be a conjurer, that led to his 'exile'. Furthermore, Manchester was not a complete backwater - its woollen goods were famous throughout England and were transported to London even in the winter months, which illustrates that the town was not inaccessible.

One character who grew rich from the textile trade was Elias Hall: Manchester's first recorded prophet. There may have been earlier prophets, and there were almost certainly earlier mystics and apocalyptical characters, who looked for omens and portents. There would also have been other Edmund Hartley-type wise-folk, who mixed astrology with healing and created herbal potions. But unlike Elias, they did not have the means to publish books, and so their stories were lost.

Born in 1502, Elias was said to have been a 'different child': a loner who was persecuted because he favoured 'abstinence and solitude' and was 'given to prayer'. As a young adult, he worked as a domestic servant and then made a fortune by trading in woollen goods. And somewhere along the way, he forgot God. God, though, did not forget him, and in April 1552 Elias heard an apocalyptical message: 'Eli the carpenter's son arise and make thine account quickly; fast and pray, for the day draweth near'. After this was repeated three times, a Christ-like figure, which was bathed in 'great light' and displayed stigmata, appeared in Elias's room. It then disappeared into heaven, 'which opened to receive him'.

Most people would have obeyed the voice, but Elias paid it little heed and got on with everyday life. Soon, though, the voice returned. As he lay ill in bed, the voice informed him that he was 'elect and chosen of God to declare and pronounce unto his people His word'. Elias protested that he was unlearned, but God was unmoved and ordered him to:

Write of the revelation that thou hast seen of baptism, repentance and amendment of life, and show it to the magistrates and rulers, and that which thou shalt write shall be put into thy head by the Holy Ghost.

Then Elias disappeared. 'For two nights', claimed one writer, 'he was absent and not seen of any man'. Cynics might suggest he was hiding in a cupboard or a barn, but Elias swore that he went on a guided tour of heaven and hell on the 9th and 10th of April.

The trip convinced him to accept God's job offer, and he wrote two accounts of his adventures. Then, wearing his best camel hair suit, he set off for London to inform everyone that he was a 'messenger from God'.

Prophets such as Elias popped up throughout the Tudor era. Ropemakers, shoemakers, sailors, and other characters appeared and declared that they had been in touch with God.

Ralph Durden claimed he was the 'Lord of Lords and King of Kings', who would lead the saints to Jerusalem; John Moore and William Jeffrey announced they were Christ and the disciple Peter; John White claimed to be John the Baptist, and William Hackett decided he was the King of Europe and proclaimed that he had the power to produce plagues. He also boasted he could foretell the future, and that God had given him the right to judge the world.

The Elizabethan authorities could be tolerant of such characters. Often they considered them to be 'holy imbeciles' or 'brainsyck' and locked them up for just a short time. But if a prophet was a political threat then he was punished - and this was the case with Elias. They accused him of 'attracting great attention' in the capital and charged him with 'seducinge the people by publyshyng ffalce revelaceons'. After being found guilty, he ended up in the pillory at Cheape and received capital punishment from two ministers. He died the following year whilst still incarcerated.

Another notable rebel, who lived in Manchester a couple of decades after Elias, was a cobbler whose name has been lost. What is known, though, is that he was a member of a sect called the Family of Love, which was founded around 1540 by the Dutchman Hendrik Niclaes. We also know that he was rumoured to have been a polygamist, which was a Family of Love trait. Other traits included the belief that the Bible was allegorical; a healthy disdain for the clergy; and a conviction that man could achieve Christ-like perfection: an idea which proved popular in Manchester during the following centuries. Familists were also associated with the 'dark arts' of alchemy, astrology, and cabalism. Consequently, John Dee has been linked with them, although there is no evidence that he was ever a member.

The Labyrinth

It would have suited Dee if Manchester offered only textile merchants and the odd prophet. But if he hoped for a sleepy little town, where he could quietly continue his quest for the philosopher's stone, then he would have been disappointed - for Manchester, although only home to approximately four thousand souls, was a cauldron of intrigue. Dee admitted as much in a letter to a friend, written in 1597, in which he confided that he had wandered into 'ex Mancestrano labyrintho' - a Manchester labyrinth.

His main problem was that he was the warden of a collegiate church which he felt was: 'almost no college'. The Stanley family had bought several of the institution's buildings in the 1540s, during the dissolution of the monasteries, and more were sold during the 1560s and 70s by the warden Thomas Herle, who was rumoured to be a forger. He also leased out farms which already had tenants, and was so poor at running the college that the fellows had to take second jobs.

The buildings which remained, as Dee soon discovered, were in a sorry state. The chancel had been neglected for over twenty years and was simply a mess, and one of the college gatehouses was so ramshackle that it collapsed after a storm in February 1598.

What made it worse for Dee was the fact that the fellows of the college were Puritans. This crew exerted a doleful influence for decades - during the 1570s, a Puritan commission headed by William Chaderton, Dee's predecessor as warden, issued a killjoy injunction against: 'pipers and minstrels playing... on Sundays, or any other days in time of divine service or sermons'. The commission also railed against 'superfluous and superstitious singing, and wakes and common feasts', and claimed that the town's drinking dens were 'nurseries of all malefactors, and the harbourers of all lewd and disorderly persons'.

By the 1580s, the town's reputation was such that it drew in Puritans from other places. John Bruen, a layman who lived in a village outside Chester, regularly travelled thirty miles to Manchester to hear sermons - or as his biographer put it: he journeyed such a distance to 'gather manna where he knew it would rain down'. Bruen ended up marrying a Manchester woman and lived in the area for a year.

In 1589, Manchester's links with Puritanism caught the attention of the nation during the Martin Marprelate controversy. This affair began after Archbishop Whitgift sought to silence both Catholic and Puritan dissidents by confining the use of printing presses to London and the two university towns. In response, the Puritans created a mobile press produced several pamphlets, purportedly by Martin Marprelate, that wittily and scurrilously ripped into the Church of England and its bishops.

The main men behind the press were two preachers who had worked in Kingston-upon-Thames: John Udall, who was a Puritan and an inveterate critic of bishops, and John Penry, who was a follower of Robert Browne - a preacher who believed churches should be independent. Also involved, amongst others, was a printer called John Hodgkinson.

Whitgift became desperate to track the press down because the tracts proved to be popular, whilst the Anglican pamphlets produced in response were flops. With the heat on, the press moved through a couple of towns before arriving, under the direction of Hodgkinson, at Newton Lane - today's Oldham Road.

Why the press ended up in Manchester has never been satisfactorily explained. Some claimed that Hodgkinson headed to the town simply because he was Mancunian, although there is no evidence he was. Another theory is that the town's reputation for radicalism and Puritanism attracted them.

What we can be sure of is that Hodgkinson regretted the move - for whilst a tract called *More Work for Cooper* was printing, Lord Stanley's men seized the press and arrested the team.

The capture of the press was a triumph for Whitgift over Puritanism, but the year later he suffered a reverse when his envoy, the Archbishop of York, failed to impose religious conformity on Manchester. Eleven local Puritan preachers, including Oliver Carter, who was one of Dee's future enemies, resisted the Archbishop - and even fired off a letter of protest to Whitgift. It was an early sign of the town's independent spirit; an early indication that Manchester would become a hotbed of nonconformism.

Six years later, Dee arrived in Manchester and soon found himself fighting to be accepted by the Puritans. It was a fight he was not fated to win: for unlike his predecessor, William Chaderton, he did not have a reputation for religious purity. Rather, it had long been rumoured that the Catholically ordained Dee remained sympathetic to the old faith. This was not true - he was only catholic in the fundamental sense that he was willing to embrace a wide range of views. But this meant he held beliefs which the fellows would not tolerate: for instance, he considered making the sign of the cross to be a sacred and solemn act, whereas the Puritans sneered at it as 'papist'.

The Puritans may have also taken against Dee because of his occult past - although several scholars dispute this. They speculate that the fellows may not have been aware, or at least fully aware, of the controversy that dogged their new warden. The stories of Dee's experiments with skryers and angel magic, they argued, may not have made it as far north as Manchester. However, as we have noted, the town was not completely isolated and insular, despite what the Bishop of Chester claimed; and the fellows of the Collegiate Church were not unworldly and untraveled. Oliver Carter was a Cambridge graduate, and even those who were not so well educated may have read *Acts and Monuments* - perhaps for details of the execution of the Mancunian John Bradford - and may have learned that Dee was a 'great conjuror'. Furthermore, they would have soon found out about his occult interests because when he rolled into the town for the first time he brought with him - along with domestic staff, his wife, and seven children - two skryers. And because Dee saw nothing un-Christian in his attempts to communicate with angels, the skryers may not have concealed their duties.

Manchester may have been Puritan, but the surrounding county was not: for Lancashire was infamous as the corner of England which most resisted the Reformation. London eyed it with constant suspicion, believing that any Catholic uprising would begin in the county and that any invading Spanish force would land there. And this was not merely paranoia - for the powers in Madrid *did* consider the county to be a good place for an invasion to begin.

Lancashire was able to resist the Reformation because its palatine system, which dated back to the Plantagenet era, meant the crown had less of a hold over it than other counties. The historian Richard Wilson went as far as to describe it as a 'semi-independent anomalous appendage of the English nation-state. . . (which was) ruled by a handful of feudal lords'. Consequently, Lancashire's most powerful families - such as the Stanleys and the Hoghtons - were able to hold on to their old faith; and those who paid them homage followed suit.

This is not to say that the prominent families overtly defied London - for the Stanleys paid lip service by staging a purge of the county's recusants, which involved the removal of 'seditious books' from the great houses and over eight hundred people appearing before a Lancaster court. But nobody was fooled - mainly because the court fined only a dozen or so people, and found the rest not guilty.

Manchester's Puritans, of course, were more enthusiastic in their attacks on recusants. One of their schemes saw them forcing children from the most prominent Catholic families into the town's college, where they were subjected to relentless indoctrination by the likes of Oliver Carter.

Carter was particularly paranoid about the threat from the county's Catholics and tended to see priests everywhere. He called them 'secret enemies' and claimed they 'wandered abroad in corners and seduced the simple by wicked doctrine'. He also claimed his neighbours were only too willing to be seduced: 'They embrace', he wrote, 'everie fonde idolatrous tradition'.

Some Lancashire Catholics responded to the persecution by exiling themselves to Prague, where they moved in circles which gathered around Edward Kelley. One such character was Richard Hesketh, who was an alchemist and a friend of John Dee's.

He not only dreamt of transforming base metal to gold but also of turning England back to Catholicism by placing Ferdinando Stanley on the throne. Hesketh left Prague for Lancashire in 1593 and delivered a letter to Ferdinando which enquired about his attitude towards a coup. After some prevarication, Ferdinando turned Hesketh over to the authorities, who hung him. Soon after, Ferdinando died in excruciating pain. He was most likely poisoned in revenge.

William Stanley

So this was the 'Manchester labyrinth' which welcomed Dee. It was a complex mess of recusant intrigue; of land disputes and legal battles; and of Puritans who were determined to make his stay in the town anything but easy. Dee, though, was not without allies: one powerful contact was William Stanley, Ferdinando's brother, who rented to Dee Alport Lodge and gave him a letter of introduction which eased him into Manchester society. In return, Dee cast horoscopes for Stanley's daughters.

The two men were friendly enough to share the odd social occasion. On June 26th 1597, along with 'a large party of ladies and gentlemen', they enjoyed a 'scholar's collation' at Alport Lodge. If we are to subscribe to certain theories then Prospero and Shakespeare were present at that merry get-together near Deansgate:

for some believe Stanley was Shakespeare, and many others, more reasonably, have argued that Prospero was based on Dee.

The idea that Stanley was Shakespeare was first put forward in 1891 by James H. Greenstreet, who noted that in 1599 a Jesuit spy claimed Stanley was 'too busy penning plays for the common players' to become involved in restoring Catholicism to England. Greenstreet died before he could fully develop the idea that the plays Stanley was 'too busy penning' were Shakespeare's, but others took the baton. In 1918, for example, the French scholar Abel Lefranc identified elements of Stanley's life in plays such as *Love's Labour Lost*, *Twelfth Night* and *Hamlet*. Lefranc also argued that Stanley's marriage to Elizabeth de Vere. inspired *Midsummer Night's Dream*. It was flimsy stuff, but the notion that Dee was the model for the magician in the *Tempest* was more convincing. The *Encyclopaedia Britannica* claimed it was 'almost certainly the case'.

Although Stanley was a good contact for Dee, he was not a permanent resident of the town and was not on hand to lend support. Dee, though, had other allies - such as the Prestwichs, a prominent family which his son married into; and some figures respected him because of his occult knowledge, such as Edmund Hopwood, who was Stanley's deputy lieutenant and a magistrate. Hopwood borrowed several of Dee's books, including Johan Weir's *On the Deceits of Demons*, and Reginald Scot's *Discovery of Witchcraft*.

The End of Hartley

Edmund Hopwood was not alone in seeking out Dee for his occult know-how. Another Manchester gentleman enquired if his astrological skills could be used to identify a thief; and then there was Nicholas Starkie, who arrived in Manchester hoping that Dee might be persuaded to use his powers as an exorcist to bring an end to the madness at Cleworth Hall.

Dee was reluctant to get involved. He may have felt that the last thing he needed, given his reputation, was to become embroiled in a controversial case of witchcraft and demonic possession. But if he was looking to avoid such cases then he was in the wrong county - for Lancashire, even before the famous Pendle trial of 1612, had a reputation for witchcraft. It was a reputation strengthened by the likes of a curate from just outside Bolton, who was warned by church authorities in 1571 against using 'predictions, divinations, sorceries, charmings or enchantments'; and further strengthened by what the historian Christopher Haigh has called 'a minor witch craze' in Rochdale, which occurred in the 1590s. Even the death of Ferdinando Stanley was linked to witchcraft: for it was rumoured that a 'little image made of wax', which included a strand of hair the same colour as his, was found in his chamber shortly after he died.

Another episode with overtones of witchcraft, which coincided with Dee's residence in the area, attracted much attention. John Bruen, a Puritan and ex-Manchester resident, investigated the case - which involved a twelve-year-old Northwich boy called Thomas Harrison. The boy, who was feeble and slight, was said to have suffered from fits which made him so strong that grown men found it impossible to restrain him. He was also said to have 'howled like a dog, mewed like a cat, roared like a bear, and frothed and foamed like a boar'. He did not, though, merely make unintelligible noises - for he also ranted about Lucifer and papists.

Bruen, who was part of a group assigned to pray for the boy, believed he was witnessing a case of diabolic possession. And the boy seemed to confirm this by ripping up any bible which he laid his hands on; by revealing that Christ had whispered in his ear that three devils possessed him; and by reacting violently whenever preachers prayed in his presence.

The affair ended positively when the boy's fits petered out after about two years. But Dee's most recent cases, which involved Ann Leke and Winifred Goose, had not ended well - which may have made him reluctant to offer Starkie his services as an exorcist. Leke, who was a nurse in Dee's Mortlake house, needed his help because she had 'long been tempted by an evil spirit', and had finally become 'possessed of him'. After Dee anointed her with holy oil, the 'wicked one did resist for a while', but soon after she tried to drown herself in a well. Dee saved her on that occasion, but later he wrote that she 'rattled in her own blood' when she committed suicide by cutting her throat. Two years later, in 1592, he treated Winifred Goose, who was said to be 'evilly tempted' because of the death of her son. Once again he used holy oil, but could not prevent the woman from giving in to her 'old melancholic pangs' and she killed herself.

And now, four years later in a strange little town, Dee was confronted with a case which promised to be more fraught and complex because it involved seven possessed people and a meddling wise-man. Although he refused to become fully involved in the matter, he did assist Starkie by reprimanding Edmund Hartley, and he also met the Starkie children after they journeyed to the town with the wise-man. Hartley was said to have forbidden the meeting, and to have warned the children it would have 'been better for them not to have changed an old friend for new'. He then mumbled menacingly and left them in Manchester.

Hartley was finally accused of diabolic deeds after he visited Margaret Byrom in Salford. The woman was said to have been attacked once again by an invisible force, and to have produced a 'loud noise in her belly, like that in the belly of a great trotting horse'. Her friends, along with Hartley and a clergyman who happened to be John Dee's curate, gathered around her bed and prayed. The curate considered Hartley's prayers to be unorthodox and reported him to the Justices of the Peace. They imprisoned the wise-man and the 'Seven in Lancashire', as Ben Johnson called them, were summoned for questioning.

Before they quizzed Margaret Byrom, she claimed 'the devil in the likeness of Hartley' appeared on consecutive nights and offered her gold and silver not to testify. And when questioned, she repeatedly fell to the ground and revealed that a 'great black dog with a monstrous tail, a long chain, and open mouth' was coming towards her. She also claimed to see a large black cat and 'a big mouse'.

The children refused to testify against Hartley., but Jane Ashton began to bark, which prompted one of the children to say: 'Ah, Edmund, dost thou trouble her now, when she testify against thee?'

John Dee

Despite the silence of the children, Hartley was found guilty. The court based its decision on Nicholas Starkie's claim that a circle had been made in the woods, and the wise-man was sentenced to death for the felony of conjuring spirits. After being taken to the gallows and strung up, he fell to the ground when the rope broke. He took this as a sign from God that he should confess and admitted to making the circle. He was then successfully hung.

The children, though, still acted strangely - so Starkie took Dee's advice and sought out two Presbyterian ministers, George More and John Darrel.

The ministers spent the first night at Cleworth in prayer and then took the demons on. - by reading the scriptures out loud. The children howled, shrieked, convulsed, and finally fell unconscious. When they woke the evil spirits were gone - or so the story went.

There was closure for the Starkie family, but for Darrell and

Dee the trouble continued - because Archbishop Whitgift used the case as an opportunity to attack the Puritans and Presbyterians. He argued that Darrell's exorcisms were a sham and merely a way to regain the credit that the Puritan and nonconformist camp lost when the Martin Marprelate project failed. Whitgift also made much of Dee's role in the case, in an attempt to discredit his adversaries by associating them with un-Christian magic.

The authorities arrested Darrel after he travelled to Nottingham to perform another exorcism. At his trial, which was said to have been 'talked about in the streets and taverns', he was found guilty of carrying out a false exorcism and was jailed. He served, though, little more than a year. Meanwhile, Dee attempted to clear his name by publishing a *Letter Apologetical*, in which he stressed that his magic was merely an expression of Christianity. But not everyone was convinced, and one critic, John Chamberlain, claimed the text was the 'ridiculous babble of an old imposturing juggler'.

The Philosopher's Stone

Six months after Hartley's execution, Dee was visited in his dreams by an old man. 'Sir, you are hartly welcomed to these parties', said Dee, and then the old man pulled him close, kissed him on the mouth, and breathed into him. It was, Dee thought, 'spiraculum vitae' - the breath of life. [2]

The dream probably indicated that he was unconsciously mulling over the madness at Cleworth Hall: 'you are 'hartly' welcomed', may have been a reference to the deceased wise-man. It was also, though, a dream of alchemy. The old man's gift of spiraculum vitae mirrored Dee's belief that the philosopher's stone was a 'great elixir', which would banish corruption and disease. Dee certainly thought he was dreaming of the stone and recorded the details in his notes about alchemy. [3]

Those who seek to give a nuanced account of alchemy stress that the true practitioner, rather than being solely a materialist, was engaged in a 'great work' which involved striving to be closer to God by gaining an understanding of His creation. The true alchemist sought, as Peter French put it, 'to transmute the human spirit through gnosis'. [4]

Plenty of alchemists, though, had not shared these lofty ideals. Thomas Assherton, of Ashton, and Sir Edmund de Trafford, of Trafford and Stretford, were motivated by the desire to gain unlimited wealth. The pair were engaged by the debt-ridden Henry VI to 'work upon certain metals, to transmute them by their said art or science, as they say, into perfect gold or silver'. They conducted their experiments in the fortified towers of Ashton Hall and informed the monarch that they were extremely close to success. The King then announced he would soon be able to pay off his debts by 'means of the stone'. But after it became clear that the base metals could not be changed, he was forced to 'pawn the revenue of his Duchy of Lancaster'.

Dee's alchemy may have been more philosophical than Assherton's and de Trafford's, but he was not above hoping that he too would be able to pay off his debts by means of the stone; and whilst in Manchester he engaged in alchemical experiments which intrigued the townsfolk, who claimed to have seen eerie lights emanating from his quarters, and to have heard explosions.

Dee was also not above asking the angels for help with his finances, and he requested they point out 'some portion of hidden treasure', so he could 'pay debts . . . and buy things necessary'. These communications were made possible by the two skryers, Bartholomew Hickman and Francis Nichol, who were part of his entourage. Later, another skryer appeared unannounced and offered 'his faithful and diligent care and help, to the best of his skills and power, in the processes chymicall'. Dee had long known this character, called Roger Cook, and considered him to be 'melancholy'. He also noted that the skryer was 'ungrateful', and had once seemed about to 'lay violent hands on me'. These tensions seemed to have returned in Manchester, for Dee's son, Arthur, claimed to have found evidence of a plot against his father in Cook's notes. But the dispute was quickly resolved.

Despite the efforts of the three skryers, Dee found the angelic communications to be unsatisfactory. He dismissed Hickman's visions and considered his 'many reports of sight and hering spirituall' to be untrue. On Michaelmas Day, in the year 1600, he made a bonfire of the Hickman transcriptions and stood before it with his wife and a small group of friends. Some of the papers were taken by the wind, only to be collected and returned to Dee. Which begs the question: What would the Puritans, had they found the strange documents, have made of them?

They would most probably have used them in their campaign against Dee. By 1604, the campaign was so advanced that the college fellows named William Bourne, a Cambridge graduate and Puritan, as his replacement; and they had the backing of the Bishop of Chester, who publically proclaimed that Dee was 'no preacher'.

As preparations were made for a battle in London's courts, the plague hit Manchester. The Puritan Oliver Carter was one of its early victims, and Dee's wife, Jane, was also taken. Sickened with grief, Dee neglected his diary for over a year - so we do not know whether he spent any further time in Manchester. With Jane gone, though, and with his position effectively filled by Bourne, the place must have held little attraction for him. Furthermore, many had fled the town, and society collapsed to such an extent that Bourne abandoned the Collegiate Church and preached in the fields. Also in the fields, around Collyhurst, were wooden cabins in which the infected were interned. The only people left in Manchester, claimed one writer, were 'covertly rascals and slaves'; although rather than being criminal, they may merely have lacked the means to escape.

Dee died in 1608.

Reputation and Legacy

Just as it had during his life, Dee's reputation fluctuated after he died. Initially, the Rosicrucians, who were concerned with alchemy, astrology and Hermeticism, were inspired by him. Eight years after his death, they included his esoteric symbol, the Monas Hieroglyphic, on the frontispiece of their manifesto.

During the early 1650s, Elias Ashmole, who was a Rosicrucianist and an associate of Dee's grandson Rowland, wrote favourably of him in his *Chemicum Brittanicum*. Towards the end of the decade, though, an Oxford scholar called Meric Casaubon claimed that Dee's attempt to communicate with angels had been a 'work of darkness', and this set the tone for many years.

In the Manchester area, myths and folklore developed which portrayed him as a bogeyman, or even as a kind of Satanist. At Worsley's Kempnough Hall, where he stayed, Dee was blamed for leaving behind an 'atmosphere of evil', and for inspiring, somehow, a subsequent tenant to go berserk and hack his wife and son to death. Other legends, though, suggest that the forces of light reclaimed the house: for years later, tales circulated of a little girl who saw a praying angel and a crucifix in the hall, which nobody else could see.

Generations of Manchester Grammar School boys kept the legend of the diabolic Dee alive by telling new students that a hoof-shaped scorch mark on a desk was made when he conjured up the Devil.

In 1840 came William Harrison Ainsworth's *Guy Fawkes*, a novel which connected Manchester's prominent Catholic families to the Gun Powder Plot, and which strongly reinforced Dee's reputation as a necromancer. Ainsworth, who was a popular writer and a friend of Charles Dickens, jumped on the romantic bandwagon with *Guy Fawkes*. He packed it with gothic tales of executions and secret passages, and with eerie descriptions of Chat Moss, which he claimed had once been a 'druid-haunted' forest, and which he populated with will-o'-the wisps, or as he called them: 'weird children of the waste'. He also included a 'half-crazed' prophetess called Elizabeth Orton, who lived in Odin's Cave on the banks of the Irwell. She was probably based on a young Flintshire prophet of the same name, who revealed in 1580 that purgatory was a realm of 'blue fires'.

Dee and Kelly indulging in a spot of necromancy

The darkest sections of the novel involved Dee and Edward Kelley: for Ainsworth overlooked the fact that the alchemist had fallen to his death in Most and had him 'secretly joining' his old master in Manchester. Their antics in *Guy Fawkes* echoed a legend which had Kelley resurrecting a corpse in a Walton-le-Dale graveyard. Ainsworth transferred the action to Manchester, where the pair dug up the 'half-crazed prophetess' and carried her corpse into a charnel house. With a nod to

Mary Shelly, Ainsworth had Dee reanimating the corpse. But whereas Victor Frankenstein utilised modern science to bring his monster to life, Dee was shown to rely on ancient techniques which included muttering incantations and directing 'ruddy currents' of blood on to the body. This conjured up, wrote Ainsworth, 'a stream of dazzling lightning' which 'shot down upon the corpse' and reanimated it.

As well as being armed with incantations and deep occult know-how, Dee also possessed material weapons - such as a traditional wizard's wand; vials of powder which rendered assailants as immovable as a 'marble statue'; and most impressively, a 'Holy Stone', which was a skryer's crystal ball that displayed scenes from the future after Dee primed it by burning certain herbs and by muttering arcane phrases.

Despite the gore and the occult shenanigans, Dee was not unsympathetically portrayed - rather, he was a positive force in the novel. 'Dr Dee', stated one character, 'is a wonderful person, and has made many discoveries in medicine and in other sciences'. It was the necromancy, though, which made the greatest impression on the public.

Ainsworth's readers, it could be argued, were sophisticated enough to have realised that such supernaturalism was bunkum and that the novel was merely a romantic romp. The *Manchester Times*, during the decade after the book was published, certainly argued that the city was no longer superstitious: 'the old dread of witchcraft', it claimed, 'has been abandoned'.

Yet this was patently untrue: many Mancunians clung to the old beliefs and fears. The city's hawkers and costers decorated their barrows with various 'bones, tails and claws', as well as 'moles feet and curved teeth', to ward off the 'Evil Eye'; and in the same decade that the *Manchester Times* trumpeted the rationality of the townsfolk, a Droylsden man, known only as 'J. W.', was tasked with combating evil entities. John Harland, the first journalist to work for the *Manchester Guardian*, described him as 'the last of the ancient race of Boggart-seers'.

This character must have been busy because Manchester's eastern hinterlands, if we are to believe folklore, had a greater population of supernatural creatures than Middle-earth or Narnia.

The world's first modern city was, then, a deeply superstitious place - and many Mancunians would simply have believed the tales of Dee's involvement with dark and supernatural forces. F. R. Raines, the author of *The Rectors of Manchester, and the Wardens of the Collegiate Church of that Town* (1885), certainly believed he was a diabolical creature. He claimed Dee was more depraved than the 'vampires and ghouls of eastern stories', and he echoed Ainsworth by contending that he had desecrated graves when attempting to have 'conversations and intercourse with spiritual essences and departed beings'.

In 1909, though, Charlotte Fell Smith restored his reputation with a largely sympathetic biography. Whilst she lingered on his exploits with Edward Kelley, and on his attempts to commune with angels, she stressed that these factors should not overshadow his 'sincere and good intentions, his personal piety, and his uncommon purity of mind'.

By the second half of the 20th-century, he was lauded as an important figure in the English Renaissance, and his influence on the sciences, mathematics, geography, and navigation was acknowledged.

As far as this account is concerned, it would be unwise to place too much emphasis on Dee's role in Manchester's mystical history. Unlike the 18th-century sects and the 19th-century astrologers, skryers, and occultists, he was not attracted to the town because of its strong tradition of mysticism and religious dissent. If not for the machinations of Archbishop Whitgift, he would probably never have set foot in Manchester.

He did, though, inspire several of the town's mystics and occultists: such as John Byrom, who studied similar alchemic and esoteric subjects during the first half of the eighteenth century. Furthermore, Dee's Enochian system, for which we must also give Edward Kelley credit, was adopted in the late nineteenth century by the Hermetic Order of the Golden Dawn, which included magicians associated with Manchester; and it was also studied by a coven of Mancunian witches in the 1960s.

CHAPTER TWO

Sects and the City

Manchester has long been distinguished as possessing a greater dissenting population than that of any other town in the kingdom. *Black's Picaresque Tourist and Road Book,* 1843.

Edmund Hopwood, the magistrate who had asked John Dee for advice on witchcraft, took a dim view of affairs in the Manchester area. In 1609, he complained that the town was such a hotbed of nonconformism that it attracted rebellious preachers who had been kicked out of other places. 'All the fanatical and schismatical preachers', he lamented, 'resort into this corner of Lancashire'.

Yet Hopwood's era was tame in comparison with the Civil War, which was the golden age of fanatics and schismatics. Prophets, holy fools, and a bewildering variety of sects emerged during the war because the state church was too weak to resist them.

Edmund Hartley, had he lived during this era, would still have been punished for drawing his magic circle in the woods - for witchcraft, along with Catholicism and atheism, continued to be prohibited. Manchester's other Tudor characters, though, would have enjoyed more freedom. Elias Hall would not have been beaten by ministers and would have been left to attract as many followers as he could, and John Dee would have enjoyed greater leeway to pursue both his Hermetic studies and astrology - for there was an upsurge of interest in such pursuits. In fact, the Mancunian astrologer John Booker was employed to raise the morale of Parliamentary forces during the protracted siege of Colchester in 1648.

Manchester's mysterious Family of Love cobbler would also have been more comfortable during the Civil War years because the Familists enjoyed a comeback. Books by the movement's founder, Hendrick Niclaes, were republished and several new sects were influenced by him.

The sects that emerged during this period were particularly millenarian - which is understandable for it seemed, as the historian Christopher Hill put it, as if the 'world was turned upside down'. The age-old deference shown to the upper classes was dissipating; and there was much talk of land reform, democracy, and the creation of an equal society. And it was all so unprecedented that for many it could only mean they were living through the climax of history.

It was particularly easy for Mancunians to believe this because these were strange days indeed for the town. Not only did it experience the realities of war but it was also disturbed by a succession of troubling events and seemingly supernatural occurrences.

The first event began on 15 July 1642 when Lord Strange, who was the son of William Stanley, arrived in Manchester intending to seize the town's gunpowder. The town resisted Strange because its Puritan sympathies had led it to declare for Parliament. A skirmish ensued and a Levenshulme linen weaver called Richard Perceval lost his life - and became the first casualty of a war that was to claim almost 186 000 others.

Strange and his men left without the ammunition but returned in September and established themselves in Alport Lodge - the old Stanley property which John Dee had rented from Strange's father. From the Lodge, Strange orchestrated a siege of the town - which lasted for a week and saw cannon attacks on the Parliamentarians. One attack destroyed several roofs and shredded tiles were blasted about - resulting in the death of a youth. Later, the Puritans claimed that the lack of significant casualties during the shelling proved that God was on their side. As for the unfortunate youth - well, 'he was a wicked child who had overrun his parents', and therefore deserved his fate.

There were further attacks but the town's defences had been well organised by a German soldier, Colonel John Rosworm, and the Royalists were ultimately frustrated. After incurring the loss of approximately 200 men - to Manchester's 20 - the Royalists abandoned the siege. Strange, who did not return to the town, later played a part in the Massacre of Bolton - a particularly grizzly event which saw Royalist forces kill, if we are to believe Parliament's statistics, up to 1600 people. Parliamentary forces caught him in Nantwich and beheaded him in Bolton in 1651.

Manchester, after the siege, played no further part in the war - but it still faced traumatic times. In 1645, it suffered once more from the plague. For forty years it had been free from the disease, but constant reminders of it were found in the plague stones that were dotted around the landscape. They evoked epidemics such as that of 1605, which carried off John Dee's wife. The stones, though, were not mere memorials. Rather, they marked the edge of where Mancunians could roam when the town was afflicted, and they were meeting points where traders from the hinterlands could hand over goods. The bowl shape in the Great Stone in Stretford was said to have been hollowed out and filled with liquid - either water, holy water, or vinegar - so coins could be placed in it and purified before the traders handled them.

The town was laid so low by the plague of 1645 that its plight was raised in Parliament, which heard that the Manchester-area was a 'miserably wasted country'; that it was 'full of merchants who were ruined in their estates'; and that families 'were likely to perish for want'.

Some of the pious believed that Manchester suffered because it was sinful. As the Puritans had said, there were too many drinking dens, too many scoundrels, and too many houses of ill repute.

And many believed the town made a grave mistake by supporting a parliament which rid itself of the king - for as everyone knew, monarchs ruled by divine right.

Four years later, in January 1649, the situation was made immeasurably worse when Charles I was executed. According to the nineteenth-century antiquarian Samuel Hibbert-Ware, the regicide caused a 'sort of panic to pervade most classes of society' in Manchester; a panic which increased after clergymen 'announced that the fiercest vial of God's wrath would be poured out in judgment for the sins of the people'. And as if to prove this was true, the town was flooded. The rain, wrote Richard Hollingworth, who was a fellow of the Collegiate Church, 'was sudden and terrible'; it came down, he continued, 'on the Lord's day, in two hours, and filled the cellars in the market place, and these channels ran down the streets like large rivers, so as to be able in some places to bear a large vessel'. Charles Henry Timperley, who compiled the *Annals of Manchester*, noted that the 'unusually heavy rain' was indeed regarded as 'special evidence of God's resentment'.

The townsfolk, Hollingworth explained, began to look for more 'supernatural omens to prove that the great day of the Lord was at hand'; and on February 24th, they seemed to find one: 'There was observed by hundreds of people in the market square', he wrote, 'three perihelion's about ten o'clock before noon, which vanished away one after another, so that at eleven o'clock none were seen – I saw two of them myself'. Hibbert-Ware claimed this strange phenomenon caused 'the stoutest hearts to tremble'.

Another unnerving event occurred the following year when a strange and bloody crop was found in Blakely. Hollingworth described it this way:

> *In one John Pendelton's ground, as one was reaping, the corne being cut, seemed to bleede; drops fell out of it like bloud: multitudes of people went to see it, and the strawes thereof, though of a kindly colour without, were within reddish, and as it were, bloudy.*

The year before, the town was afflicted by 'a violent fever and smallpox', and for the Presbyterian church authorities, this was a further sign of God's disapprobation. Consequently, a public fast, known as a 'day of humiliation', was declared by Richard Heyricke, who was the warden of the Collegiate Church.

There was another reason for the Presbyterians to believe that God had turned against them: for in 1649, they were shut out of the Collegiate Church by Cromwell's government, which ruled that the town's religious buildings belonged to the Commonwealth. Soldiers and sectarians who were loyal to Cromwell, and commanded by a local Colonel called Thomas Birch, took over the buildings and smashed several stained glass windows which depicted the saints. This was, claimed Hibbert-Ware, the action of 'misguided fanatics'. It was also the action of millenarians: for they believed that by destroying the windows, and any other 'popish' remnants, they were preparing the way for the return of Christ.

Sects, Sects, Sects

For the warden, Richard Heyricke, the destruction of the windows was traumatic. Also disturbing for him was the fact that many members of different sects took part in the vandalism: for Heyricke, like Edmund Hopwood before him, was irritated by Manchester's varied religious tastes. Just two years before the attack, he criticised the area's Brownists and also denounced the Anabaptists - who believed, amongst other things, that babies should not be baptised, and that it should be left to the adult to decide if he or she should undergo the ritual. These sects, claimed Heyricke, were comprised of 'blasphemers and heretics'.

Two years later, he had to contend with more than just Brownists and Anabaptists, for according to Samuel Hibbert the takeover of the college involved: 'Levellers, Fifth Monarchy men, Seekers, Ranters, and other violent enthusiasts'.

Some of these groups, such as the Seekers and the Ranters, who were both inspired by the Family of Love, did not have a concrete presence in Manchester - for they were loose associations of like-minded individuals, and were opposed to formal religious structures. The Levellers, though, were more organised and campaigned for social equality. But just as they were poised to prosper in the North West, they met their end when Cromwell turned on them in 1649.

The Fifth Monarchists were also more organised than the Seekers and Ranters, and they were more millenarian. They believed that Christ and the saints would soon return to begin a 'fifth monarchy', which would succeed the Assyrian, Persian, Grecian and Roman monarchies discussed in the *Book of Daniel*. The year of His return, many Fifth Monarchists claimed, would be 1666, which they equated with the Number of the Beast mentioned in Revelation.

The sect was mostly southern-based, but there were a few northern outposts, and there was said to have been an 'isolated congregation' in Manchester. The most prominent Fifth Monarchist in the area was John Wigan. He first appears in the records in 1642, as a preacher in Gorton, where he strongly promoted congregational independence. After a stint preaching in the Birch area of south Manchester, he joined the New Model Army and became a colonel. In 1654, though, he lost his commission because he couldn't accept Cromwell as the 'Lord Protectorate'. England's only ruler, he insisted, like a good Fifth Monarchist, was Christ. In 1664, after the Restoration, Wigan was accused of plotting against the government and imprisoned in Lancaster jail. He shared the prison with several Quakers and entered into religious debates with them, known as 'disputations', which were lively affairs that sometimes ended in violence.

One of his Quaker opponents, George Fox, was a founder of the sect and often preached in the Manchester area. Local legend had it that he began his career in Dukinfield after he travelled there to visit a holy woman who endured a fast that lasted twenty-two days. On his arrival, he found that the woman was 'under temptation', but he took the opportunity to preach, or 'declare the truth', to her neighbours. Later, he visited Manchester and found it was a raucous town. As he preached, the public threw 'clods, water, dirt and stones at him', and other preachers contradicted his beliefs. His beliefs, though, were not unfamiliar to the town - for like so many of the area's independents he was convinced that preachers were superfluous; that God was within the believer; and that men and women could become perfect holy beings.

It was after Fox refused to swear an oath of allegiance to Charles II that he found himself in Lancaster jail, and engaged in a theological battle with John Wigan. It is hard to say who won the disputation, for both men left biased accounts of it. Ultimately, though, Fox outlasted the Fifth Monarchy man, and when he heard that Wigan had been taken by the plague in London in 1665, he claimed it was God's judgment.

The fevered millenarian climate calmed down after the Restoration - even 1666 came and went without any great upheaval. Although, as George Fox noted, the Fifth Monarchists spent the year watching the sky during thunderstorms in the anticipation of His return. 1666 was certainly quiet in Manchester. There were no bleeding crops or strange sights in the sky. In fact, in his *Annals of Manchester*, Timperley missed out the year and jumped from mentioning that Chetham's Hospital was made a corporate body in 1665, to noting the death of the astrologer John Booker in 1667.

By this time, many of the Civil War sects were defunct. 'The Levellers, Ranters and Fifth Monarchists,' wrote Christopher Hill, 'disappeared, leaving hardly a trace'. Yet Hill also noted that 'nothing ever wholly dies', and claimed their spirit lived on in the Shakers, an eighteenth-century Manchester sect.

The spirit also lived on in the Quakers, who continued to prosper in Manchester, and during the decades to come, the town attracted and produced other new sects and prophets. One prophet, who emerged in 1679, was an infant called Charles Bennett. Several pamphlets told the child's story, although only one, a farfetched affair called *The Miraculous Child: or Wonderful News from Manchester*, seems to have survived.

Charles was the son of Thomas Bennett - 'an honest, poor, industrious man from the town of Manchester'. It is a sign of those times that the name of his mother was not mentioned in the pamphlet. She was, though, said to have had 'several very strange dreams when she was big' with Charles; dreams which 'denoted what a famous child she would bring into the world'.

Charles seems to have been a normal and healthy toddler. He developed language skills quickly but also indulged in what his parents thought was 'childish gibberish' until a relative claimed he was speaking a foreign language. The pamphlet's author described it this way:

> *He was heard by several that understood him to speak words of Latine, at which the hearers were not a little surprised, both because of his age and education; and upon a second demand in Latine, receiving a sensible and plain answer, they were more concerned; and when on further tryal, he was found not only to understand Latine, but likewise Greek and Hebrew too, they were wholly astonished.*

After news of this strange child spread throughout the country, 'an abundance of Ministers, Physicians, and Gentlemen that are scholars' visited the Bennett family'; and none of them, it was claimed, left disappointed.

Some, though, were disturbed by Charles. 'Even those that would seem very wise', felt he was possessed by 'some evil spirit' which 'supplied him with the knowledge of languages'. This annoyed the author. He stressed that Charles was no spawn of the Devil, and definitely not possessed: 'I can by no means yield to this uncharitable opinion . . . because possessions are always attended with some kind of pain, or disorder of the body, and often the countenance is disturbed'. Charles, in contrast, had a composed countenance and was not inclined to behave mischievously. In the following paragraph, the author described just what a little cherub he was:

> *When this child speaks he tends to promote piety and virtue and discourages all kinds of wickedness. For his chief discourse is to admon-*

ish men to repent, and amend their lives . . . we do therefore esteem it rather as an extraordinary gift from God; and hope it will be a means to advance His glory; and that those who will not be reclaimed from their ill lives by ordinary Ministers of the church, may at least be startled and awakened from their sins, and to face this young miraculous preacher, sent to call them to repentance.

The author stopped short of calling Charles a prophet, but fuelled the matter by claiming: 'several things that he hath said have afterwards come to pass'. He also noted that Ambrose Merlin prophesied from an early age, and that 'God doth often reveal his strength and his power out of the mouth of babes and sucklings'.

The story ended in a suitably strange way when Charles requested, in Latin, asked his parents to take him to the King. At first, they ignored him, but after he repeated his request, in Greek and Hebrew, his parents listened to him. When they asked why he wanted to see the King, he only revealed that he had something to say to him in private.

Charles' journey to London was slow because he was waylaid by a 'multitude of onlookers'. These curious souls were not, claimed the author, purely the masses: they were also 'persons of quality' who invited him to their houses, and he was met by the town's magistrates when he arrived in Coventry. Eventually, in London, he lodged with 'Mr Nightingale at the Bear Inn, in West Smithfield' and received 'hundreds of visitors'.

The author completed the pamphlet as Charles stayed in London, and so it did not reveal if he ever got to deliver his mysterious message to the King.

The French Prophets

Ten years before Charles' adventure, several child and adolescent prophets emerged in France. They were connected to a sect known as the Camisards, or the French Prophets, which would eventually establish itself in Manchester around 1710.

Some conspiracy theorists have claimed the sect can be traced back to 12th century France. They see the Prophets as a late flourishing, or at least the spiritual ancestors, of the Cathars. Leigh, Lincoln and Baigent, the authors of *The Holy Blood and the Holy Grail,* speculated that the Cathars passed onto the Camisards secret knowledge concerning the survival of Christ's bloodline; and that Sir Isaac Newton, who was also said to possess this knowledge, had affection for the sect because of this.

In 1689, Louis XIII decided to suppress Protestantism - which seriously threatened the Camisards. Before this, the Edict of Nantes guaranteed their rights, but now they were forced to convert or face persecution. Consequently, many became radicalised and fought back, and they believed they were ushering in the millennium.

The movement seems in retrospect to have been deeply gothic: tales circulated of infants preaching from their cribs; of true believers weeping tears of blood and walking on fire; and of young Prophets trying to convert others by blowing into their mouths and uttering: 'receive the Holy Ghost'.

Some of the Prophets viewed martyrdom as attractive. - more attractive than apostasy, and those who converted to Catholicism were despised. To avoid changing their faith, as many as 150 000 left France. They headed for Germany, Switzerland, and Holland, and in the process lost much of their apocalyptical vibrancy, or as one opponent of the sect put it: 'these countries extinguished their pretend spirits and laid their oracles silent'.

In England it was different: Prophets such as Elie Marion, Durand Fage and Jason Cavalier found an audience. Although some in the crowds indulged in a little heckling, and on one occasion threw 'excrement, dogs, dead cats and stones', others were taken with this strange French group. They joined the sect and were said to have inherited 'holy gifts', such as the ability to heal and to speak in tongues. They were probably more successful at this than Durand Fage, who could only manage 'tring, trang, swing, swang, ling, lang'.

One of the new English Prophets was Dr Thomas Emes.

He was a high profile convert: a chosen one who was expected to serve in the New Jerusalem. So when he fell seriously ill it was a blow to the sect's credibility. It was an even greater blow when he died because the Prophets had boasted that he would survive. Then they made the situation worse by announcing that the Lord would resurrect him on 25th May 1708, at Bunhill Fields. Some of the Prophets, obviously those with the gift of foresight, had misgivings about the whole affair. Others, though, were exhilarated and renewed their efforts to convert England, and missionaries were sent to far-flung towns, including Manchester.

Back in London, on 25th May, a huge crowd waited for Emes to rise. Riots ensued and graves were damaged when he stayed in the ground.

The failure was seen as a 'disconfirmation' of the Prophets - as a sign that they had no holy powers - and it led to the publication of pamphlets and tracts that were critical of the sect: such as Richard Kingston's *Enthusiastick Imposters no Divinely Inspired Prophets,* which appeared in 1709. The leaders of the sect answered the critics by blaming the failure on 'the fact of some unfaithful person looking on'. They also reassured their members that God was still with them and claimed He would send new spiritual gifts.

For a time, the sect flourished again and it gained a foothold in Manchester. Little is known, though, about its exploits in the town - for references are limited to footnotes in obscure texts. For instance, the Reverend Charles Owen, in *Scenes of Delusion Opened*, noted: 'the secret meetings of some prophets' in Manchester in 1712, but he didn't record any details.

What we do know is that a year before the meeting, two high profile Prophets, John Lacy and Elizabeth Gray, left London after causing a scandal and moved to the North West. Lacy had been a wealthy Justice of the Peace and a leading member of Westminster Presbyterian Chapel, but when he heard the Prophets preach everything changed. He felt they were touched by 'the truth of Divine Inspiration', and he was converted. So converted that his hands automatically wrote divine warnings, and he fell into trances and thrashed about. It was, he felt, 'exhilarating' and a process that 'sensibly refreshed the body'.

Lacy, who was married, also found Elizabeth Gray refreshing, which is how the scandal arose. Gray was an impressive performer: when the spirit took her she gyrated in a wild fashion, her eyes rolled in the back of her head, and she probably made some suitable noises. It was all too much for Lacy. 'When that girl has visions', he said, 'I partake of the joy of them'.

Some members of the sect were outraged, but one Prophet claimed that the Holy Ghost instructed him to give the couple permission to be together, and in the summer of 1711 Lacy left his wife for Gray. The pair are then said to have moved north, perhaps to distance themselves from a furious Mrs Lacy.

It is possible that they visited Manchester and attended the secret meetings which the Reverend Owen mentioned, but the nearest we can place them is the village of Great Budworth, between Northwich and Knutsford, where a small bunch of the Prophets met under the guidance of Thomas Dutton.

On a national level, the sect began to decline. Prophet turned against Prophet, each claiming the other was false, and by 1737 it was said that 'the spirit in its Public Manifestation has been gradually withdrawn'. There was no danger, though, of Manchester running out of sects - new groups continued to emerge. One interesting outfit was the British Orthodox Church, which claimed to offer a pre-Constantine version of Christianity. It differed to the town's other sects by being a closed shop - in fact, one contemporary observer likened it to a secret society and noted that members took an oath of discretion. The secrecy was due to the sect being Jacobite - which meant it supported the House of Stuart, and believed there was nothing glorious about the 'Glorious Revolution' of 1688, which dethroned James II.

The British Orthodox Church was not alone in supporting the Stuarts - for many in Manchester were fervent Jacobites; and as the next chapter reveals, the most intriguing of them was a gentleman called John Byrom.

CHAPTER THREE

The Machinations of John Byrom

St. John's Street dates from the 1770s, a good address for the gentry, beautifully proportioned town houses, like Bath or Edinburgh. Laid out on land owned by the Byrom family, the run of elegant proportions, brass plated and polished to mirror-like sheen, is end stopped by Byrom Street. I investigated the small park where St. John's church once stood. A stumpy Celtic cross, surrounded by spiky plants, acknowledges the scattered remains of twenty two thousand Manchester people . . . We stumbled on something too rich to be untangled in a few hours. The ghosts are toying with us. Solicitors and discreet medics, golden plaques with burnished name plates turn St. John's Street into an alchemical ditch, the Prague of the North. *Iain Sinclair.*

John Byrom's biographer, Joy Hancox, described him as 'an enigma: a playboy, a philosopher, a poet, and possibly a spy'. We could also add that he was a mystic with a deep interest in occult matters and the cabala. He shared these interests with various friends, such as William Stukeley, who was known as the 'Arch-Druid' because of his obsession with Stonehenge; and the Anglican priest William Law, who Byrom discussed the philosopher's stone with.

Byrom maintained a library stocked with occult classics: such as Reuchlin's *De Arte Cabbalistica*, Hermes Trismegistus' *The Divine Pymander*, John Baptist Porta's *Natural Magik*, Henry Cornelius Agrippa's *De Occulta Philosophia*, and John Dee's *Monas Hieroglyphica*. He also owned several works on alchemy and Rosicrucianism; a volume by the French Prophet John Lacy, which he found boring; and the manuscript of a 16th-century grimoire called *Tractus de Nigromancia*, which was mostly concerned with necromancy.

Also part of his library was John Falconer's study of codes and cyphers: *Cryptomenysis Patefacta*. This reflected Byrom's predilection for subterfuge - for he developed a system of coded writing, joined several secret societies, and even had an intriguing nom de plume - John Shadow. His most secretive activities, though, were carried out to further the Jacobite cause.

When Byrom was born, in 1692, Manchester was immersed in Jacobite intrigue. Just three years earlier, the authorities accused several prominent Jacobites of conspiring against King William and demanded they attended a hearing in the town. As the meeting got underway, the supporters of the Stuarts wandered the streets and distributed pamphlets which criticised the Glorious Revolution. Five years later, there was a full-scale trial of Jacobites which became known as 'The Lancashire Plot'. The trial collapsed through a lack of evidence, but Manchester's reputation as a treacherous place was reinforced. It was further strengthened by Richard Kingston, who would later attack the French Prophets and John Lacy. In a tract about the Lancashire Plot, he claimed that 'the Popish mob in Manchester had resolved to prevent the trials of the prisoners, by stoning the King's evidence to death as they came into town'.

The adolescent John Byrom may have identified with the prominent Jacobite families who were involved in the plot because his clan was part of the same elite. Ralph Byrom, who settled in Manchester in the 1480s, established the family's fortune when he became a successful wool merchant; and later Byroms added to the estate by purchasing significant properties around the town, including the Shambles and Kersal Cell. But it was not all good fortune for the family - for as noted, Margaret Byrom was caught up in the witchcraft controversy at Cleworth Hall during the 1590s.

On the whole, though, the family prospered and were wealthy enough to provide Byrom with a privileged education. He attended King's School in Chester, Merchant Taylor's School in London, and then Cambridge, where he read Classics and excelled in several languages. It was at Cambridge that his Jacobite views came to the fore.

Byrom supported the Stuarts for several reasons. He believed - like Sir Oswald Mosley and other prominent Manchester men - that monarchs were divinely appointed, and that it had not been the business of mere mortals to depose James II. He may also have felt attracted to the Stuarts because he shared their philosophic views: for as Marsha Keith Schuchard revealed in *Restoring the Temple of Vision: Cabalistic Freemasonry and Stuart Culture*, the family had a mystical bent.

It is more likely, though, that Byrom's support for the Stuarts was political: for like many Jacobites he was a Tory, and he despised the Whigs - who he believed were the 'gothic enemies of liberty'. Therefore, the Glorious Revolution, which he saw as a Whiggish revolution, was to be opposed. In fact, Byrom's willingness to oppose the Whigs at all opportunities led him to campaign against plans to establish a workhouse in Manchester, simply because it was a Whig project.

Supporting the Stuarts would, at times, prove costly for Byrom. For instance, in 1715, after being accepted as a Senior Fellow at Cambridge, he was compelled to leave the college because he refused to sign an oath of loyalty to the Hanoverians. This was the start of his life as a 'non-juror'.

For the Jacobites back in Manchester, 1715 was also a portentous year. In June, a group led by a blacksmith called Thomas Siddall demolished the Presbyterian Chapel on Cross Street. They were incensed by the King's decision to uphold the Toleration Act, which they believed tolerated Protestant dissenters but not

Catholics. Siddall was arrested after the riot and imprisoned in Lancaster. He was soon freed, though, by the Jacobite army. It had marched from Scotland and Northumberland, with the intention of placing the 'Old Pretender' - James Francis Edward Stuart, who was the son of the deposed James II - on to the throne. In response, Hanoverian forces marched north to meet the rebels at Preston. They were careful, though, to secure Manchester first: for the town's reputation for dissent and disloyalty was as strong as ever, and so its leading Jacobites were rounded up, and a force was garrisoned in the area to prevent an uprising.

The king's forces defeated the Jacobites at Preston and amongst those captured were Siddall, and Charles and James Radclyffe, who were cousins of the Old Pretender, and part of a prominent family which owned Ordsall Hall. Charles was imprisoned in the Tower but managed to escape to Paris after he got his jailers drunk and slipped out of the main door when a guard mistook him for a visitor. James had no such luck and was beheaded on Tower Hill.

In Manchester, at Knott Mill, Siddall was also executed, and as a warning to any future rebels, the authorities fixed his head to the cross in the Market Place. The Jacobites, though, were not cowed. In fact, Manchester went on to gain a reputation as the most Jacobite town in England; and Siddalls son, who probably witnessed the gruesome remains of his father, grew up to be a fervent supporter of the Stuarts.

Of course, the town was not exclusively the domain of Jacobites - there was a healthy Whig contingent which was more than happy that the Stuarts were in exile. There was even a branch of a national society, known as the Calve's Head Club, which celebrated the execution of Charles I. It became notorious after a pamphlet, *The Secret History of the Calve's Head Club,* which attempted to expose the 'plots and conspiracies of the Whiggish factions', was published. It revealed that the club made toasts 'to those worthy patriots who killed the tyrant', and burnt copies of the *Eikon Basilike,* which was a 'spiritual account' of the King's life. Such activities became risky after the Restoration, and so the club began to meet in secret. Its presence in Manchester was revealed by the wig-maker Edmund Harrold, in a diary which he kept from 1712-15. (The diary, which was retrieved from a bookstall in the 1800s, delighted Victorian Mancunians. Before it was published, though, it was heavily censored because Harrold had a habit of recording when he had sex with his wife, and included details of positions and places: 'did wife standing at the back of the shop').

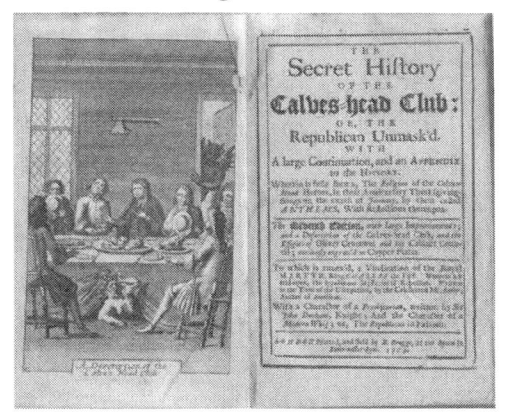

To return to the town's Jacobites - their number was boosted with the arrival of Lady Barbara Fitzroy, who was a member of the aristocracy. One theory has her as the daughter of Charles I and his mistress Barbara Palmer, whilst another maintains that her father was the Duke of Marlborough. Either way, she was of such blue blood that her presence was seen as a mystery. Observers such as W. E. A. Axon, the antiquarian and *Manchester Guardian* journalist, could not understand what 'induced' her to settle in the town, for she was accustomed to much grander places - such as Paris, where she attended the Immaculate Conception of Our Lady convent. Furthermore, it was not as if Manchester was home to other nobles who would make her feel at home.

What the town did offer, of course, was a tight-knit elite which fervently supported her family's cause. It included the Dawsons, who Lady Barbara lived with, and who were related to the Byroms; and John Clayton, who would go on to establish Saint Cyprians, also known as Salford Grammar School, which catered for the sons of the most prominent Jacobite families.

The Deacon family was also part of the elite and was headed by Thomas Deacon, who was a physician and a high profile non-juror bishop. He was the founder of the Orthodox British Church, which was said by James Ray, who was a contemporary historian, to be a clandestine outfit. Ray claimed that the worshippers 'do not allow any to come amongst them but such as their own sort'. He also revealed that they were 'under oath not to divulge what is transacted there except it be to a just and lawful Jacobite'; and he concluded that the sect was 'like the more worshipful society of Freemasons'.

Lady Fitzroy would also have been welcomed by John Byrom and would have had much to talk over with him - for he travelled to France in 1717, and met the crème of the Stuart court. He even met the Old Pretender himself, and years later he confided to a friend that he kissed his hand.

Secret Societies

According to Joy Hancox, Byrom joined a secret society whilst in France. She believed it was the Ordre du Temple - a Templar-style outfit which only accepted nobility as members. Next to nothing, though, is known about his association with the order.

Back in England, Byrom joined a Masonic lodge. Once again, little is known about his activities with the group - although we can presume that like all the 'Brothers' he was obliged to declare a belief in God, or 'the Great Architect of the Universe' and that he acted out, or 'worked', various rituals based on biblical legends.

According to some, Freemasonry - or the 'Craft' - was as old as the legends. John Yarker, who was Manchester's foremost Freemason and occultist in the last quarter of the nineteenth century, claimed that the roots of the Craft went back to Atlantis. In several books, he argued that the rites and rituals were passed through the ages by the mystery schools, the

Knights Templar, and all manner of mages and sages. He also reckoned that the stonemasons who constructed buildings such as the Manchester Cathedral in the 14th century were well versed in esoteric subjects.

Byrom also believed that Freemasons could be linked with the ancient world, and claimed: 'if thou consultest the Freemasons thou wilt find in them certain remains of the ancient Cabbala'. Thomas De Quincey, though, did not see them as particularly ancient. In an article for the *London Magazine*, he claimed 'the original Freemasons' were a society which 'arose out of the Rosicrucian mania'. Many others take a similar line and argue that Freemasonry became injected, or infected, with mysticism during the 1600s. Before this, the organisation was simply a guild; and the members, retrospectively called 'operative' Masons, were more concerned with construction than cabalism or any other form of mysticism.

The change in the organisation occurred when non-tradesmen were admitted to the guilds. They were known as 'speculative' Masons, and one of the earliest in England was Elias Ashmole - a keen alchemist and astrologer, who was a devotee of John Dee and an acquaintance of John Booker.

On 16th October 1646, Ashmole noted in his diary that he had been 'made a free mason at Warrington in Lancashire'. Which begs the question: was the Warrington lodge the only one in the area, or did others exist?

Similar speculative Freemasons may have been present in Manchester. However, this cannot be proven because the early Brothers did not keep scrupulous records. The first mention of a lodge in the Manchester area came in 1725 when the Grand Lodge in London acknowledged an outfit in Salford, which met at the King's Head pub. This group, though, may have been established years before 1725.

As for Byrom - the lodge he joined, which was based in London, had a Jacobite flavour: for many of the leading Masons, both in England and on the continent, supported the Stuart cause. One of the most prominent was Charles Radclyffe, who established the first lodge in Paris and introduced the 'Scottish Rite': a form of the Craft with more than the three standard degrees, which was said to possess profound ancient knowledge that had been preserved in Scotland.

Much to the annoyance of Quatuor Coronati, the Freemason research lodge, Byrom only briefly referred to the Craft in his journal. One reference, for March 11th 1725, revealed that he discussed 'Masonry and shorthand' whilst sharing a coach with a few eminent gentlemen. Shorthand was discussed because Byrom had developed a new system, which he made a living from; and in February 1726, he founded the Shorthand Society.

The Quatuor Coronati researchers claimed the society had a 'quasi-Masonic character', and noted that new members were 'initiated'; that they addressed each other as 'Brother'; that they were pledged to secrecy concerning the system; and that the organisation styled itself an 'order'.

Also Masonic in character were the titles of the society's administrators: Byrom was the 'Grand Master'; his sister, Phebe, was its 'Grand Mistress'; and Thomas Deacon, of the Orthodox British Church, was referred to as 'Grand Warden'.

Byrom taught the system in the town, and also established an order of the society close to Altrincham, but interest was limited due to the relatively small population of the Manchester area. In London, though, demand was high, and Byrom taught luminaries such as the scientist James Jurin, Horace Walpole, and both John and Charles Wesley. Lord Baltimore enquired about lessons for Prince Frederick, and there were hints of interest from other royals. The system also led to Byrom joining the prestigious Royal Society in March 1724, which meant he regularly rubbed shoulders with the likes of Sir Isaac Newton.

The Royal Society, which was founded in 1660, became a bastion of science and reason. In its early days, though, it was tinged with mysticism and was initially known as the 'Invisible College' - a term lifted from the Rosicrucian literature of fifty-odd years before. Amongst its founding members were mystical-minded characters such as the Freemasons Sir Robert Moray and Elias Ashmole, and the alchemist Robert Boyle. By the time Byrom joined, more emphasis was put on empirical methods and the 'new science', but there remained members who had a taste for mysticism - such as the 'arch-druid' William Stukeley; John Theophilus Desaguliers, who was the Grand Master of England's Freemasons; and Isaac Newton, who, as Robert Lomas noted: 'wrote three times as many words about the sacred geometry of King Solomon's Temple as he did about physics.' And of course, there was Byrom himself, whose interest in such themes was so strong that he proposed the founding of a Cabala Club.

The cabala was an ancient form of Jewish mysticism, which was given a Christian spin by the Franciscan Ramon Llull during the 1200s, and by others during the Renaissance. It was complex and varied but was often interpreted as an attempt to become closer to God. Indeed, John Dee's attempts to converse with angels have been viewed as 'practical cabalism'.

Byrom wrote very little about his Cabala Club. He mentioned it so fleetingly in his journal that some, such as the Freemason Trevor McKeown, have wondered if he ever got around to founding it. McKeown criticised Joy Hancox for presuming that Byrom did create the club. 'She doesn't consider the possibility', he wrote, 'that the club never existed except in casual remarks by Byrom to his friends'.

Hancox, though, argued that it met in London from 1725 to 1735. The lack of discussion about it in the journals, she reasoned, was the result of censorship: for *The Private Journal and Literary Remains of John Byrom* was carefully edited before it was published in 1854, probably on the orders of Byrom's granddaughter, Eleanor Atherton. Furthermore, a letter which was written by the Manchester Canon F. R. Raines - (the same F. R. Raines who compared John Dee to a ghoul from an 'eastern story') - revealed that the original papers were burnt. All this may have been done, Hancox claimed, 'for prudential reasons'. Although what the prudential reasons were is not clear.

Another who believed the Cabala Club existed was the Freemason Trevor Stewart. He claimed that fourteen Freemasons, 'from ten different lodges', attended its meetings; that it was founded before 1724, and that it 'was not Byrom's creation'. Stewart, though, was probably conflating the Cabala Club with the Sun Club - yet another of Byrom's societies, which discussed, according to Joy Hancox: 'every imaginable subject: metaphysics, the notion of infinity, shorthand and ciphers, hydraulics, mechanics and the art of memory'.

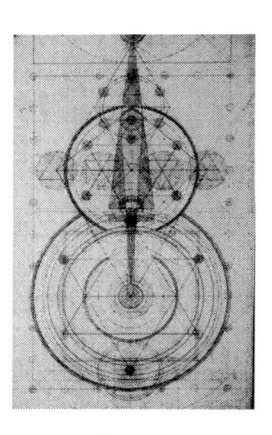

Some of the discussions at the Cabala Club concerned a group of 516 strange, geometric drawings. These intricate and beautiful designs included a smorgasbord of cabalistic and Rosicrucian references. John Dee's Monas Hieroglyphica was in the mix, as well as versions of the Tree of Life, and also plans for London's Temple Church, which was built in the twelfth century and based on the Church of the Holy Sepulchre in Jerusalem. Other pieces revealed the ground plan of Westminster Abbey and contained geometric patterns which are the same as the Sanctuary's Cosmati pavement. Also, the names of several mystics, scientists, and natural philosophers were written on the drawings, including Robert Fludd, Jacob Boehme, and Michael Maier, who was a German alchemist.

The provenance of the collection is unclear. Hancox believed that certain pieces were made for the Sun Club and that others were purchased from a member of the Royal Society called Mr Falkner. Before Falkner, Hancox claimed, the drawings may have belonged to the Le Blon family, who were renowned for producing 'esoteric engravings and publishings'. According to Vincent Bridges, an occult scholar and writer, the drawings belonged to a 'magical society' which was formed sometime in the 1590s.

Most of Byrom's secret society shenanigans occurred during the 1720s and 30s, but he was also involved with at least one 'mock corporation' in Rochdale during the 40s, and possibly with another in Ardwick. These organisations, which were peculiar to Lancashire and Staffordshire, were the domain of Tories and Jacobites - for they were a reaction to the Whigs pre-eminence in borough corporations. They satirised the offices of local government by giving their own officials titles such as 'slut-kisser' and 'house-groper; and the name of one Manchester society - the Ancient and Loyal Corporation of Ardwick - also had a contemptuous quality, for as well as not being a corporation, the organisation was neither ancient or loyal - or at least it was not loyal to the government or monarchy. Just how ancient the Ardwick society was has been a matter for debate. Some claim it began in 1714, whilst others date it to 1746 and argue that it was founded to celebrate the Young Pretender, Charles Edward Stuart, who passed through Manchester the year before, during the second Jacobite uprising. Furthermore, they state that a chair was kept empty for the Prince at every meeting.

The '45

Byrom was back in Manchester during the '45, and according to Joy Hancox, he was involved in laying the foundations for the uprising. She believed that his tour through Yorkshire and Derbyshire in 1744, which he claimed was to promote his shorthand system, was really undertaken to survey the attitudes of local clergymen and gentry towards the Young Pretender. Other Manchester men, such as the Reverend Deacon, and a businessman called Richard Jackson, were also said to be involved. They were, Hancox stressed, part of a spy network that stretched between Manchester and Scotland.

If we are to believe a local legend, then the ultimate Jacobite, the Young Pretender himself, was part of the Manchester network during the year before the uprising. This tale originated with Sir Oswald Mosley, who claimed in his *Family Memoirs* that his passionate belief in the divine right of kings compelled him to put the Prince up at Ancoats Hall. His presence was kept secret, even though he regularly left the hall to visit Mr Bradbury, who ran the Bulls Head, so he could 'peruse the London papers'.

The following year, after he raised the standard in the Scottish Highlands and defeated government forces at Prestonpans, near Edinburgh, the Young Pretender once more headed for Manchester. John Byrom's daughter, Beppy, who was a committed Jacobite, kept a diary in which she described the panic of the Whigs as the army drew near: 'there is hardly any family left but ours and our kin; they have all shut up shop, and all the warehouses in town almost are empty . . . Everybody is going out of town and sending their effects away'.

Everybody, though, didn't mean everybody - Beppy only counted the town's more illustrious residents. The lower orders, and those with nowhere to scurry off to, would have stayed. It is likely that the Lee family, of the less than salubrious Toad Lane, (now known as Todd Lane, near Victoria Station), remained in the town; and nine-year-old Ann Lee, who was later lauded as the female Christ, may have witnessed the arrival of the army. She may have seen the town illuminated as householders obeyed orders to burn candles for the Young Pretender; she may have seen the bonfires and heard the church bells and the proclamations that Charles Edward Stuart was the King of England and Scotland; and she may also have seen the Manchester men readying themselves to greet the prince and sign up for the fight - men such as James Dawson, whose family Lady Barbara Fitzroy had stayed with; Thomas, Robert, and Charles Deacon, who were the sons of the Reverend Deacon of the Orthodox British Church; and Thomas Siddall junior, whose father was beheaded for his part in the '15 uprising.

The army left the town and headed south. But just over a week after he enlisted, Thomas Siddall arrived back from Derby to try and drum up more recruits. Soon he was followed by the entire Jacobite army, because its commanders had heard tales of a far superior Hanoverian force in London, and decided a temporary retreat would be prudent. The retreat, though, turned out to be permanent, and the dream of reinstalling the Stuart monarchy died at Culloden in April 1746. The Manchester men - Dawson, Thomas Deacon, Siddall and several others - also died. They were beheaded, and their hearts and bowels were ripped out and burnt. Siddall's head, just like his father's had after the '15, was displayed in Manchester. Along with Deacon's, it was fixed to the roof of the Exchange building. Joy Hancox revealed that Siddall's widow, who was pregnant, was protected from the spectacle: 'To preserve her life and that of her unborn babe, friends boarded up her bedroom window so that she could not see her husband's head decaying in the summer air'. [1]

The heads stayed there for three years and then disappeared. Where they went, claimed the writer Edward Mansfield Brockbank, 'was a mystery that was not dispelled for about 100 years'. The figure, to be more accurate, was 82 years: for in 1828 an elderly lady called Frances revealed to Dr James Lomax Bardsley that her brother, Edward Hall, removed the heads. Hall, who was a medical student, a Jacobite, and a member of the Ancient and Loyal Corporation of Ardwick, fixed a plank from Mrs Raffald's coffee shop, which was next to the Exchange, and crawled across it to gain the heads. He then buried them in his father's garden, where they stayed until his sister revealed the spot. Finally, they were reinterred in the consecrated ground of St. Ann's.

Another who lost his head during the '45 was Charles Radclyffe. The Royal Navy intercepted his ship as it made for Scotland, and he was arrested and found guilty of treason. Cool to the end, he forgave his executioner and tipped him ten gold guineas.

Byrom's head, though, stayed resolutely on his shoulders - for during the '45 he was careful not to be seen as too much the Jacobite. So when the Young Pretender arrived in Manchester, Byrom made it look as if he was forced to meet him. But not all were fooled, and in 1748, Josiah Owen, a Presbyterian preacher from Rochdale, published a pamphlet in which he denounced Byrom as the 'master tool' of the Jacobites. Owen's claims, though, did not lead to any action, and a year later another pamphlet, *Manchester Vindicated*, exonerated the town's Jacobites.

In 1763, Byrom was buried in his family's chapel in Manchester Cathedral, after a life which had been remarkable by most standards. It was made even more remarkable, though, by Joy Hancox in her 1992 book: *The Queen's Chameleon*. In her hands, he became not only an 'enigma, a playboy, a philosopher, a poet, and possibly a spy', but also a serial killer.

Joy Hancox

Hancox's interest in Byrom began after she bought a house on Singleton Road, Salford, in 1965. She was drawn to its 'old world charm', and to an atmosphere of seclusion and rusticity, which belied its proximity to the city. The mystique of the place increased four years later when builders found a 'vast cavity' behind the chimney, and also 'a chamber with a flight of stone steps disappearing into a brick wall', which was uncovered 'under the floorboards at the back of the house'. This chimed with tales she had heard of 'a passage going from the house under the road towards Manchester'.

After delving into the building's history, she discovered

that Thomas Siddall lived there from 1729 to 45. Further research led her to Jacobite Manchester and John Byrom - who fascinated her. His public image, she believed, was 'far too good to be true', and in the early 90s, she attempted to reveal his true self in *The Queen's Chameleon*.

The gist of the criticism of the book was that Hancox, in her efforts not to portray Byrom as 'far too good to be true', constructed a tale which was too far-fetched to be true. It was a fair point because Hancox claimed that Byrom had conducted an affair with Queen Caroline and was the father of Prince William the Duke of Cumberland, and she also sounded less than credible when she argued that he played an integral part in a plot that resulted in the death of George I.

Hancox became convinced of his role in the regicide after she read his notebooks and found he had written: 'The K.G.B died at Osn', which meant 'the King of Great Britain died at Osnabruck'. She then noticed that on the opposite page Byrom had scribbled 'antinomy', which is a tasteless but lethal element, and 'anodyne', which is a painkiller. The King may have been given this poison, she speculated, whilst on the royal yacht, four days before his death. The man said to have done the deed was 'Mr Guy', who was the captain of the yacht. Byrom, Hancox revealed, met Mr Guy in Manchester. She also thought it was significant that the yacht's surgeon, Dr Beale, who Byrom knew from the Freemasons, was not present on the trip.

Hancox directly linked the poison to the triumvirate of Byrom, Dr Deacon, and Henry Salkeld - a Catholic doctor from Northumberland who was distantly related through marriage to Byrom. She believed it may have been in a box which Deacon, in the following missive, instructed Byrom to give to Salkeld: 'Dear Grand Master, you are to get the box and everything in it to him, and he is to take care of it till I send him further instructions'.

Deacon noted that his friend would be frightened to handle the box, and Byrom replied:

Dear Doctor, I had your last post, in which you tell me I shall perhaps be frightened because of your box; now I tell you that there is no perhaps in the case, for I am frightened out of my wits quite and clear, and shall not be my own man again these seven years. But to be serious, you did not do well to alter your mind and send this packet to me, for it is the only way to discover one of the triumvirate, that is to say, myself.

The murder of King George may have been the first that Byrom was involved with, but Hancox implied it was far from the last. She revealed that 'over many months Byrom became obsessed with the possibility of death by poison'; and noted that around 1742, eleven people who were connected to him passed away. Some were advanced in years, but others were young and died suddenly, and many possessed potentially damaging information about Byrom's personal life and political allegiances. Their deaths, she reckoned, were 'highly convenient'.

Hancox's theory was, needless to say, speculative. And when we note that luminaries such as Queen Caroline and Horace Walpole were said to be amongst his victims, the theory seems simply outlandish.

It is likely, then, that Byrom's acquaintances simply died of natural causes - especially when we consider that medical science was in its infancy and that the average person only reached their 30s throughout the 1700s.

(The 1725 Mary Toft affair, which Byrom's friends investigated, illustrates just how limited medical knowledge was - for Toft's claim to have given birth to rabbits was believed by many doctors, who spouted nonsense about 'maternal imprinting', which meant she thought of the animal when pregnant. William Whiston, who was one of Stephen Hawkins' predecessors in the Lucasian seat at Cambridge, and an acquaintance of Byrom's, also believed her and claimed that the monstrous pregnancy fulfilled the biblical prophecies of Esdras, which meant the apocalypse was nigh. Byrom's friends, though, considered Toft's claim to be comical. And every year they celebrated the strange affair by sending Byrom a rabbit).

The Priory of Sion

Hancox was also criticized for linking Byrom to the Priory of Sion - for this society did not have the historic pedigree that was claimed for it. Rather, it sprung from the fevered imagination of an eccentric Frenchman. It was simply a post-war hoax.

The Priory, though, still has its believers - they claim it was a chivalric Catholic order, founded on Mount Zion in 1099 by the French Crusader Godfrey of Bouillon. And they stress that it remained underground until it was registered in France in 1956 and that it became visible during the 60s when it was linked to the mystery surrounding Berenger Sauniere.

This character, who was the priest of a small French village, Rennes-le-Chateau, was said to have become suddenly and unaccountably rich in the late 1880s. Noel Corbu, a 1950s restaurateur from Rennes-le-Chateau, claimed that Berenger found treasure. This tale was embellished by the surrealist author Gérard de Sède in *The Templars are Amongst Us* (1962) and *The Accursed Treasure* (1967). In the books, he claimed Berenger discovered genealogical documents which proved the Merovingian royal lineage had not, as was previously thought, died out. The priest was said to have used this knowledge to extract a fortune from the French establishment, which feared that the information, if it became public, would lead to a popular movement calling for the reinstallation of the Merovingians. The Priory of Sion was included in this yarn as the body which protected the Merovingians throughout the centuries.

In 1969, an English writer called Henry Lincoln read *The Accursed Treasure* whilst on holiday in France and was intrigued. With the help of Michael Baigent and Richard Leigh, he took de Sède's tale and injected it with a potent dose of religious conspiracy in *The Holy Blood and the Holy Grail* (1982). Sauniere's wealth, they argued, had not come from the discovery of treasure, or the French establishment, but from the Vatican, which paid the priest a fortune to keep quiet after he discovered parchments which proved that Christ, rather than dying on the cross, had lived on and fathered children. The Vatican, they claimed, was well used to suppressing this knowledge and persecuted those who were privy to the secret, such as the Cathars of Southern France. And they maintained that the Priory of Sion, which was depicted as the custodian of the secret, remained underground to avoid such trouble.

Those who didn't believe in the secret society easily demonstrated that such claims were untrue. They showed that the Priory was created in 1956 by Pierre Plantard, who fantasised about restoring the Merovingian monarchy, with himself as the leader. Plantard was revealed to have faked documents which were supposed to be ancient proofs of the Priory's past and to have deposited them in institutions such as the French national library. The most famous was *Dossiers Secrets d'Henri Lobineau*, which included a list of the society's Grand Masters. Plantard was also shown to have collaborated with Gérard de Sède on both *The Templars Are Amongst Us* and *The Accursed Treasure*, which were mostly fictional.

However, the believers in the Priory of Sion were a resilient bunch who were not to be shaken by such facts. De Sède and Plantard may well have been fantasists, they argued, but the Priory existed independently of them and was indeed an ancient organisation.

In 1992, Joy Hancox gave the believers a boost when she published *The Queen's Chameleon*, which included the following paragraph linking Byrom to the mysteries of Rennes-le-Chateau and the Priory of Sion:

In unravelling all the complexities of Byrom's story certain names of people and places recur like themes in music, some more clearly than others . . . some of these echoes are coincidental, others are part of a much larger pattern. That pattern extends to events in France which began in 1891 in the tiny French village of Rennes-le Chateau.[2]

Byrom, she explained, was connected to five of the Priory's Grand Masters: Robert Fludd, J. Valentin Andrea, Robert Boyle, Isaac Newton and Charles Radclyffe, who presided over the society, one after the other, between 1595 and 1746. Some of the connections were through Byrom's collection of geometric drawings - Robert Boyle was said to have possessed 'companion pieces', and J. Valentin Andrea's book, *Mathematicum Memoriale*, was shown to contain material which had 'an unmistakable relationship' to the pieces. Similarly, Robert Flood - who took over John Dee's mantle as England's most prominent hermetic philosopher – was connected through a drawing which referred to him and his work *The Microcosm*.

These connections were not particularly strong, but the links to the other Grandmasters were more convincing: as we have noted, Byrom regularly rubbed shoulders with Isaac Newton during Royal Society meetings, and he knew Charles Radclyffe through their shared devotion to the Jacobite cause.

The Priory believers saw the 'Byrom connection' as independent corroboration of the society's ancient pedigree. That a gentleman from the 18th century was linked to so many of the Grand Masters - and by an author who was not part of the 'Priory of Sion debate' - proved, to them, that the society was not dreamt up during the 1950s. And although Hancox did not explicitly state that the Manchester man, or his secret societies, had communicated with the Priory, this did not stop the believers making such a claim. For example, John Howells, who was the author of *Inside the Priory of Sion*, asserted that Byrom's societies and the Priory had been 'in contact with one another'.

For the Priory-deniers this was bunkum. That Byrom could be linked to five of the so-called Grand Masters, they argued, meant nothing: for Plantard simply choose them from a historical pool of prominent people connected with cabalism, alchemy, and other Hermetic pursuits. Therefore it was no surprise that these characters could be associated with a series of drawings dealing with such subjects.

This was a persuasive argument, and given that Plantard was comprehensively shown to be a charlatan, the matter seemed to be closed. But *The Messianic Legacy*, which was Baigent, Leigh and Lincoln's sequel to *The Holy Blood*, threw up another intriguing Byrom connection which seemed more concrete.

The International League of Antiquarian Booksellers

When reading *The Messianic Legacy*, Hancox came to believe that a descendant of Byrom had bought Sauniere's parchments in the 1950s. This was several decades before the priest and the Priory of Sion came to the attention of the public, so it was thought that the relative must have been privy to the secret of the parchments.

Details of the sale were revealed to Baigent, Leigh and Lincoln in 1983 by Pierre Plantard. He showed them documents stamped by an English notary called P. J. F. Freeman, which revealed that Sauniere's niece, Mme James, sold the parchments to a group of Englishmen. This group consisted of the Earl of Selborne, Captain Ronald Stansmore Nutting, Viscount Leathers, and Major Hugh Murchison Clowes, who were all representatives of the International League of Antiquarian Booksellers. The League was then said to have applied to the Consulate General of France for permission to export the documents. Eventually, they were deposited with Lloyds Bank Europe.

This tale may have had a ring of truth because the sale of the parchments was publically noted years before Plantard's meeting with Baigent, Leigh and Lincoln. It was mentioned, for instance, in 1978, in *L'Enigme de Rennes*, which was written by the Marquis Philippe de Cherisey.

Baigent, Leigh and Lincoln were intrigued by this new 'British connection', and investigated the names mentioned in the documents. They found that between 1942 and 1945, the Earl of Selborne was the Minister of Economic Warfare and the head of the Special Operations Executive, which worked closely with the French Resistance and the proto-CIA. They also discovered that Stansmore Nutting was an operative for MI5; that Viscount Leathers 'was a close personal friend of Churchill's' and served as Minister of War Transport; and that Major Hugh Murchison Clowes was a lawyer who had been active in his family's printing business, which specialised in bibles.

At first glance, Murchison Clowes seemed the least noteworthy of the group. For Joy Hancox, though, he was the most interesting because he was related to John Byrom. She felt this may have had some bearing on Murchison Clowe's decision to purchase Sauniere's documents in the 1950s. Some secret knowledge, she speculated, may have been passed through the generations from Byrom to his twentieth-century relative. And Murchison Clowes, it was argued, may have been cognizant of this knowledge because he was a Freemason. The insights he gained as a Mason, Hancox felt, 'may have been relevant to the mysteries surrounding the genealogies from France'.

Hancox revealed that the first to receive Byrom's knowledge, or secret, was his cousin Joseph Clowes - a barrister from Manchester who kept chambers in London. The two men were 'constant companions' and Byrom used Joseph's chambers when he stayed in London. They also shared friends, such as Charles Radclyffe, and Byrom confided in Joseph to such an extent that he made him privy to the business of the Cabala Club.

Joseph Clowes was said to have passed the knowledge to John Clowes, who was his son. John, Hancox noted, received Byrom's papers, diary extracts, manuscripts, letters about the Cabala, and possibly 'other material dealing with the same tradition which has not survived, or which is still waiting to be discovered'. The next recipient was William Clowes - who was 'banished' from Manchester after an unsuitable marriage, and could have headed south. This may, Hancox speculated, 'have been the means whereby certain knowledge was transmitted to the southern branch of the family from which Hugh Murchison Clowes sprang'.

This tale of Freemasons and secrets passed through the centuries was seductive: especially because the Clowes family, as is noted in Chapter Five, played a significant part in Manchester's occult history. Ultimately, though, it did not amount to much: for there was no connection between the Priory of Sion and Hugh Murchison Clowes. Baigent, Leigh and Lincoln realised as much when they discovered that the documents which purported to confirm the sale of the parchments to Murchison Clowes and the International League of Antiquarian Booksellers were false. This was confirmed when they interviewed the notary mentioned on the forms, who stressed he had no recognition of dealing with such a case. They also discovered that the signatures of Murchison Clowes, Stansmore, Leather, and the Earl of Selborne were forged; and they noted that Lloyds bank of Europe, where the parchments were supposed to have been deposited, did not trade under such a name until the mid-1960s.

In 1983, Plantard admitted that at least one of the documents was false, although he did not admit to being the forger. Ten years later, though, whilst under oath, he confessed that the entire business was fabricated. The Priory of Sion, Sauniere's parchments, and the tales of Merovingian bloodlines were simply the invention of a man who dreamt of being installed as the Merovingian king of France.

Co-opting the International League of Antiquarian Booksellers into the tale was a typical Plantard ploy: for he often wove real organisations into his fantasies. For instance, the year after he produced the papers signed by Murchison Clowes and the others, he showed Henry Lincoln and his colleagues documents from the First National Bank of Chicago - in an attempt to prove some point concerning to 'Priory archives' - which were signed by Gaylord Freeman, who was a director of the bank. The papers turned out to be false, and when he was interviewed Gaylord Freeman revealed that he had never heard of the Priory of Sion or Pierre Plantard. Hugh Murchison Clowes, had he been alive and asked the same question, would doubtless have made a similar answer: for it was merely a coincidence that he been roped into the affair.

For the believers in the Priory of Sion, though, the confessions of Plantard, and the debunking of the Murchison-Clowes connection, changed little. They argued that Plantard simply introduced deceptions to obscure the truth. They also had no time for talk of coincidences. Such talk was dismissed as too naive and too ignorant of the hidden patterns of history. It was no coincidence, they claimed, that Byrom had known or been linked with five of the Grand Masters; and it was certainly no coincidence that a relative of his appeared, two hundred years later, and purchased documents relating to the Grand Masters. They saw this as proof that Byrom and his family were members of a shadowy, cabalistic network which spanned the centuries and which was still in existence.

Symbolic Numbers

In 2011, Joy Hancox made the extraordinary claim that such a shadowy organisation, or individual, interfered with the publishing process of *The Queen's Chameleon* - her biography of Byrom. She believed that a passage which revealed that the Young Pretender, flanked by the Dukes of Athos and Perth, rode into Manchester at 3 'o clock on 28th September 1745, was altered. The '3', she claimed, was removed.

It would seem obvious that this was simply a printing error - Hancox's editor certainly felt it was - but the author was not convinced. 'At the time', she wrote, 'I felt that this was not carelessness because the omission was not a question of a compositor *forgetting* that the number had been left out, but of someone *deliberately taking out something already correctly in place*. The '3' had been removed'.

Hancox claimed she 'might have dismissed the irritation caused by the missing 3', but was not inclined to because there had been other strange occurrences. On these occasions, the number 72 was involved - which she believed was no ordinary number. It has had, she explained 'a symbolic weight for mystics and hermeticists for many centuries'. One such mystic, Hancox noted, was Pico della Mirandola, who drew up his account of Christian cabalism in *'72 Conclusions'*; and it was no coincidence, she argued, that Byrom's poem, *The Session of the Critics* - which she believed revealed 'important truths' to 'the adepts close to him' - consisted of 72 lines. She also noted that the modern mystic, John Michell, revealed that the word 'truth' had a cabalistic value of 72.

Furthermore, Hancox discovered that '72 was a unit of measure regularly used in the Byrom collection of geometric drawings'; and she claimed that as a consequence the number 'has had a certain fascination for me', and also that it came to feel 'ubiquitous'. One occasion when the number popped up was in 2001 when a colleague sent her *The Arcadian Cipher*, which was a *Holy Blood, Holy Grail*-style book that promised to reveal 'Christianity's Greatest Secret'. It contained, wrote Hancox, a 'tribute to the importance of John Byrom's collection of geometric drawings', which appeared as 'a single, substantial entry on page 72'.

A few years later, Hancox worked on *The Hidden Chapter*, a book which documented her search for the origin of brass plates connected to the Byrom drawings, and which led her to speculate about the Templars, and a certain grave marker and headstone. As she considered these factors, a fellow author directed her to chapter 72 of Dan Brown's *The Da Vinci Code*, which concerned the Templars, a grave marker and a headstone.

'Another coincidence no doubt', wrote Hancox, 'and it made me smile until I checked the printer of the book'. The same firm published all three books - *The Da Vinci Code, The Arcadian Cipher* and *The Queen's Chameleon*. 'Fanciful though it seemed', she wrote, 'it was as if someone was playing a game with me'.

Hancox was probably not too disturbed by these 'intrigues',

for in the mid-80s she was advised to be cautious when researching the provenance and meaning of the drawings in the Byrom Collection. The man who gave her the advice, Dr Ryan - who worked for the Warburg Institute, which focuses on classical antiquities - explained that such material 'attracted more than a few eccentrics'; and these characters, he stressed, had interests which 'were in no way compatible' with those of Hancox. 'This was the first hint', she wrote, 'of the dark side of the occult tradition in connection with the drawings'.

One of the characters who got in touch with Hancox did not represent the 'dark side', but he was certainly intriguing. Over five or so years, he sent the author several poems which concerned the geometric drawings, particularly those examples which represented Elizabethan playhouses. The verses were, claimed Hancox, 'so allusive and enigmatic that they required considerable time and skill to decode'.

The versifier adopted several pseudonyms, including 'Janus', and never disclosed his name. Hancox, though, concluded that he was a man of status. 'I became convinced', she wrote, 'that the writer was so close to the centre of power at the time that he felt unable to reveal his true identity'.

It is easy to be sceptical about this. Rather than being a powerful figure, such as a cabinet minister, the poet may have been a cabinet maker who happened to have an interest in sacred geometry and Elizabethan playhouses. Sceptics would also question Hancox's fixation with 72. It would seem to them that she had spent too long immersed in Byrom's world of cyphers and intrigue.

Byrom's Legacy

Hancox's controversial theories changed the perception of Byrom. Prior to her books, he was remembered as a poet and a composer of hymns such as *Christians Awake*: Hancox's work, though, exposed him to a wider public and placed him firmly in the sights of conspiracy theorists. Their ears pricked up at the mention of his interest in Freemasonry, the Cabala, and Rosicrucianism, and they soon installed him as a fully paid-up member of the 'Illuminati' and included him in farfetched books about elite bloodlines and holy grails.

As far as this book is concerned, Byrom was merely a gentleman with an interest in esoteric subjects, who represents the cerebral side of Manchester's mystical tradition.

A tangible part of his legacy was St. John's church, which was built in his honour after he died in 1763. It was led by the son of Joseph Clowes, the Reverend John Clowes, who was a mystic. He claimed to have been visited by Christ, and this helped him attract a congregation which was said to communicate with the dead and to have been visited by angels.

CHAPTER FOUR

A Mancunian Messiah

> The first in America who received the testimony of the Gospel, were satisfied that it was the truth of God against all sin, and that in faithful obedience thereunto, they should find that salvation and deliverance from the power of sin, for which sincerely panted. And being made partakers of the glorious liberty of the sons of God, it was a matter of no importance with them from whence the means of deliverance came, whether from a stable in *Bethlehem*, or from *Toad-lane* in Manchester.
>
> The United Society Called Shakers, *Testimony of Christ's Second Appearance*

During John Byrom's later years, a new millenarian sect called the Shakers emerged - and its members came to believe that the Second Coming occurred in Manchester. The new Christ, they claimed, was born on February 29th 1736, in a house on Toad Lane. And this time He was a She: a blacksmith's daughter called Ann Lee.

There was something about 1736. Several figures who predated the Shakers were fixated on the year. Cotton Mather, who was a New England Puritan, predicted it would be the year the world ended; as did John Byrom's acquaintance, William Whiston, who claimed the year would see a deluge that would wipe out mankind. Whiston, as we have noted, had a history of such predictions. He interpreted Mary Toft's monstrous 'pregnancy' as a sign of the end of days and also claimed that a comet would arrive in 1712 and curtail human life. Cotton Mather also had a history of erroneous prophecy: before becoming obsessed with 1736, he earmarked both 1697 and 1712 as the years of doom.

Joseph Mede, who was born in 1586, was another with 1736-fever. His works, which were edited by John Worthington, a Mancunian who was a member of a group of mystics based in Cambridge, included a prophecy which claimed the anti-Christ would fall and Christ would rise in that year.

It is not known if the Shakers knew of these predictions. They may not have cared if they did, for they believed that Ann Lee's birth was predicted by no less an authority than the Bible. In *A Summary View of the Millennial Church*, published in 1823, Calvin Young and Seth Green quoted *Revelation* xi, 3, which explains that for 42-months the Holy City was subjugated by the Gentiles. Forty-two months, noted Young and Green, equalled 1,278 days. They also noted that in prophetic language days equal years, and so, they concluded, the Bible was speaking of the year 1278. To this figure, they added 457, which was the year of the accession of Pope Leo I, who they believed had inaugurated the dark era prophesized in Revelation when he established papal supremacy, and the result was 1735. [1]

1735 was, of course, the year before Ann's birth - which must have frustrated Young and Seth. Perhaps they considered arguing that the millennium began when Ann was conceived in 1735. In the end, though, they simply stated: 'it was a remarkable circumstance that Ann Lee was born the very next year, 1736'.

A Child Visionary

The little we know of Ann's early life is garnered from an 1816 Shaker book called: *Testimonies of the life, character, revelation, and doctrines of Mother Ann Lee, and the Elders with her, through who the world of Eternal Life, was opened in this day of Christ's Second Coming, collected from living witnesses in Union with the Church.*

As to be expected from a tract written by the sect, it contained a hefty dose of propaganda - and so Ann was never depicted as a less than an exemplary child. She was never a pest and never mischievous, and she was said to have eschewed 'trifling toys' because her mind was too 'taken up by the things of God'. She was also portrayed as a child visionary who watched enjoyable biblical scenes unfold before her eyes, as she lay in the dark in the house on Toad Lane. But not all of her visions were pleasant: for she saw, later in life, a crowd of Manchester's lost souls who were 'clothed with blackness and darkness'.

Several authors portrayed Ann as a slum child. They placed her firmly in the grime of Cottonopolis and claimed that the communalistic ethos of the Shakers was a reaction to the privations she suffered in the industrial town. Maggi Smith-Dalton, for instance, noted that Ann's 'budding youth' was spent 'imprisoned in the industrial workspaces of Manchester'; and Roger Dobson stated that Blake's vision of diabolical industrialisation was a 'sad and sordid reality' for her.

Yet just a glance at the facts reveals that the town of her childhood was not yet a place of 'dark Satanic mills'. Large factories had yet to replace the tumbledown Tudor buildings, and Manchester remained fairly picaresque and rural. Just a few minutes from Ann's neighbourhood were open fields, and the houses along Deansgate had gardens which led down to the river.

Ann's father was called John Lees. For some reason, the 's' was lost along the way - as were almost all the details of Ann's early history - and so we don't know her mother's name, and we cannot be sure of the family's religious inclinations. Ann may have attended Anglican services as a child, but she formed no lasting attachment to the church. It is hard to imagine her sitting quietly on a cold pew whilst listening to an uninspiring vicar - but if she did, then she only put up with it until her teens, and then she took off in search of a more raw and vital kind of faith.

Shaking up the Shakers

Luckily for Ann, Manchester still served up this sort of religion. It still produced sects, prophets, visionaries and mystics. One such mystic was a woman who roamed the streets in the 1740s and 50s and irritated the established preachers. Also present were several groups devoted to the study of the 17th-century German shoemaker and mystic Jakob Böhme. There was so much interest in him that the *Manchester Mercury* serialised his book *The Way of Christ Discovered*.

Itinerant preachers could also be found. The Moravians regularly visited and eventually settled in Dukinfield and Fairfield; Arian and Socinian preachers, who rejected the Trinity and the notion of original sin, also passed through; and those pejoratively referred to as 'Antinomians', who believed that to simply have faith in God was enough to bring salvation, were frequent visitors.

The most high-profile preacher to stay in the town during this era was Charles Wesley, who was one of the founders of Methodism. He did not approve of Manchester. For him, the town was too volatile and had too much of a taste for mysticism. And so he took action - he expelled six men from the town's Methodist society because of their adherence to Böhme; he denounced the itinerant female mystic; he clashed with John Byrom, who was a friend, but who held mystical views which Wesley found unacceptable; and he even prayed that God would 'take vengeance' on rival preachers, particularly a couple of Arian and Socinians who were staying at 'Mr Phillips' guest house' at the same time as him.

Wesley was so shaken by Manchester that he felt compelled to stay in the town for longer than he intended - because he feared that his followers, as soon as he had left, would 'run into a thousand sects and a thousand errors'.

Although Ann did not quite have a thousand sects to choose from, she was not without choice. For a time she showed an interest in George Whitefield, who was another leading Methodist. He probably appealed to her because he was passionate and dramatic, and perhaps because he talked of the 'New Birth' – which was a perfectionist notion that the Holy Spirit merged with the soul of those who turned against sin. Ultimately, though, Ann turned against Whitefield. As Richard Francis noted in *Ann the Word*, she felt that he lost credibility after he sought the King's protection from the mobs that harassed him in London. A truly powerful leader, she believed, would seek only the protection of God.

The sect which Ann finally chose to join was known as the Wardley Society. It was obscure but was becoming increasingly noticeable because of its noisy night-long meetings, which were said to have: 'kept the neighbourhood awake for some considerable distance'.

John and Jane Wardley rolled into town from Bolton during the 1740s. One theory has them as Quakers who left the sect after Jane experienced a vision; whilst another claims they were directly influenced by the French Prophets. A small pocket of the Prophets was said to have survived, and to have held 'secret meetings' with the Wardleys. Most commentators, though, believe the Prophets had fizzled out by this period, so it is more likely that the Wardleys were turned on to the sect by its literature, or simply by its reputation.

As well as being known as the Wardley Society, the early sect was also called the Millennium Church, and in true millenarian style, its members often saw omens and harbingers. One Shaker historian claimed that they felt 'great fear and anxiety' after seeing 'many terrible signs and wonders appear in the heavens'. (One of these 'signs' may have been the comet of 1754, which Axon described as 'a remarkable phenomenon, resembling a large ball of fire, with a tail to it, which hovered in the air').

John and Jane Wardley delivered their powerful millenarian sermons from the Canon Street house of one of their followers. They informed their small flock that Jesus would soon be back and implored them to be ready. They probably didn't realise, though, just how soon the Messiah would be back; and they definitely didn't realise she was a Mancunian who lived a few minutes away on Toad Lane.

After joining the Shakers, Ann experienced much hardship. She married a blacksmith called Abraham Standish and gave birth four times. All the children died in their infancy and she fell into a deep depression. After starving herself and praying continuously, she was finally committed to the local bedlam in Piccadilly. This may not have been a place where the patients were neglected: for, as Richard Francis noted, the staff seemed to have cured her through therapeutic methods.

Soon after, Ann claimed to have experienced a mystical conversion. Shaker texts claimed the conversion - which transformed her into the holy being known as 'Mother Ann' - took place after she was persecuted and jailed by the Mancunian authorities. Richard Francis, though, reasoned that it was more likely to have taken place in the Piccadilly bedlam. If so, then this was nicely apposite, for 'Bedlam' derives from 'Bethlehem'.

The strangeness of the notion that the Second Coming occurred in 18th-century Manchester led several scholars to ask if the Shakers really believed this. They reasoned that Ann was considered to be holy and Christ-like, rather than the second version of Him.

To some extent, they were right. Shaker authors such as Amos Taylor stressed that: 'Christ will never make any public appearance as a single person'. But others certainly believed in the divinity of Ann. In the early 19th-century, an elder of the sect proclaimed: 'Yea, Christ through her is born again'. And the following piece, which was part of a tract published in 1816, makes it clear that Ann was the second Christ:

> God, in all his wise providence had laid the foundation of man's re-
> demption in Judea, among the Jews, who were called his Chosen People.
> It was there the First Born of the New Creation, who was to be the
> Saviour of the world, was first revealed . . . When the time was fully
> come, according to the appointment of God, Christ was again revealed,
> not in Judea, to the Jews, nor in the person of a male; but in England,
> to a Gentile nation, and in the person of a female. This extraordinary
> woman, whom her followers believe God has chosen, and in whom
> Christ did visibly make his second appearing, was Ann Lee.

The Woman Clothed with the Sun

Ann was not only seen as an incarnation of Christ, but also as the 'Woman clothed with the Sun', or the 'Woman of the Apocalypse', from Revelation. It was a coveted role for those with an apocalyptical bent, and approximately five French Prophets had claimed it. The most interesting of these figures was Dorothy Harling. She attracted disciples despite – or perhaps because of – her practice of whipping sinners and then urinating on the offending parts of their bodies. Others who claimed the title included Joanna Southcote, who declared she was pregnant with Christ's child; Mary Ann Girling, who would lead the New Forest Shakers; a mysterious figure known only as 'Mother', who appeared on the South Coast in 1877 and was said to have saved a house from a storm; and Elspeth Buchan, who predicted the Second Coming would occur during July 1876. Buchan's followers stood on a hilltop platform, shaved their heads, and left little tufts of hair so the angels could tug them up to heaven.

Ann Lee was the most successful of these women, and this was partly because she was relatively subtle. When she emerged from her stay in the infirmary she didn't earn any scorn or contempt by declaring that she was the reincarnation of Jesus. She was not a crackpot like Nathaniel Smith, an American contemporary who wore a cap inscribed with GOD. She did, though, make sure the Shakers knew she had changed. 'It is not I that speaks', she told them, 'it is Christ who dwells within me'; and occasionally she demonstrated her powers by passing on messages from the dead, and by claiming to see angels.

Shaker histories claim the sect was overjoyed to hear of Ann's experience. Her revelations were said to have 'moved them with the most astonishing power of God', and to have inspired the Wardleys to 'resign their office in her favour and to call her 'Mother', thereby placing her at the head of affairs'.

But were the Wardleys so accommodating? Perhaps Mother Jane rued the day that Ann stepped into the house on Cannon St; perhaps she secretly saw her as a false messiah who had stolen her sect.

After becoming the leader, Ann transformed the Shakers from a harmless, albeit noisy bunch, into a more radical group which disrupted Anglican services. On one occasion, as the *Manchester Mercury* reported, Ann and several others were arrested and fined £20 for 'wilfully and contemptuously disturbing the congregation then assembled for Morning Prayer'. Later, possibly because she did not pay the fine, she was imprisoned.

Later generations of Shakers mythologized these events. They claimed that Ann's experiences were analogous to the sufferings of Jesus, and biblical stories were recreated against the backdrop of eighteenth-century Manchester. For example, Ann's imprisonment was portrayed as an attempt on her life. The Shakers claimed the jailers starved her for a fortnight and 'fully expected to find a corpse on entering the cell'. She was said to have been saved, though, by a disciple who piped a mixture of milk and wine through the door: an act which has been seen as a parallel to 'Jesus being given a sponge of vinegar to drink on the cross'. [2]

Another tale, which echoed the fable of the Good Samaritan, revealed that the Shakers were attacked by a mob whilst travelling away from Manchester at night. Simultaneously, some miles away, a nobleman felt uneasy and had an urge to go somewhere. He ordered that his horse be saddled and rode out into the country. When he found Ann, who was being chased along a road, he rescued her.

Other tales revealed that Ann had divine protection. God was said to have saved her as she lay all night on a frozen pond to avoid her persecutors. Rather than feel the cold, she felt 'great peace and consolation'. He was also said to have intervened and ensured no one was seriously injured when the sect was being stoned by yet another Mancunian mob.

The New World

Some American accounts exaggerated the influence that the Shakers had on Manchester. A verse printed in 1813, for instance, claimed:

> *At Manchester, in England*
> *The blessed fire began*
> *And like a flame in stubble*
> *From house to house it ran*
> *A few at first received it*
> *And did their lusts forsake*
> *And soon their inward power*
> *Brought on a mighty shake.*

But the flame did not touch many houses, and there was no 'mighty shake' - for at most the sect had a membership of around sixty. And it was this indifference, rather than persecution, which drove them out of the town.

The Shakers, though, claimed that God told them to leave England. They believed He inspired them, through dreams, prophecies, and visions, to leave for the New World.

Ann recounted that one of her visions revealed to her 'the lost situation of the people there', and she claimed to know that the Americans would 'come and embrace the gospel'. Another

Shaker had a vision of America as a burning tree, which was so vivid it left him temporarily blind: 'I saw a large tree, and every leaf thereof shone with such a brightness as made it seem like a burning torch'.

In May 1774, Ann and eight others, including her husband, sailed for New York. She was not the first Mancunian religious rebel to make the journey to the New World. Samuel Gorton, who was a scion of a family that had lived in Gorton since at least the 1330s, crossed the Atlantic in the 1630s as part of the Great Migration. Whilst in Massachusetts he was sentenced to death for heresy and sedition. This was later reduced to banishment, and Samuel relocated to Rhode Island, where he established a sect known as the 'Gortonites'.

The Gortonites were not a particular success, but the Shakers were. They established around twenty settlements and attracted thousands of converts throughout the next century. When Ann died, in 1784, she was safe in the knowledge that her sect was in much better shape than it had been in Manchester.

After her death, the local paper referred to Ann as the 'Elect Lady', and one of her followers claimed that 'when the breath left her body I saw in a vision a golden chariot, drawn by four white horses which received and wafted her soul to heaven'.

Of course, it could not end there, for Ann was a female Christ, and so in true messianic style, she returned. In the 1840s, a fourteen-year-old girl from New England saw herself in a room in which Mother Ann was sat on a throne. Before long, others were claiming to have had similar visions, and the sect underwent a spiritual revival which came to be called 'Mother Ann's Work'. Strange rituals evolved, such as the 'Midnight Cry' and 'Mother Ann's Sweeping Gift', which combined physical and spiritual cleansing and were meant to reinforce the Shaker's devotion to Ann. Those taking part in the rituals also danced, got drunk on invisible wine, adorned themselves with spiritual jewellery, laughed 'for hours', built fountains which never saw water but were meant to channel spirits, and spoke to dead Indians and began pow wows which consisted of 'whooping, yelling and strong antics'.

The Shakers continued to grow for decades after Ann's death, peaking at approximately 6 000 in the 1840s; and during the 1870s the leader of the sect, Frederick Evans, toured England and held successful public meetings in Manchester. The twentieth century, though, saw the sect gradually decline, and by 2010 there remained only a handful of believers.

In the years after the Shakers departed, Manchester continued to produce children who were as intensely religious as the young Ann Lee. In *Museum Europaeum* (1798), Charles Hulbert recounted the antics of Elizabeth Bradbury, who was an infant preacher. She was said to have read at twelve months, and like Charles Bennett before her, to have learnt Latin at a very young age. When she was three years old, she preached from a table at the pulpit of the Methodist Chapel in Middleton, and some of the congregation were reported to have fainted as she spoke. Subsequently, claimed Hulbert, she was inundated by crowds seeking to witness her 'miraculous gifts'. Sadly, Elizabeth was to see tough times. When she reached five years, her father began taking her around pubs, and it was in the Bulls Head in Swinton that Hulbert saw her. 'She was', he wrote, 'exhibited for the amusement of the public house company'.

Manchester also continued to produce those who, like the Shakers, were fixated on the millennium. One such character was Dr John Mitchell, who worked at the Infirmary and wrote a book called: '*The First of the New Exposition of the Revelation of the Apostle John, containing the sealed-book Prophecy, or the eleven first chapters, by J. M, M. D*'. Published in the 1780s, it revealed how great historical events, such as the fall of the Roman Empire, were foretold in the *Book of Revelation*.

Despite the taste for revelations and millenarianism remaining in the town, the sect which was left behind by Ann Lee withered. According to a Shaker text commonly known as *The Secret Book of the Elders*, the members 'lost their powers and fell into the common course of the world'. As for John and Jane Wardley, they did not experience the distinguished end that was afforded to 'Mother Ann'. They were not heralded as the founders of the sect and instead spent their final years in an Alms House somewhere in Manchester.

CHAPTER FIVE

The Occult History of the Peterloo Massacre

> I am well aware that many will say that no one can possibly speak with spirits and angels so long as he lives in the body; and many will say that it is all fancy. *Emanuel Swedenborg.*

During the autumn of 1773, as Ann Lee planned to leave for America, the Reverend John Clowes claimed to have been visited by Jesus Christ. This inspired him to create a new sect, which proved to be popular in the town. Soon, Clowes' followers were seeing angels, and in the years to come, the movement produced a band of mystic vegetarians and an eccentric cotton spinner who believed that the Peterloo Massacre was mirrored by trouble in the spirit world.

Clowes, who was the rector at St. John's, the church built by John Byrom's son, experienced the holy visitation when staying in Yorkshire. It began as he flipped through a friend's copy of a tract by Emanuel Swedenborg, which Clowes also owned but never read because he found the style disagreeable. On this occasion, though, the book grabbed him, and the phrase 'divinum humanum' caught his eye; some said it illuminated the page.

Clowes felt ecstatic when he awoke the next morning. 'My

mind', he wrote, 'was suddenly and powerfully drawn into a state of inward recollection, attended with inexpressible calm and composure, into which was instilled a tranquillity and peace and heavenly joy, such as I had never before experienced'. This event grew even more remarkable, because as he lay there, 'musing on this strange and delightful harmony', he became aware of a presence which stayed for an hour, and he believed it was Christ.

John Clowes

The presence returned the following day, and Clowes claimed it was of 'increased splendour'. It instilled in him an 'almost irresistible desire' to return to Manchester, so he could 'enter upon a serious and attentive perusal' of his volume of Swedenborg's book. This was awkward because he was scheduled to stay with his friend for a fortnight longer. He made an excuse, though, and hurried home. The journey, he recalled, 'was made more with the impetuosity of a lover than with the sedateness of a man who had no other object of pursuit but to consult the pages of an unknown and hitherto slighted book'.

Swedenborg, who was born in 1688, was a Swedish scientist, philosopher, and mystic. He enjoyed a strange childhood, during which he played in a summer house with boys who told him things which astonished his parents. His playmates, though, proved to be elusive. Swedenborg's parents never caught a glimpse of them, so the boys were considered to be angels.

The adult Swedenborg worked as an engineer and dabbled with inventing. In a letter to his brother-in-law, he claimed to have devised both a submarine and a flying machine. The 'inventions', though, turned out to be merely sketches. The matter of propulsion wasn't addressed, and the flying machine seems to have been powered by oars.

During the 1740s, Swedenborg began to have mystical experiences, which included an Elias Hall-style trip to both heaven and hell; but whereas Hall was only given a guided tour, the Swedish mystic seemed to have been given access to all areas, and was granted the right to talk to spirits, angels, and even demons. Also like Hall, he was instructed to write about his experiences. In the books that followed, he described the afterlife in detail and laid out his theory of 'correspondences' - in which he maintained that the material world was a reflection of the heavenly one and that earthly happenings are symbolic of spiritual realities.

Swedenborg produced a large body of work, but it was his final book, *Vera Christiano Religio*, that gripped John Clowes. After he read it he declared himself to be a convert, and 'his name', wrote the scholar William M. White, 'was blazed about Manchester as a Swedenborgian'.

It was no surprise, given the town's enthusiasm for Böhme, who is often seen as a precursor to Swedenborg, that many Mancunians wanted to hear Clowes' thoughts. His house 'thronged with people seeking information', and he was compelled to deliver 'formal lectures' and to create societies devoted to the mystic in the town and the surrounding areas.

Tales of this strange new sect spread through the country. John Augustus Tulk, who mixed with William Blake in London's Swedenborgian circles, informed a friend that 'several persons in Manchester are having open communication with the spiritual world', and he believed the happenings in the town were 'ocular and auricular proofs of the statements of Swedenborg'.

The group continued to grow throughout the 1780s, and by the 90s there was even a Swedish Swedenborgian presence in Manchester, when C. B Wadstrom and the Nordenskjold brothers, who were involved in the cotton trade, attended meetings and lectures.

Clowes' enthusiasm for Swedenborg, however, was not welcomed by everyone. Thomas De Quincey, a friend of Clowes, called the Swedish mystic 'gross', and could not fathom what the attraction was. Others accused Clowes of heresy - mostly because Swedenborg had denied the Trinity.

The Swedish mystic claimed to have 'often talked with angels' about the Trinity, and to have been invariably told that it was impossible to 'divide the Divine into three'. This contradicted Anglicanism, and so Clowes was summoned to appear before Beilby Porteus, who was the Bishop of Chester. However, those who hoped that Clowes would be kicked out of the church were disappointed - for Porteus proved, in this instance, to be fairly liberal. He merely advised Clowes to 'be on guard against his adversaries' and allowed him to remain within the Church of England.

Clowes stayed loyal to the state church for the rest of his life, but many of his fellow Swedenborgians felt their New Church should be entirely independent, and in true Manchester-style, they split into several sects. The first split occurred in 1793 when the New Jerusalem Temple was built on Peter Street, and William Cowherd, an ex-curate of the New Church, was invited to be the minister. In 1809, Cowherd moved on again and established the Bible Christians in Salford. In 1820, yet another split occurred when a female Swedenborgian attempted to found a sect called The New Church New, in order to distinguish it from The New Church. This woman was said to have had 'open communication with heaven', and to have 'frequently seen and conversed with the Lord Himself'. During her chats with God, it was claimed, she was 'expressly commanded by Him to establish a New Church'. But after gathering several converts, she was persuaded by Clowes to stay within the fold.

William Cowherd was by far the most influential of Clowes' rivals. His followers were given science and religious instruction, and they had access to an observatory which was incorporated into the Bible Christian's chapel. The students were also encouraged to abstain from eating meat, which Cowherd believed was a holy thing to do. He claimed that meat-eating was evidence of mankind's fallen state, and believed abstinence was promoted in chapter nine of Genesis:

> *Every moving thing that liveth shall be meant for you; even as the green herb have I given you all things. But flesh with the life thereof, which is the blood thereof, shall ye not eat.*

After he died in 1816, Cowherd's ministry was taken over by Joseph Brotherton, who became Salford's first MP. Brotherton, along with several others in his circle, also abstained from eating flesh. His wife, Martha, published a book of recipes for meat-free meals; and with John Kay, who was the mayor of Salford, he established the Vegetarian Society.

Cowherd and Brotherton, along with many other Swedenborgians, also promoted progressive politics, and from their stable emerged several prominent characters who were devoted to both mysticism and radicalism. One such figure was Rowland Detrosier, a charismatic young activist who preached to devoted crowds at a Swedenborgian chapel in Brinksway, Stockport. Another was Elijah Dixon, who began his religious life as a Bible Christian and then moved from sect to sect. He was a verbose back street prophet who bewildered his audiences with fevered ramblings. According to the radical publisher Richard Carlisle, so much 'insane mysticism' poured out of Dixon that the listener became lost in a 'labyrinth of words', and was unable to 'fix any one sentence for criticism'.

Peterloo: A Battle in Heaven

More significant than both Detrossier and Dixon, in regard to Manchester's mystical history, was a radical called James Johnston, who was another member of Cowherds' flock. He was Scottish but had lived in Manchester and Salford for decades, and was a cotton-spinner and a self-proclaimed prophet.

In his *Diary Spiritual and Earthly*, which was published posthumously, he claimed to have communicated with spirits for 24 years. He began the diary by explaining that the dead first appeared before him wearing either blue, white or crimson robes. Initially, they were silent and he was unsure of 'whether they were good or otherwise'. After he asked them to identify themselves he was given a note which stated: 'their names are secret'. But things soon grew less mysterious: the visitors began to speak, the spirit of Reverend Cowherd popped by to say hello, and arrangements were made for Johnston to meet them regularly.

The spirits asked him to begin each meeting by informing them of events on earth, and so he read to them articles from the *Times*, the *Manchester Guardian*, and the *Manchester and Salford Advertiser*. Although they relied on Johnston as their link to the earth, the spirits did have other forms of contact with the planet and could see spheres over places where significant events had occurred. One sphere, which was 'very dark and doleful', appeared over a Calvinist Church school in Rusholme, but the spirits didn't have the power to see what had happened, so Johnston told them there had been a sex scandal.

On other occasions, they seemed to have some influence on earthly matters. St. John, for instance, rescued Johnston's son, James, who fell into a canal lock. The 'first man on earth' informed Johnston that the saint kept James afloat until 'a man came along with a long hook and pulled him out'.

The spirits also informed Johnston of the latest news: 'St. John came and informed that on the railroad between Manchester and Liverpool an accident has taken place by the bursting of the boiler, and sixteen persons were killed thereby'.

One Swedenborgian dismissed Johnston's diary as the 'product of a diseased imagination'. Yet it could also be seen as a product of Manchester's diseased political and economic system - because Johnston created a fantasy world in the diary which gave him refuge from the grim realities of industrial life. And he would not be the only person to seek such refuge - for many Victorian Mancunians did the same. In fact, the whole 'Occult Revival', which was particularly vibrant in Manchester, has been seen as a response to industrialism.

Johnston responded to the humdrum nature of life in the mills by reinventing himself as the 'natural representative' of the spirits. Now, rather than being a mere cotton-spinner, he was the confidant of figures from the bible, of other historical characters, and of royalty - such as the recently deceased Princess Charlotte, who told him she was: 'glad to have the honour of speaking with a man living on earth'.

Also transformed in Johnston's mystical world was the status of Manchester's workers - for they now had powerful allies in the spirits. Johnston knew from bitter experience that they needed such allies because in August 1819 he attended a rally with the workers at St. Peter's Field which turned into a massacre.

The organisers stressed that it was to be a peaceful gathering, which was meant to highlight the need for working-class representation at Westminster. Henry Hunt, the principal speaker, appealed for the crowd to be 'armed with no other weapon but that of a self-approving conscience'. The sheer number of protestors, though, panicked the magistrates, who issued an order for Hunt's arrest. The Manchester Yeomanry attempted to get to him by hacking their way through the crowd, and at least 15 people were killed and hundreds were injured.

Although the dates in his diary show that he began his entries during the months before the massacre, Johnston probably took up his pen after Peterloo. And he probably did so because it was cathartic: a way of coming to terms with the slaughter he witnessed; and a way of dealing with the realisation that he, and the rest of the working classes, would have no voice for the foreseeable future.

Whereas the massacre was the immediate catalyst for Johnston to begin writing, Swedenborg was his long term influence. The diary was a homage to him, in which Johnston utilised the mystic's spirit world framework. He used, for instance, Swedenborg's doctrine of correspondences when describing Peterloo - by having a simultaneous event occur in the spirit world.

Johnston may also have been inspired by romantic fiction because the diary included several gothic scenes. The most notable involved a strange beast called 'Lumdale', which appeared in the spirit-world during the months before the massacre. Initially, it was not fully formed, but it slowly evolved as the fateful day drew closer, and a spirit informed Johnston of its progress:

Its body is somewhat like a whale, its head like that of a man, but black; the face, like a man, is also white; its teeth are also like a man's teeth, but it has no tongue. It makes a strange noise through its throat; on its head there are two large horns, black till near the point, where each is white; it also has a sharp sting in its tail.

On August 15th, the day before Peterloo, the spirit revealed that Lumdale had grown legs, and could 'make a noise through its throat, though it had no tongue'. It was also said to be 'very unsettled'.

Meanwhile, back in reality, a crowd which included the mystic Elijah Dixon made its way to St. Peter's Field. Johnston also attended but did not record the details of the massacre. He merely claimed to have informed the spirits of the tragedy:

'I gave them a true statement of everything that I could recollect relative to the meeting and the murders up to last night'.

He also stated that the 'angel Nixon', who was the spirit of a medieval Cheshire prophet, had stood before him, 'with a drawn sword', and revealed that the massacre had been mirrored by trouble in the after-life. The spirits, Nixon explained, had defended 'the New Church all the past week from the fury of the dragonists (the evil forces); and that even now they were in the utmost rage'.

The government responded to the massacre by imprisoning Henry Hunt. Johnston claimed that the spirits observed him in jail, and witnessed the authorities making attempts on his life.

The government also passed legislation which suppressed various types of public meetings and affected Manchester's Freemasons. Masonic organisations in the town had diversified since the days of the Salford Lodge, which met at the King's Head a century before. That outfit evolved into the Lodge of Integrity, and several new lodges had appeared, such as the 'Jerusalem Encampment', which was founded in 1786. It styled itself on the Knights Templar and held an annual feast to honour Jacques de Molay - the Templar Grand Master who was put to death in the 1300s after Pope Clement V instigated the dissolution of the order.

The Jerusalem Encampment was no threat to the authorities, but leading Masons feared it might be construed as such. And so in 1819, Brother James Lazarus Threlfall burnt material - said to be 'interesting Templar documents' - in the stable yard of the Old Boars Head in the Hyde's Cross area of the city, not far from Long Millgate.

The legislation that followed Peterloo may have intimidated secret societies such as the Jerusalem Encampment, but it did not prevent a group of London-based radicals hatching a plot to take revenge for the massacre. This affair, known as the Cato Street Conspiracy, was led by Arthur Thistlewood, who informed his comrades that 'high treason was committed against the people at

Manchester'. He also argued that 'the lives of the instigators of the massacre should atone for the souls of the murdered innocents'.

Along with other radicals, Thistlewood hatched a plan to bomb the Prime Minister and the cabinet. Several men were arrested, though, before they could implement the plot, and Thistlewood fled after killing a policeman. He was eventually found 'in some obscure lodgings' by Stephen Lavender, a Bow Street officer who replaced the notorious Joseph Nadin as the Deputy Constable of Manchester.

The spirits, James Johnston claimed, monitored the Cato Street Conspiracy, and the spirit of Joshua told him that Lavender orchestrated the whole affair. 'When the plot was gone as far as (Lavender) thought proper', wrote Johnston, 'then he got Thistlewood and others put to death. The blood is on his head'. And this operation, Johnston believed, secured Lavender the 'office of Manchester thief-taker'.

Another rascal connected to Peterloo was the Prince Regent, who became George IV in 1820. He was despised because he thanked the militia for preserving the public peace after the massacre, and on the day of his coronation there was a protest in Manchester. 'The radicals', wrote Johnston, 'walked in mourning, waving a black flag with a picture of a coffin on it', and they carried 'sticks with herrings, cabbage leaves and potatoes on the end of them'.

The new king was not only hated for his stance on Peterloo, but also because of his immorality - he was a womanizer, a glutton, a drunk, and an opium user. Consequently, when his marriage to Queen Caroline fell apart, the public sympathised with her. Johnston reflected the public mood by including conspiracy theories about the monarch in his diaries. George, he revealed, was not just louche and self-indulgent, but was a full-blown-evil character who treated his wife badly and murdered his daughter, Princess Charlotte, in 1817.

The spirit of Charlotte appeared only briefly in the *Diary Spiritual and Earthly*, but Caroline, who died in 1821, had a larger role as a member of a heavenly governing assembly, which also included the Reverend Cowherd, John Wesley, and other figures who were prominent when alive.

Johnston was not the only mystic preoccupied with Caroline - for a self-proclaimed prophet called John Wroe was also interested in her and claimed to have met and unnerved her.

Wroe's sect, which the mystic Elijah Dixon joined after his stint in the Bible Christians, was called the Christian Israelites, and in 1829, Johnston decided to call on their stronghold in Ashton-under-Lyne. He claimed to have been divinely instructed to 'visit the synagogue of those who call themselves the Israelites', but in reality, his interest may have been piqued by the media attention that the sect was receiving - for Wroe's outlandish millenarian schemes, such as his ambition to enclose Ashton with a wall and turn it into the New Jerusalem, were considered entertaining by the press.

A Pilgrimage to the New Jerusalem

The Christian Israelites did not initially go by that name and the sect was not the creation of John Wroe. Rather, it was founded by a prophet called Joanna Southcott, and its members were colloquially known as 'Southcottians'.

Southcott was born in Devon in 1750, and the first 40 years of her life, during which she worked as a domestic help, were fairly mundane. In the 1790s, though, things began to change. She claimed to have been chosen by God to be a prophet, and over the following decades, she stressed many times that the millennium was imminent. England, in particular, was said to face a mighty upheaval.

Southcott tapped into the zeitgeist when making these statements: for these were uncertain times. The country was suffering economically because of the wars with France; the ruling elite feared that English radicals would emulate their French counterparts and revolt, and there were constant rumours that Napoleon's armies would soon be crossing the channel.

Any disasters or out of the ordinary occurrences were interpreted as omens and were reported in a plethora of almanacks and pamphlets. A fire in 1801, which killed 23 people and destroyed Littlewood and Kirkby's mill on the banks of the Irwell, was certainly seen as an omen. According to a London almanack called '*Strange and Wonderful prophecies for 1801, foretelling all the alarming events of battles on land and sea; plagues, earthquakes, etc*, those who witnessed the fire saw 'the remarkable appearance of the word, God, during that shocking conflagration'.

Unusually harsh weather was also interpreted as a harbinger or a sign. Southcott, in her 1803 book *Divine and Spiritual Communications*, argued that storms and floods in Manchester, which she reckoned were 'more awful and tremendous than any experienced in the memory of the oldest person living', were part of a general upheaval that heralded the Second Coming.

Manchester, of course, was unable to resist such mysticism, and Southcott gained followers in the town - such as an accountant called William Harrison, who was converted in 1805 by his grandfather, and who became a prominent figure in the sect. By 1812, there was enough interest for a Southcottian 'Millennium Chapel' to be established, and another appeared in Salford in 1813.

During the following year, Southcott amazed her followers, and many others, when she revealed she was pregnant with the Shiloh. '*The spirit*', she claimed, informed her that: '*this year . . . . thoult shall have a son, by the power of the MOST HIGH*'. Such claims were not unique - during the Interregnum, several Ranters claimed to be carrying Christ's child. Yet Southcott's case was a little stranger because she was a known virgin; she was well past childbearing age, and seventeen doctors confirmed that she was indeed pregnant.

As the news spread, the sect attracted new followers and Southcott was inundated with gifts - mostly she was given money, but she also received valuable objects, such as a gold inlaid satinwood crib worth over £200. The attention, though, was not all positive - her house was besieged by a mob, and she was subjected to incessant heckling. She was also extensively attacked in the press.

One of the most effective attacks appeared in the *Manchester Gazette,* under the headline *Deplorable Effects of Religious Delusion.* The article began by describing a local mill worker's decent circumstances - he was said to have been 'contented', 'comfortable' in his job, and well-liked by his employers. His life, though, was reported to have changed in just one 'evil hour,' which he spent at a Southcottian chapel, where a visiting preacher infected him with such zeal that he emerged convinced that 'the time was near'.

Against the advice of his family and friends, he quit his job and set off on foot to London, in order to witness the coming of the Shiloh. Over a week later, with little money and looking dishevelled, he arrived in the capital. After a search, he found the home of the preacher who had convinced him that he was living through the end of days, and he was 'full of expectation' as he introduced himself. The preacher, though, turned him away as a stranger, and he was left to wander the streets until he was taken in by charity workers who realised he had a 'diseased mind'.

The journalist stressed that the mill worker would have been treated very differently if he had been affluent and proffered 'gifts of gold for the little Shiloh', and he concluded by lamenting that 'thousands are daily verging on the same point of fanatical idiocy' as the Manchester man.

Those who eagerly awaited the birth of the new messiah were disappointed when Southcott died in December 1814. A coroner found no signs of pregnancy and concluded that she had suffered from dropsy.

After her death, Manchester-based William Harrison remained devoted to Southcott, and as late as 1842 he published a pamphlet in which he argued that she had been a true prophet. Harrison was not alone in staying loyal, and Southcottian sects remained intact throughout the country - although the issue of who was to guide them proved to be a thorny one. Those who staked leadership claims included George Turner, who was an early devotee of Southcott; a character called Zebulon, who organized his flock into twelve tribes; Mary Boon, an illiterate peasant with one eye and a cleft lip, who heard Southcott's voice and dictated her messages to a local stonemason; and of course there was John Wroe, who was to prove the most successful post-Southcott leader in the North West.

Wroe, who was born in Yorkshire in 1782, did not become a prophet until his late 30s. It was after a serious illness, he claimed, that he began to slip into trances and have visions. They were epic affairs involving angels and Old Testament characters such as Moses and Aaron, and on one occasion he even witnessed Christ on the cross. When he emerged from the trances, he was said to recite, word for word, chapters of the Bible which he had never read.

Accounts of these experiences were published and he attracted a following. His neighbours, though, were not inclined to jump on board and criticised him for making money from his trances - for visitors were expected to put money in a bucket. The neighbours also discovered that he was faking the trances after one young man sneaked into the house, whilst Wroe was supposedly still under, and found him 'sat up eating beefsteak, pickled cabbage and oatcake'.

This early controversy did not seriously harm Wroe, and soon after he made more strange claims. For instance, he announced he had seen: 'Rabbi, Rabbi, Rabbi', written in gilt letters on a board near his bed. Initially, he believed Rabbi was the name of a place but soon concluded that he must 'testify to, and join the Jews'.

With no money or supplies, or as Wroe put it: 'without anything but which covered my nakedness', he walked to Manchester. The landlord of his lodging house, Mr Morrison, recognised him and did not charge him rent. He also gave Wroe an early taste of the city by revealing that he too had visions.

At a watchmakers shop in Shude Hill, Wroe told two Jewish men that God had sent him to inform them that: 'He would set his hand the second time to the covenant which He made with Abraham and He would cause those which were joined against the Gentiles to come and join them'. The men laughed at him and offered to pay for his circumcision. Then, possibly to get rid of him, they gave him a shilling, which he spent on a ticket to Liverpool.

A few months later, he was back in Manchester and back with the Jewish gentlemen. He told them he had heard a great rushing of the wind and a voice which said 'go to the Jews at London, and declare my words that I shall give thee', and once again they paid his fare.

We do not know if he bothered London's Jewish community, but it was on this occasion that he unnerved, or so he claimed, Queen Caroline. He boasted that he gave her a copy of his book of visions and sneaked away before he could be apprehended. The Queen, he wrote, 'turned as pale as a whitened wall, and trembled like an aspen leaf'.

It was at this point that Wroe joined the Southcottians, and soon after he began jostling with the other candidates to assume the leadership of the sect. His most serious rival, George Turner, had a habit of making reckless prophecies. He let it be known that the earthquake mentioned in Revelation 6:12 would happen on 28th January 1817. The sun, he claimed, would turn black, other stars would plummet from the sky, and all the heathens who had laughed at him would meet a sticky end. On top of this, he began giving specific dates for the Second Coming, and revealed that God had commanded him 'to marry a common strumpet'. Turner, being a God-fearing man, promptly did so.

As he carried on like this, Wroe sniped from the sidelines and criticised him for making rash predictions. When another of his prophesized dates for the return of Christ came and went, Turner was devastated; nothing could console him, not even the common strumpet, and he was dead within a year.

The way was now open for Wroe, and so he launched a charm offensive which involved much religious theatre and dramatics, and which won him control of the Yorkshire Southcottians. Eventually, doubtful congregations such as Stockport and Ashton also fell in line. The Ashtonians went as far as to declare that he was 'the instrument whom God has chosen to lead his people'.

After he assumed power, Wroe began to change the Southcottians into the Christian Israelites - a sect predicated on the belief that the British were descended from one of the 12 lost tribes of Israel. For some Southcottians, especially a few Manchester businessmen, this idea was not unfamiliar - for they had followed an ex-naval officer called Richard Brothers who popularized the notion in the 1790s. After his behaviour grew too eccentric - he not only claimed to have persuaded God not to destroy London but also declared he was the 'Prince of Hebrews' and the 'Ruler of the World' - many of his flock deserted him for Southcott.

Whilst infusing the sect with Brother's ideas, Wroe also found the time to pull off a series of publicity stunts. One caper saw him claim that God instructed him to live rough in the hills above Ashton for two weeks. On another occasion, a public baptism in Yorkshire turned chaotic as rumours spread that he would attempt to walk on water.

His next escapade attracted considerably more attention: for he announced that he had been divinely inspired to sire the Second Coming and that a female from the sect would be chosen to give birth to Him. Incredibly, his Ashton congregation went along with the plan. They declared that the female to be 'honoured' was Sarah Lees, who was from a wealthy family. Sarah's feelings about the affair were not made public, so it is impossible to know if she indulged in megalomaniac fantasies and was fully committed to the scheme, or if she was coerced into sleeping with Wroe - who was not a physically attractive specimen.

After a formal ceremony was held, a crib was delivered to the Lees' family home in Henry Square and preparations were made for His arrival. He, though, turned out to be a She, and because there was no contingency plan, which might have seen the girl used as an Ann Lee-style Shiloh, the project was ruined.

Soon after the birth, Wroe fled to Manchester - where, according to the *Times*, the 'prophet was soon afterwards detected in a house of ill-fame'. Other accounts embellished the tale and had him consoling himself by drinking 'hot whisky and water' with two prostitutes.

Wroe showed no interest in the child. His name was absent from the birth certificate, and the girl was brought up by her mother and a step-father. It is not known if she was protected from the madness that surrounded her birth, or if she was told who her biological father was. But we do know that her identity was kept a secret to shield her from gossip. Local historians, even during the 1960s, declined to name her. She was, wrote one observer, 'a respected and capable lady', and the matter was left alone. It wasn't until the 1970s that a student from Manchester University revealed that she was called Sarah; that she lived in Henrietta St and Albermarle Terrace; and that she died, unwed, in 1907 at the age of 83.

In 1830, the year after James Johnston made the trip to Ashton, the *Voice of the People*, a Manchester paper, revealed Wroe's latest scheme:

> *In the course of a presumed visitation, Wroe brought forth several commands, in the name of the God of Israel, stating that he was to have seven young females, who should, on strict examination, be proved to be virgins, that they should wait upon, nourish and comfort him, and be as wives to him.*

To justify this, Wroe claimed the process would help purify the sect because 'he would not carnally know (the virgins), and the act would be a kind of sign of the new Kingdom of God'. He also argued that as he overcame the 'lust of the flesh', so would 'the whole of the House of Israel'. Once again, the Christian Israelites gave their blessing to a highly dodgy scheme, which, when we consider that Wroe was already rumoured to have mistreated a young female servant, seems incredible.

The seven virgins were selected from girls around the country and were initiated in a kind of millenarian ceremony. *Wheeler's Manchester Chronicle* described the event:

> *The appointment of the seven to this holy calling took place on the 'feast of the full moon', when the high priest delivered a discourse on the 'coming of the Shiloh' and his reign upon earth. The believers were also informed that if they had faith they should not die, but where to inherit Shiloh's kingdom, which was near at hand, where they would behold the seven virgins 'walking amongst the seven golden candlesticks in the New Jerusalem.' The ladies were entrusted by the committee to the prophet, who was to take care that they were kept free from the world and all its impurities, and the elect were favoured with a communication every morning as to their condition and feelings.*

During the summer of 1830, rumours that Wroe had misbehaved began to circulate, and the *Manchester Mercury* and other papers claimed the town might soon witness three Shilohs. Although none of the girls turned out to be pregnant, they did make accusations against Wroe to elder members of the sect. He had promised, they said, that the Second Coming would soon occur and that he 'was to be honoured as the holy instrument for bringing about this glorious event'. Wroe was also said to have warned the girls that they would face a 'terrible judgment' if they spoke of this revelation.

Later, the *Voice of the People* revealed the sexual relations that the prophet had with the girls. The article was surprisingly forthright and hinted at Wroe's enjoyment of flagellation. One observer claimed the punishment 'was inflicted by the women with rods'. Sarah Pile, one of the virgins, confirmed this when she revealed that Wroe forced her to 'inflict a peculiar punishment upon him, which he had appointed for disobedient and offending females'.

After a prolonged process, which included fights, riots, and a strenuous effort by Wroe to retain his position, the sect finally rid itself of him, and Ashton symbolically took its revenge by hanging and shooting an effigy of him. The town, though, had not quite seen the back of him because he returned several times in the 1830s and 40s, and even conducted marriage ceremonies in Manchester. Finally, he left for Australia and set up another branch of Christian Israelites.

Consequently, Ashton never became the Holy City and was never enclosed with walls. But James Johnston, during his 1829 visit, would still have seen signs of the New Jerusalem: several gatehouses - known as the 'Gates of the Temple of the Children of Israel' - were built, and there were also shops with 'Israelite' inscribed above the doors. Furthermore, there was a school which taught Hebrew, and on the streets were Christian Israelites who were compelled to dress in a certain way: women had to wear only specific colours, mainly blue and green, and were to avoid black, red and yellow. They were also forbidden to mix materials and were instructed to wear veils. Men had to wear collarless coats with seams on one side; hats had to be broad-brimmed with a green lining; jackets had to be buttoned up to the throat, and to be single-breast, and shirts had to be made of linen and have a ruffle. Men were also told to grow beards, although this proved controversial because it was a relatively clean-shaven era. After some debate, it was agreed that those who attended the stock exchange in Manchester were exempt.

The most impressive of the sect's buildings was the Sanctuary, which was the main place of worship. It was a colossally expensive construction which reflected the obsession with all things Hebrew: the Star of Judah was carved into a huge stone slab over one of the main entrances, and the organ, which cost over £600, had twelve sides, each one representing one of the lost tribes. Although the building's exterior was plain and functional, the inside indicated the wealth of the sect: the seats and furnishings were made from oak and mahogany, the fittings were silver and bronze, and set in the roof were two glass domes.

James Johnston did not mention in his *Diaries* that he met Wroe when he visited the Sanctuary, but he did meet some unspecified Christian Israelites, and he revealed that the spirits of St. John and Abraham watched over the meeting. They had 'heard and seen', he noted, 'all that had passed on both sides'.

The Most Wicked Town

Come the apocalypse, believed the Christian Israelites, the elect would gather inside Ashton's walls as they prepared to be saved. Gathering outside, presumably, would have been the damned of Manchester: all those drunken, opium-addled, and sexually wanton creatures who were the products of the new industrial age.

Johnston would have identified with this, for he believed Manchester to be the 'most wicked' town in the country. He also considered England to be the country with 'the glory of God least in its heart', and held it responsible for 'all the evil in the Christian Church'.

The spirits, claimed Johnston, agreed with him. Noah, an ex-boat owner, revealed that: 'I have been looking at the state of your town and country, and I see that the greater part of the working class are actually in a state of starvation; even children'; and Cain, of Cain and Abel fame, was said to have been disgusted by Manchester's loose morals:

> *I have spent part of my time this morning in looking through your town, and I am disgusted to see in almost every street such numbers of public-houses; and even yesterday I saw many drunkards that could hardly stand on their feet, and all this in a land of Bibles – I cannot call it a land of Christians; and I say if they acted according to divine law, a drunkard ought to be stoned to death.*

For Johnston, this all meant he was living through the end of days, and he noted signs and omens in the news, such as a 'woman with two heads' and several 'monsters born of women', which signified the coming apocalypse. He also claimed the spirits had informed him that 'some great evil is about to be put down in the natural world'.

Towards the end of his life, Johnston revealed that the spirits ordered him to carry out strange rituals. At midnight on the 9th of June 1833, for instance, he was to walk 'three times round the 'old church, as it is called in Manchester'. He was to repeat this on the following two Sundays, whilst wearing a 'new black hat, red and white neck cloth, black coat and vest, brown trousers, and black gloves'. In August, he was told to circle other churches: 'I have received the following orders: go round the Temple in Peter Street once, at twelve o'clock at noon; and at twelve o'clock the same night go around the oldest Calvinistic Church in Manchester once'.

On other occasions, the spirits involved Johnston's adult sons in the rituals:

> *You are to buy a hat for your son James, let it be quite new, and to save expense let the price be low, and on Sunday you are to cut some hair from his head. This you are to divide into two parts by cutting it in the middle. The root part he is to eat, and the top part you must burn in the fire. All of this you must perform in a solemn and rational view of its sign and significance, because the hair of the head corresponds to the divine wisdom.*

Other rituals involved the drawing of blood and were meant to symbolize Christ's suffering on the cross. But apart from one occasion in 1837, when Johnston was ordered to 'draw blood from the heel', he never seemed to be the donor, and the honour was mostly given to his son.

Johnston used a lance to cut his son's side and then used the blood to write the first verse of one of the psalms. These bloody notes were either kept in his son's hat for a year or longer - or delivered to one of Manchester or Salford's 'false preachers'. On another occasion, Johnston had to collect blood from a lamb, a horse and a cow, and then 'buy three shirt-fronts of linen' and dip the corner of each in the fluid.

Johnston was said to have attracted a following, yet it is more likely that he gathered around him just a few friends, for he was never recognised as a prophet, and his diaries remained unpublished in his lifetime. After he died in 1840, he was regarded as just another working man, rather than the 'natural representative' of the spirits.

Swedenborg and the occult

In contrast to Johnston, with his homespun and naive take on Swedenborg, were more intellectual characters who emphasized the mystic's occult leanings. They belonged to Masonic outfits and other esoteric societies, such as the Illumines d'Avignon - a French group who studied 'renaissance alchemy, hermetic authors, the divine science of numbers and the mystical interpretation of dreams'.

For John Clowes, whose interpretation of Swedenborg was narrow and conservative, the claims of the occultists were unacceptable. Occultism was also unacceptable to Robert Hindmarsh, who was the minister of the New Jerusalem church in Salford for ten years, and who wrote the following attack:

> *The divinatory arts are unreliable, otherwise we should find their practitioners becoming very rich. Astrology and magic doubtless have their foundation in truth, but as used today they are perversions of the divine order. There is nothing to be gained in paying attention to whatever influences the stars and planets may have. If we believe that God governs all things, then they are governed by love and wisdom.*

Palmistry was another pursuit which Hindmarsh disapproved of. He noted with satisfaction that a palm reader, who studied his hand and predicted he would die in twelve months, dropped dead himself within a year. [4]

The Illumines d'Avignon also came under Hindmarsh's fire. He mocked one of their leaders, the Polish Count Thaddeus Leszczy, for claiming to be 'in possession of a grand secret which was the crown and summit of all mysteries; the key to all wisdom; and the perfection of revelation'; and he scorned the group for carrying out a ritual which required one of their number to dress in 'purple garments' and pretend to be 'the actual and personal presence of the Lord'.

Yet despite the denials of Clowes and Hindmarsh, Swedenborg *was* steeped in the occult. Not only did he claim to have conversed with spirits, but he also studied Rosicrucianism and the Cabala with Rabbi Dr Hayyim Samuel Jacob Faulk, who had an alchemical lab on London Bridge.

Although Faulk was a man of mystery, he could not match the reputation of his student - for rumours of Swedenborg's strange powers abounded. One tale had him detecting a fire in his neighbourhood in Stockholm, even though he was 300 miles away in Gothenburg; and it was believed that he announced the death of Peter the Third of Russia before it was made public. He was also thought to have stunned the Queen of Sweden by passing on information from her deceased brother, the Prince Royal of Prussia, that he could not possibly have known.

According to Joscelyn Godwin, the prolific writer on mystery schools and esotericism, such supernatural happenings meant that: 'Swedenborg was every inch a magician'; and Gary Lachman, another writer on esoteric matters, argued that Hindmarsh's New Church may not have existed if Swedenborg had not sat at the feet of Faulk and developed an interest in the occult.

This may have been an uncomfortable truth for Hindmarsh, but others, such as Augustus Nordenskjold, who was one of the Swedish businessmen trading in Manchester in the 1790s, had no problem accepting Swedenborg's occult leanings. In fact, Nordenskjold revelled in esoteric matters: for he was a Freemason and an alchemist who endeavoured to produce gold from base metal for King Gustav III. He also dreamt of travelling to Africa in a hot air balloon to establish a Swedenborgian 'free love' society.

Samuel Beswick was another champion of the occult aspects

of Swedenborg's philosophy. This intriguing character was born in Stockport in 1822 and raised in the New Church. He claimed to have studied privately with John Dalton and to have 'introduced Swedenborg's work on chemistry to his attention'. Dalton, he wrote, felt the philosopher's scientific work was 'singular and wonderful'.

During the late 1840s, Beswick became the leader of the Haslingden New Church Society and the principal of the Salford and Manchester New Church Day School. He also found time to publish his first book, *How are Worlds Made? Being a System of Cosmognical Philosophy*, in which he tackled the origins of the universe.

Once that subject was done and dusted, he headed for Ireland and then emigrated to the United States, where he led an adventurous life. He became an associate editor of the New York Post, 'one of the pioneers in the construction of the Illinois Central Railroad', a bookkeeper in New Jersey, a church leader in Ontario, and the editor of the Tyrone Daily Herald. He was also instrumental in founding the Swedenborg Masonic Rite; and at some point, he travelled to Jerusalem and later boasted to have made important archaeological discoveries which would 'set to rest all the disputed points now occupying the attention of modern scholars'.

Through it all, he continued to publish books, including a biography of Cagliostro, who was an eighteenth-century alchemist, forger, occultist, and Freemason. Beswick also wrote a volume called *Swedenborg and Phremasonry*. The unorthodox spelling, he explained, was a conflation of 'two ancient words: Phre or Pi - re, meaning light, and Mason'. The 'ancient brethren', he claimed, used it to describe 'a poor blind candidate, or one in darkness, who is feeling his way in search of light'. For one Mason this was the most 'utterly preposterous and absurd etymology ever proposed'.

Other Masons were irritated by more than his creative grammar. They claimed that Swedenborg was never a Mason; that Beswick himself was not initiated; and that he had not studied with

John Dalton. R. A. Gilbert, a modern writer, stressed that: 'Almost everything about (Beswick's) life in England involves contradictions and conjecture'. The 'only thing that was certain', he continued, 'was his birth date'.

Some of the gripes were justified. The Freemasons were right to doubt that he made important discoveries in Jerusalem, but Beswick's other claims were more credible. It is entirely possible that he studied privately with John Dalton. Students were often found at the scientist's house on George Street - James Joules being one of them. In fact, Joules put Beswick forward for membership of Manchester's Philosophical and Literary Society - perhaps after the two men met as students at Dalton's house.

The Freemasons were also wrong to dismiss the idea that Swedenborg had joined them. They made this mistake because they relied on Whig accounts of the craft, which scrubbed Jacobite influences from Masonic history. Consequently, they overlooked the fact that Swedenborg joined a Jacobite lodge in 1710.

So how was Beswick aware of Swedenborg's membership of the craft? Marsha Keith Schuchard, in her 800-page tome, *Swedenborg Secret Agent on Earth and in Heaven*, speculated that Manchester's Swedish contingent, C. B. Wadstrom and Augustus Nordenskjold, may have 'provided information on Swedenborg's Masonic association to friends in the city' and that Beswick may have been privy to this knowledge during the following century.

Swedenborg's legacy in Manchester

Both strands of Swedenborgianism - the conservative interpretation of Clowes and Hindmarsh, and the occult and Masonic perspective of Samuel Beswick and others - were to become influential in Manchester during the second half of the nineteenth century.

Beswick's Swedenborgian Rite certainly influenced John

Yarker - one of the city's most renowned occultists. He installed himself as the Worshipful Master of the rite and announced that the headquarters would be in Manchester.

The Clowes' strand, though, was more influential. Clowes' belief that: 'Everyman hath communication and association with the Invisible World, whether he knows it or not', set the scene for the town's obsession with spiritualism. But before examining Manchester's many mediums and table-rappers, we will meet the mesmerists - a group who influenced spiritualism just as much as the Swedenborgians.

CHAPTER SIX

The Battle of the Mesmerists

In 1849, Dr Joseph W. Haddock, who often worked in Manchester, published *Somnolism and Psycheism*, which was said by the Reverend George Sandby to have scientifically proven the existence of Swedenborg's spirit world. Haddock claimed to have contacted spirits via a domestic servant, who he put in a trance by using a force known as 'animal magnetism', which was thought to emit from living things. This force, claimed the doctor, not only allowed the 'magnetics' to speak to and observe the dead, but also to identify images and objects without looking at them; to diagnose illnesses, and to connect with people around the globe.

The belief that mysterious forces affected people was not new. After Manchester was hit by an earthquake in 1777, some claimed that such a force was unleashed upon the town. The physician Thomas Henry revealed that 'many people complained of nervous pains and hysteric affections, and of sensations similar to those of people who have been strongly electrified'.

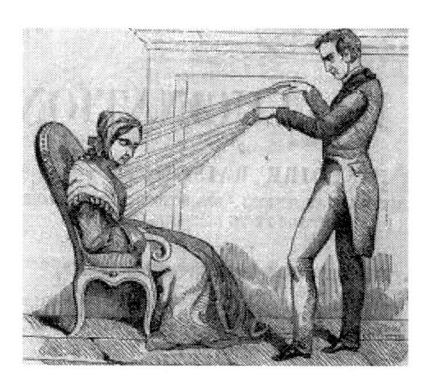

Two years later, Franz Mesmer introduced animal magnetism to the world, and during the following decades, many came to believe in the force. By the mid-nineteenth century, Manchester was home to a flourishing mesmerist scene: lectures and public demonstrations were common; several of the city's practitioners contributed to a journal called the *Zoist*, which was devoted to the subject; and some in the town claimed that certain adepts could see the force. Dr Haddock, in a journal entry for February 1850, revealed that his domestic servant could see 'a fluid issuing from the points of the fingers of each hand. This fluid . . . was of an orange or reddish colour from the right hand, and greenish or bluish from the left hand'. Illustrators for the penny magazines also liked to imagine that the force was visible and often depicted lines of energy flowing from the hands of slightly sinister-looking characters.

Despite the flourishing scene, all was not well with Manchester's mesmerists - for certain figures claimed the force did not exist. The most prominent sceptic was Dr James Braid, and his most significant opponent was Charles Lafontaine - a

French actor who always dressed in black, and spoke English with such an impenetrable accent that an interpreter was required on stage.

Lafontaine arrived in Manchester in 1841 and gave six demonstrations at the Athenaeum. He proved to be popular with the public, but Braid was not impressed. He was already sceptical of characters like Lafontaine, and believed their subjects were either in on the act, or complied with the mesmerist because of their 'excited imaginations'. He called it 'collusion or delusion'. So after a friend suggested they attend Lafontaine's third demonstration, he had to be 'almost dragged' to the Athenaeum. Many other gentlemen, though, were keen to see the mysterious mesmerist, and the audience included several illustrious characters, such as the Canon of Manchester Cathedral, and Dr Kay Shuttleworth. Also present were several surgeons and Tobias Theodores, who acted as Lafontaine's interpreter, and later became the professor of Modern Languages at Owens College.

The gentlemen were treated to an impressive display - with Lafontaine putting his assistant in such a deep trance that he didn't flinch when a member of the public pushed a pin into his eyelid. Some of the audience, though, did more than flinch; in fact, several ladies were said to have 'become so faint as to make them quit the place'. But Braid remained unimpressed, and claimed to have 'seen nothing to diminish' his 'previous prejudices'.

Yet he must have seen something of interest because he attended the next demonstration. The *Manchester Guardian* reported that the audience was a thousand strong and raucous. Braid added to the spectacle by shouting for Lafontaine to use fresh subjects, instead of those who had been put under on previous nights, and the audience responded by telling him to sit down and stop interrupting. Some even called for him to be 'turned out'. After a woman was put in a trance, Braid and two other surgeons climbed on stage and checked her. They pushed pins under her fingernails, and although she felt a sensation, she did not react as she would in normal conditions. Once again, Braid was not convinced, and the evening ended in chaos as groups argued and shouted.

A reporter for the *Manchester Guardian* was not impressed. He claimed Lafontaine had been 'badgered', and he believed that 'any rational and reflecting person present must have felt ashamed at the rude demeanour and great discourtesy shown by Englishmen to a stranger and a foreigner'. He also asked how Englishmen would feel if one of their lecturers had been treated similarly in France, and concluded that he would be sorry if even a charlatan - although he doubted such a word could be applied to the Frenchman - was so badly treated.

The reporter would have been more unimpressed if he had known that Braid sent a letter to Lafontaine in which he stressed that the subjects were merely playing along with his act. He may also have frowned on Braid's intention to attend that evening's demonstration with several of Manchester's men of science, who also had a dim view of Lafontaine's trade. The group included Dr William Crawford Williamson, who was a paleobiologist and the curator of natural history at the museum; Dr Wilson, who was a prominent eye specialist; Mr Smith, who was a surgeon; and several others who were members of the Wernerian Society, which was dedicated to natural history, and was named after Abraham Gottlob Werner, a German geologist.

Before Lafontaine had a chance to begin, Braid read out his letter and demanded to know why the mesmerist hadn't replied. Lafontaine claimed the messenger told him no reply was necessary. Then, sensing that the evening was going to become chaotic, Lafontaine appointed Dr Radford, who was a respected obstetrician, as chairman of the demonstration. Radford proceeded to declare that Braid had perpetrated the 'most unwarrantable interference with the rights and privileges of a public lecture'. Braid, though, would not be silenced, and once again called for a 'new subject' to be mesmerised. Lafontaine declined to do this, and instead put the same female volunteer from the last demonstration into a trance. Pins were stuck in her face, hands and arms, and a starting pistol was fired near her ears, but she did not react.

Charles Lafontaine

It was an impressive display, but once again Manchester's men of science voiced their disbelief. During the following debate, Dr Wilson, the eye specialist, made his opinion clear: 'The whole affair is as complete a piece of humbug as I have ever witnessed'. Lafontaine, who didn't understand the term 'humbug', took offence: 'The gentleman', he retorted, 'says it is all bog; I say it is not bog; there is no bog in it at all'.

To try and prove that it was indeed bog, the scientists climbed on stage and Dr Williamson lifted the woman's eyelids. He noticed that her pupils were contracted and suspected that she *was* asleep. Dr Wilson confirmed she was and gave a low whistle as he realised that Lafontaine was not a charlatan. Dr Smith, though, was not convinced. He argued that Dr Wilson had previously been right and dismissed it all as a 'wretched humbug'. He later fired off a letter to the *Manchester Times* in which he claimed that mesmerism, along with astrology and homoeopathy, formed a 'trinity of the credulous'.

Braid also realised, whilst stood on the stage, that the woman was in a trance - and soon after, he began to experiment with mesmerism. A friend, Mr Walker, agreed to be his first subject, and others were invited to witness the proceedings, including Captain Thomas Brown, who was a curator at the museum and would soon have the gastropod - Zebina browniana d'Orbigny - named after him.

James Braid

After successfully experimenting, Braid developed a theory which demolished the ideas of Franz Mesmer. People went into trances, he explained, because continuously staring at objects - be it watches or a mesmerist's eyes - fatigued the rectus and levator muscles. Thus he showed that tales of invisible forces, which could be channelled by magnetic individuals, were false. Consequently, a new term was needed to replace mesmerism and magnetism, and Braid came up with neurohypnology, which was sometimes spelt 'neuryhypnology', and which was derived from hypnos - the Greek word for sleep. Eventually, it was shortened to hypnology.

Less than two weeks after Lafontaine's demonstrations, Braid placed an advert in the *Manchester Guardian* which declared that he would not only reproduce the 'effects exhibited by Monsieur Lafontaine in his lectures here', but would also explain how induced trances 'have no right to be attributed to the influence of animal magnetism'.

The lecture was attended by a crowd of 700 - which included several surgeons, and worthies such as Archibald Prentice, who was the proprietor of the *Manchester Times*. There was loud applause as Braid took the stage, and the crowd was not disappointed because he not only demonstrated hypnotism but also made good on his promise to explain the physiological causes of it.

Braid could have been forgiven for feeling satisfied as he ended the demonstration and began a question and answer session. He would not, though, have felt positive had he known that hypnotism would cause him several problems in the years to come. The first problem, which took the form of Joseph Peel Catlow, manifested immediately during the session of questions. Catlow, who was the cousin of Sir Robert Peel, was a surgeon in Manchester. He claimed he was the first to discover the truth about mesmerism, and that a 'respectable gentleman' and 'two ladies', to whom he had earlier explained his theories, would testify that this was the truth. Braid was not amused and accused Catlow of 'seeking to defraud'. The spat was reported in the *Manchester Times*, which also revealed that Catlow would give his own demonstrations of mesmerism.

Soon after, Braid announced that he would give two other lectures. Meanwhile, the city's papers announced that Lafontaine, who had left the city, was to return, and called for him to be given a 'fair and dispassionate hearing'.

Braid far outstripped Lafontaine in his second and third lectures. He put more subjects in a trance than the Frenchman had, and his technique was speedier. He even offered to put Lafontaine, who attended the last lecture, into a trance - but the Frenchman refused.

Over the following two evenings, Lafontaine gave successful lectures at the Athenaeum and defended the theories of the mesmerists. 'Magnetism', he argued, 'was affected by the communication of a fluid, through the nerves, from the magnetiser to the magnetised'. He also scoffed at the notion that Braid had solved, 'in a few days', a 'mystery which, for more than a century, had occupied the attention, and baffled the powers, of some of the greatest scientific eminence in Europe'.

As Lafontaine made these points he was interrupted by Joseph Peel Catlow. In fact, the interjections were so frequent that the audience became annoyed, and Lafontaine was applauded after he claimed that the doctor was not experienced enough to give lectures on animal magnetism. Catlow, though, was not cowed and retorted that the Frenchman could only mesmerise 'those who were easily bamboozled'.

The *Manchester Guardian* frowned upon his behaviour, and reported that 'a gentleman said he considered Mr Catlow's conduct to be most un-gentlemanly'. This observer, the paper also revealed, believed that Catlow 'deserved to be bundled out of the room'.

During Lafontaine's next lecture, which was also at the Athenaeum, he was regularly interrupted by Catlow and Braid. The *Manchester Guardian* reported that Lafontaine responded by pointing out that he had politely sat through Braid's lectures and had 'made no remarks', and that he 'thought that the present interruptions were quite out of place, and hoped that the same courtesy would be extended to him'. Many in the audience loudly applauded this remark. Not all, though, were averse to Braid's interruptions, and several people called for him to speak. Lafontaine would not allow it and proceeded to give the stage to an ally of his, Dr Cantor, who argued for animal magnetism. After a lengthy speech, Cantor concluded: 'One fact that Mr Braid has shown us, that should not be lost sight of - is that the phenomena of animal magnetism is not 'humbug', but a real phenomena'. This was greeted with calls of 'hear, hear' and loud applause.

As Lafontaine brought the evening to a close, he revealed that he would leave Manchester but would return in July. He then thrilled the audience by promising he would bring subjects with him who were truly clairvoyant. They would, he declared, 'be able to distinguish an object placed in an opaque box, just by bringing their forehead into contact with it'; and the objects, he said, would be supplied 'unseen to the magnetiser or the subject' from the pockets of the audience.

But Lafontaine did not leave the city, for Braid and Catlow had got under his skin, and so he announced he would lecture on December 17th at the Mechanics Institute. This was seen as an attack on Braid, who was lecturing on the same night at the Athenaeum.

Braid began his lecture, which was said to have been 'crowded to excess', by rubbishing Lafontaine's belief in a 'certain fluid'. He then claimed that travelling entertainers should show hypnotism more respect, for it could prove to be highly beneficial to medicine. He illustrated this point with the help of a 62-year old Stockport man, who had been unable to work for thirteen years because of severe attacks of rheumatism. After hypnotic treatment, Braid revealed, the man's ailments disappeared. And then, no doubt to the delight of the audience, the man proved this point by running in a circle for a few minutes.

During the following lecture, Braid revisited the man's case: 'He came to me as a miserable wretch, leaning over his staff; and, in less than a quarter of an hour, by the agency of what I am showing you tonight, he was enabled to stoop, walk, or run, without any feeling of uneasiness'.

The audience applauded this touching story, but Catlow wasn't impressed and asked the subject several searching questions.

Continuing with the lecture, Braid claimed to have successfully treated a woman who suffered from greater incapacitation than the Stockport man. The *Manchester Guardian* detailed her case: 'Mr Braid saw, on Thursday night, a woman who had not stood on her legs for three years . . . (she was) made by such an operation, capable of standing and walking, with no other assistance than merely holding her hand.'

Lafontaine was not to be outdone. He placed an advert in the *Manchester Times* which proclaimed that he was to lecture 'positively for the last time', and on the night he performed his own miracle by restoring the hearing of a girl.

Rather than leaving the city soon after, Lafontaine waited for a full ten days to attend Braid's next demonstration. He was rewarded with an attack on his character, as Braid not only accused him of 'buffoonery' but went as far as to question his honesty. Braid then stressed that his own demonstrations were carried out with the utmost veracity:

My object is to dispel mystery, and elicit truth, in the simplest possible manner; and I pledge my word of honour, as a gentleman, that there shall not be a single attempt at illusion, or delusion, in any experiment I shall adduce to the company who have honoured me with their presence this evening.

The following demonstration was impressive. Braid began by putting his cook into a 'cataleptiform' state, then asked Dr Herbert, who was the Dean of Manchester, and Colonel Wemyss, who was the military commander for the Manchester region, to check her. They confirmed that she was indeed cataleptiform. After puncturing her head, face and hands with pins, Braid called upon John Benjamin Dancer to give her an electric shock. (Dancer, who was a prominent member of the city's scientific community, invented microphotography; developed laboratory apparatus with James Joule; and produced the first photographic image of Manchester - which was a picture from the roof of the Royal Exchange).

After Dancer shocked the cook, Braid stuck snuff and ammonia up her nostrils and she showed no response. He then hypnotised two young girls and had them walking about the stage with their arms extended. Later, one of them waltzed and sang.

After he made further criticisms of Lafontaine, Braid was met with a mixed response. Some clapped, whilst others shouted 'shame'. One man called for Lafontaine to be given a chance to speak, but Braid declined because he had not been offered the same courtesy at the Frenchman's last lecture. Then Catlow had his say, and Dr Edward lacy - a surgeon from Stockport who had been implicated in a resurrection scandal - also interrupted.

Over the following months, Catlow gave several lectures and on one evening he introduced a 'mesmeric and soporific machine'. The *Manchester Guardian* described the device: 'The instrument, which is wound up like a clock . . . made a rattling noise . . . (and incorporated) two brass cups, which cover the patient's ears, and were attached to the side of the instrument by metallic rods'. It was not a great success, and one gentleman of science called it 'useless'. Catlow must have secretly agreed, for the machine was never seen again.

By this point, Lafontaine had left Manchester. The dispute between the city's home-grown mesmerists, though, rumbled on. Then, in March 1842, the *Manchester Times* revealed that Braid was forced to confront 'an unfounded report that had circulated about him, that he had driven a patient mad'. Braid denied this and made it clear that the patient was troubled before he appeared at the surgery, and that hypnotism helped to calm him for a short while.

Despite the denials, rumours that hypnotism could induce madness persisted; and a decade later, the *Manchester Times* revealed that a sixteen-year-old called Margaret repeatedly tried to commit suicide after she was put in a trance. Margaret had worked for Mr Snowden, who owned a public house in Back Piccadilly, and was desperate to track down his wife, who had left him. He suspected that Margaret knew of her whereabouts and employed Samuel Bottomley, whose day job was at a cheese warehouse in Shudehill, to put her in a trance. His attempts were witnessed by several neighbours, who feared the girl was in trouble and intervened. Margaret was said to have acted strangely when she woke, and after several suicide attempts, she was detained in a straightjacket. During the following court case, Bottomley was warned by a magistrate that he would have been held accountable if she had died.

Another worry often voiced in the city concerned the possibility of mesmerism being used to facilitate sexual abuse. Braid addressed these concerns by developing what can only be called a 'strumpet-versus-nice-girl' experiment. The *Manchester Times* gave the details:

> *To contradict the assertions that this agency might be employed for indecent and improper purposes . . .* (Braid) *called in two girls, differently educated, who being outside could not know what were the experiments he was about to perform, and the audience should have the opportunity of judging themselves . . . One was a delicate neatly-dressed girl; the other evidently of coarser habits. They were desired to gaze at an object raised before them, and in a very short time were somnolent.*
>
> *Braid asked the girl we have last described to take off her shoe and stocking, and she stooped down instantly to commence the operation, but was stopped.*
>
> *He then repeated the same request to the other girl, who hesitated, as though unwilling, and when the request was repeated, positively refused.*
>
> *She also refused to remove her handkerchief. Mr Braid remarked that this was just the difference that existed between the girls in a natural state. They had different notions of propriety when awake, and the fact of being hypnotised made not the slightest difference.*

Soon after conducting this groundbreaking experiment, Braid lectured in various northern towns. Whilst in Liverpool, Braid and Lafontaine, who was also lecturing in the town, made a formidable enemy in the form of the Irishman Hugh M'Neile, who was the curate of St. Jude's church.

M'Neile was not your average curate. He was lauded by some, such as Disraeli, as a great orator and as one of the most dynamic characters within the Church of England. Others, though, considered him to be a demagogue and accused him of stirring up anti-Catholic prejudice.

In 1842, to a packed congregation of 1500 souls, M'Neile declared that mankind was living through the 'latter days' and that Christ would soon return to inaugurate his thousand-year reign. This was good news, but the scriptures, he explained, warned that a 'satanic agency would appear amongst men' as the Second Coming drew near. The satanic agency, he declared, was mesmerism. He then launched into a sustained personal attack on Braid and Lafontaine, in which he called them 'necromancers' and 'purveyors of witchcraft'; and he claimed to avoid their demonstrations because he feared he would not have the strength to resist the 'diabolic power' which they dabbled with. Finally, to pre-empt arguments which stressed the benefits of medical mesmerism, he noted that the Bible made it clear that the devil had the power to relieve the possessed of pain. Three weeks later, a transcription of the sermon was published in a pamphlet, and it also appeared in the *Penny Pulpit*, which was a weekly paper.

The attack damaged Lafontaine. His lecture tour of the north failed, and he was reduced to appealing to his followers for funds. He left England soon after and never returned.

Braid was not so badly affected. Unlike Lafontaine, he could argue his case as a man of science and medicine, and in a 12-page pamphlet, *Satanic Agency and Mesmerism*, he stressed that hypnotism was far from an instrument of evil and could be a useful medical technique.

At this point, Braid may have believed his battles were over. M'Neile had not responded to the booklet or launched any further attacks of any significance from the pulpit; Lafontaine was out of the country; and whilst Catlow was still sniping away, he was not a formidable enemy. The calm, though, did not last - for in June 1842, Braid was to do battle with several foes within the British Association of Science, and during the same month, a serious opponent emerged in the form of the Manchester-based surgeon Patrick Gordon Dunn.

The science association was an itinerant institution which held an annual conference. The medical section of the Manchester conference was undersubscribed, so Braid was confident that his paper: *Practical Essay on the Curative Agency of Neuryhypnotism*, would be heard. Yet there was no response after he submitted it, then he was given the run around by the association's secretaries, and finally, it was returned with 'unsuitable' stamped on the envelope. This caused a furore in the city's press, and Braid claimed the paper was rejected because of the jealousy of his rivals in the science association.

Braid decided to read his speech and to give a demonstration of hypnotism at an independent event which he advertised in the papers. He also put up placards at the various events which were held by the science association, but they were quickly torn down by his opponents.

The demonstration was well attended and the *Manchester Times* noted there were many 'eminent individuals' in the crowd, including the founder of the science association, Sir David Brewster, and the Marquis Francesco Maria Sauli, who was the Envoy Extraordinary and Minister Plenipotentiary for His Majesty the King of Sardinia.

Catlow constantly interrupted as Braid spoke and was warned he would be thrown out if he continued. Despite this, the lecture was well received: loud applause greeted Braid as he took the stage; shouts of 'shame' met his revelation that his placards had been torn down, and the Manchester papers gave him positive reviews. A few days later, though, a certain Patrick Gordon Dunn entered the fray, and Braid realised that he had another battle on his hands.

Dunn was early Victorian Manchester's version of James Randi. Not only did he delight in debunking the likes of touring clairvoyants, but he also took on the city's phrenologists and mesmerists; and like Braid and Catlow, he annoyed audiences by persistently interrupting demonstrations and lectures.

Dunn intended for his first attack on Braid to be delivered at the science conference, but the organisers refused to give him a platform. Consequently, he took the stage at a colleague's lecture and claimed that Braid had not cured any patients through hypnotism and had misrepresented the cases.

As he worked up a head of steam, Braid arrived at the venue. Dunn, though, was unconcerned: he reiterated that Braid's patients had not been cured, and Catlow piped up with a 'hear'. Dunn then went as far as to state: 'Remember this is a serious matter - it is a charge before a public audience of what I call deceit'.

Braid learnt of Dunn's next move when he saw the following advert in the *Manchester Guardian*:

> NEUROHYPNOLOGY UNMASKED: *an exposure of the claims and cures of Mr Braid, surgeon in* TWO LECTURES *to be Delivered* TONIGHT *and* TOMORROW NIGHT, *the 20th and 21st July, at the Mechanics Institute, Cooper Street, by P. G. Dunn, surgeon.*

There are no records of the lectures, but what did survive was Dunn's advert in the *Guardian*, in which it was claimed that the audience was entirely satisfied that Braid's claims to have successfully treated patients with hypnotism were false. In another advert, Dunn accused Braid of 'truly quackish' behaviour.

Braid's response, which was published in both the *Manchester Times* and *Guardian*, revealed that Dunn's attacks might have been motivated by something other than a debunker's disgust with pseudo-science. After Dunn settled in Manchester, claimed Braid:

> *He got introduced to me as a Glasgow surgeon, who was anxious to see some of my operations. After professing to leave my house he went into my waiting-room and interfered with my patients, in such a manner as to induce my servant to come and inform me of it, that I might instruct him how to act. I, of course, desired him to turn Mr Dunn out, and never to allow him again to enter my premises.*

Two weeks later, the Braid camp further dented Dunn's debunker credentials with an article by Captain Brown which was published in a local paper: 'It is not a little amusing', he began, 'that Dr Dunn, at a lecture which he himself gave at Stockport, in January last, on Neurohypnology, in which he lauded Mr Braid, and also illustrated his lecture by his theory, should now turn around and denounce both'.

This was true: Dunn *had* praised Braid and hypnotism - which begs the question: what caused him to change his mind? The answer may be that he became wary after he hypnotised a man and struggled to wake him. Braid certainly seemed to think this was the case.

For whichever reason, Dunn reinvented himself as the city's chief sceptic and was soon busy interrupting displays of clairvoyance and mesmerism. In 1843, he attended a lecture by Mr Hewes, who worked with a magnetic clairvoyant from Greenwich known only as 'Jack'. The lecture hall was packed and included 'medical men known in scientific circles in the city', most notably Professor Williamson. The professor supervised as Jack's eyes were covered with court plaster and a silk scarf. But Dunn was not satisfied and protested that Jack's eyes quivered as they were covered with plaster, making it possible for him to see. The crowd, though, didn't listen and many lined up before Jack to test his supernatural abilities. They held up watches, keys, and even 'uncommon articles,' and he correctly identified each object. 'Few', wrote one observer, 'left the hall unconvinced of the reality of clairvoyance'.

Dunn, of course, was not convinced, and he soon announced that he would replicate Jack's act at the Athenaeum. When the night came, the hall was full and many medical men attended. Jack and Mr Hewes were also present.

Dunn began by revealing the tricks and deceptions used by mesmerists. His eyes were plastered and covered with a scarf and he identified every item held before him. He rounded off the evening by demonstrating how his quivering eyeballs stopped the plaster from being effective, and he explained that the scarf was easy to see through.

Jack was, as William Smith of Mumps stated in a letter to a local paper, 'at once revealed to be an imposter'. These kind of exposures, Smith continued, 'are sufficient to make thoughtful men pause before they conclude the phenomena witnessed at these séances, through the agency of 'mediums', are of supernatural origin'.

Yet thoughtful men continued to be taken in by mesmeric clairvoyants. One such character, as already noted, was the Bolton doctor Joseph W. Haddock, who aspired to establish a 'sanative institution' in Manchester which would promote healing through mesmerism. Haddock believed his domestic servant, known only as Emma L, showed amazing powers whilst in a trance.

The Amazing Emma L

His adventure with Emma began when she revealed, after overhearing him discussing mesmerism, that she had been put into a trance by a cousin who gave her a dose of ether.

Soon after, Haddock acquired some of the gas and began putting her under. He also took Emma to Manchester to be examined by William Bally, who was a Swiss-born sculptor and a renowned phrenologist. At this point, phrenology, which posited that an individual's moral character could be discerned by the shape of their skull, was associated with mesmerism. In fact, the two pursuits merged and became known as 'phreno-magnetism' - which was promoted in Manchester by worthies such as the physician Daniel Noble, and George Falkner, who edited *Bradshaw's Manchester Journal*, which was devoted to 'art, science and literature'. William Bally, though, was the city's main phrenologist, and was famous for his 'Phrenological Gallery of Casts' on King St, which the *Manchester Guardian* claimed trumped the city's 'pantomimes and panoramas, wild beasts and circus troops, conjurors and tumblers'. It is easy to see why the paper was impressed, for Bally had two thousand models of skulls on show, including those of famous writers and scientists, and, according to the writer Benjamin Love, those of 'several idiots' and murderers. After he examined Emma's skull, Bally declared it was 'well-formed', which must have been a relief for her.

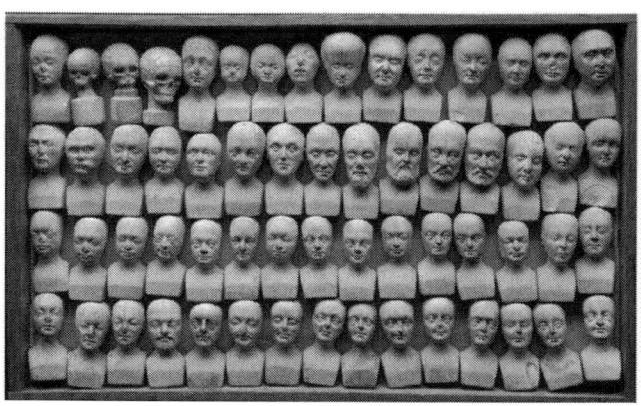

A selection of M. Bally's model skulls

Over the following weeks, Haddock continued his ether experiments with Emma, each time lowering the dose. Finally, she entered trances without taking the gas, and Haddock concluded she was sensitive to the magnetic force that flowed out of him. Emma seemed to confirm this by explaining that when she was mesmerised, she felt controlled by 'cords' which were 'wound round' her. This appealed to Haddock. He liked the idea of pulling the cords and wrote about 'sensitive subjects' being 'under the control of the operator'. He also revealed that Emma did most of the things that were suggested to her.

This all sounds, of course, drearily familiar. It sounds like just another case of a Victorian male dominating and manipulating a young female employee. But further examination of the relationship between Emma and Haddock leads to the question: who was manipulating who?

One incident early in their mesmeric adventure indicates

it was Emma who was pulling the cords. Haddock had been asked by a neighbour, who lived 'several doors away', to put him in a trance. After repeated attempts, the man remained conscious and Haddock admitted defeat. When he returned home, though, he found that Emma was comatose. No doubt she slipped into the 'trance' when she heard the door open, but Haddock didn't consider this and believed the force he directed towards his neighbour had journeyed down the street and found her.

During the following months, Haddock was led to believe that Emma possessed certain powers when she was in a trance. When he gave her a book containing an illustration, she 'placed it open over her forehead and upper part of the cranium, without the least attempt to look at it in the ordinary way', and immediately described the picture.

He also discovered that Emma had the power to diagnose illness - for she professed to see the condition of internal organs and to see blood as it circulated. Amongst those who employed her for her medical skills, revealed Haddock, 'was a highly respectable gentleman residing at, and well known in, Manchester'. The gentleman was worried about his daughter, who was seriously ill and seemed to be slipping into insanity. When he first visited Haddock, Emma was in a trance, and so he left her with 'a few pencil marks' which were made by his daughter. 'These scant marks', wrote Haddock, allowed Emma to 'describe accurately the external symptoms, and also the perception of the internal condition of the brain'.

The cure, Emma said, was to be found in a 'little bottle' for sale in a Manchester shop with a bust in its window. Initially, Haddock was puzzled, but he soon concluded that she meant Mr Turner's homoeopathic chemists, in Piccadilly. It was a shop which displayed a plaster bust of Hahnemann, the founder of homoeopathy.

The respectable Manchester gentleman bought a selection of little bottles, Emma licked the outside of them and decided that one labelled 'Ipecacuanha' contained the cure. After the girl took the 'medication', and after Haddock and Emma mesmerised her several times, she was said to be cured. 'Two years have now nearly elapsed', wrote Haddock, 'and the lady remains well'.

By early 1848, Emma and Haddock were giving public demonstrations similar to those Mr Hewes and Jack held at the Athenaeum five years earlier. Like Jack, Emma donned a blindfold and identified all the objects placed before her. She struggled, though, when the objects were placed in a box before being brought to her. Her way out of these situations was to give an obtuse and baffling description, which was often interpreted as applying to the contents of the box after it had been opened.

Another way of avoiding the box-test was for Emma to feign annoyance and exhaustion. This led Haddock to babble about clairvoyance causing fatigue because it 'powerfully affected the nervous system'. He also used an age-old excuse when he blamed her failures on the negative vibes which were caused by sceptics in the crowd.

Emma, then, was just as much a charlatan as Jack had been. Yet it is possible to sympathise with her, or at least to understand her motives: for being a clairvoyant was far more interesting than being a charlady. As a mysterious, magnetic seer, Emma not only became a local celebrity but was also mentioned in the national press; and she would have made much more money from her public appearances than she did as a domestic servant.

She may also have gained satisfaction from fooling Haddock: for he underestimated her by considering her to be too illiterate, unintelligent, and naive to be able to fake the revelations she made whilst in a trance. Others had an even dimmer view of her. Harriet Martineau, the famous writer and social commentator, described her as 'vulgar and extremely ignorant'. She also claimed Emma was 'anything but handsome', which was a little rich because Martineau was no oil painting - if Richard Evans' oil painting of her is anything to go by.

The Search for the Franklin Expedition

As Emma's profile grew, she was sought out by many people looking for missing relatives. They presented her with letters and personal items - anything that could create a 'medium of connection' - and Emma, Haddock claimed, 'frequently found people in distant parts of the globe'. One such case, which seems to have been a test rather than an attempt to find a missing person, involved 'some ladies from Manchester' who presented her with a sample of handwriting from a clergyman based in Archangel in Russia. After reading the writing, Emma was said to have described the man's 'personal appearance and little personalities', and to have accurately accounted for 'the climate and season' of Archangel.

Soon after, she became involved in a case which was to earn her, as James Braid put it, 'no ordinary degree of notoriety'. It began when Captain Alexander Maconochie contacted Haddock. Maconochie probably read about Emma in the *Times* - which printed a story about her under the headline: *An Interesting Case of Clairvoyance* - and wondered if she might be able to locate his friend, Sir John Franklin, who was missing in the Canadian Arctic.

Franklin had led a well-prepared expedition of two ships, the HMS Erebus and Terror, which were stocked with enough provisions to last three years and crewed by a total of 128 men. The aim was to fully chart the North West Passage and to open a fresh route to Asia.

The expedition left London in 1845 and was last seen by the crew of a whaling ship in Baffin Bay in late July. Fourteen years later, a note was found by a sledge team on King William Island, which revealed that the ships became ice-bound in September '46 and that Franklin died the following year. None of the crew survived. The wreck of the Erebus was finally found on 7th September 2014.

Disquiet over the expedition began after nothing was heard

from the explorers for two years. The year later, panic set in the when it was realised that the provisions would soon be exhausted. Search parties were sent and several outlandish schemes were put into action: Arctic foxes were let go with the coordinates of the rescue teams stitched into their collars; balloons bearing messages were released; Inuit children were given stuffed toys with messages on them, which it was hoped would be seen by members of the expedition; and in 1849, Emma and other mesmeric clairvoyants were urged to make contact with Franklin and his crew.

Captain Maconochie sent Emma a sample of Franklin's handwriting and a lock of his hair; and Haddock, who presumed the crew perished, was surprised when she declared the explorer was alive. 'She spoke of the snow and ice', he wrote, 'and said that many with him were dead, but that he expected to get away in about nine months, but that she could not say whether he would be able to do so, but that it appeared to her he would get home again'.

When Emma alleged to have visited Franklin, in some disembodied way, at the North Pole, it caused a media sensation and prompted Maconochie to call on her. He was amazed when he witnessed her slip into a trance and talk to the explorer. Soon after, a report on Emma and her visions was sent to the Admiralty, and samples of handwriting from other crew members were given to her. Franklin's widow was also given a full report.

For James Braid such visions were worthless. They were, he wrote, 'merely dreams, spoken and acted out, and directed and modified by the suggestions of those present'.

The Coming Storm

As Emma made her revelations, the city's chief debunker, Patrick Gordon Dunn, died at the age of 36. His death spared him from witnessing the arrival in Manchester of many spiritualists, as well as faith healers, charlatans, and myriad other chancers.

An early sign of this coming storm was the craze for table-turning. This began in the mid-1840s, and James Braid was so miffed by tales of mysteriously moving furniture that he sent a letter to the Manchester Courier in which he debunked reports of a Parisian girl who was said to move tables and chairs, as well as a heavy chest and 'two strong-men', just by lightly touching them.

A couple of years later, the activity crossed the Atlantic, and in 1853 came what Brandon Hodges, the American spiritualist historian, called 'the summer of the table'. It was a summer when both the USA and Europe were consumed by the phenomena.

In April '53, Braid wrote an article for the *Manchester Times* in which he debunked 'Mysterious Table Turning', and on June 2nd he was part of a public investigation into the matter held at the Athenaeum. Afterwards, he concluded that the tables were moved by the 'ideomotor effect', which meant that those sat at the tables produced unconscious or reflexive motions which shifted the object.

This theory, which Braid took from his friend, the physician William Benjamin Carpenter, who lectured in Manchester in 1852, was completely rational. During the coming decades, though, many in Manchester were not interested in the ideo-motor effect, for they were convinced the tables were moved by spirits.

CHAPTER SEVEN

Ghosts in the Machines

> Looping around in one more curve, the roar of the engines steadily increasing, the plane set a course across open country. By now, we should have been able to make out the sprawling mass of Manchester, yet one could see nothing but a faint glimmer, as if from a fire almost suffocated in ash. A blanket of fog that had risen out of the marshy plains that reached as far as the Irish Sea had covered the city, a city spread across a thousand square kilometres, built of countless bricks and inhabited by millions of souls, dead and alive. W G Sebald, *The Emigrants*

By the 1890s, Manchester had become a hotbed of spiritualism. It was home to a secret society, the Angelic Order of Light, which claimed to commune with spirits from earth and other planets; it was the base for the most successful spiritualist newspaper in the country, and it attracted mediums from far and wide. It was such a draw that several American mediums either stayed for a while or settled permanently. One visitor was the president of the American National Spiritualists Association: Harrison D. Barrett.

After inspecting the scene in 1896, he declared: 'The orbit of British Spiritualism, to use an astronomical simile, may be described as an ellipse, of which London and Manchester are the foci'.

The spiritualist age began in March 1848, after Margaret and Kate Fox claimed to have communicated with the dead in Hydesville, New York. In their wooden house, which was reputed to be haunted, a spirit they called 'Mr Splitfoot' rapped on the walls in response to their questions. After the girls were taken to Rochester, the rapping sounds followed and the phenomena began to attract attention. The Quakers and the Shakers were among the earliest to take notice. One Shaker declared that the rapping noises were 'the prelude to extensive manifestations of different kinds'.

In 1852, when an American medium called Mrs Hayden brought the phenomena to England, she was given a frosty reception by the press. But after she won over several eminent figures, including Robert Owen, the philanthropist mill owner who began his career in Manchester, the country became more receptive. By 1853, a dedicated spiritualist church had been opened in Keighley by David Richmond, who had spent time as a Shaker in America; and during the following decades, the movement grew steadily.

Initially, though, Manchester was underwhelmed by the phenomena. There was a sense that spiritualism offered nothing new. John Clowes' congregation had been visited by spirits at the beginning of the century; and over a decade before the Fox sisters appeared, some anonymous Swedenborgian published a pamphlet in Manchester with a very spiritualist-sounding title: *Letters to a Friend in reply to Observations respecting the possibility of Man having Intercourse with Angels and Spirits*. And of course, there had been James Johnston, who conversed with the dead for decades. His spiritualist credentials were so strong that he gained popularity with New York mediums and their followers, twenty six-years after his death. The revival began after the manuscript of his *Diaries Spiritual and Earthly* was taken to America by John Martin, who knew Johnston in Manchester. It became a word-of-mouth success, and one female medium even claimed to channel his spirit. Finally, in

1866, it was published and Johnston posthumously achieved his dream of becoming a recognised prophet.

Emma L, the mesmeric clairvoyant who 'saw' the fate of the Franklin expedition, prefigured spiritualism even more than Johnston. She introduced the concept of the 'spirit guide', although she didn't refer to her contact as that; and like many of the mediums who followed her, she manipulated people by claiming to be in touch with their relatives. She certainly manipulated Joseph W. Haddock when she claimed that her guide, known as the 'Lady', was one of his ancestors. Furthermore, in the summer of 1848, when in a trance witnessed by 'several highly respectable gentlemen from Manchester', she adumbrated the mediums of the following decades by giving a detailed description of the 'other side'.

Emma also took readings from immaterial objects, such as letters. Haddock merely referred to this process as 'creating a medium of connection', but in the years to come, as the practice became a favourite of the spiritualists, it acquired the grand title: 'Pyschometry'; and characters such as Wilfred Rook of Levenshulme, and Mrs Hyde of Ardwick, made a living by clutching a dead person's scarf, hat, or other possession, and relaying messages from the spirits.

Emma faded from view in the 1850s, and until the mid-1860s spiritualism in Manchester remained a low-key, grass-roots affair. There were no formal organisations to join, and no professional mediums were based in the city. Only a handful of professionals were found in the entire country, and most, such as Mrs Mary Marshall, were in London.

Several Mancunians made the trip to sit with Mrs Marshall - the most notable was a wealthy Didsbury businessman called Charles Blackburn. He was one of the most illustrious spiritualists in the country, but as the writer Trevor Hall noted: 'he has been forgotten in his native city of Manchester'. What we do know is that he was a widower; that he had a daughter called Eliza who was slowly going mad; and that two of his children had died.

Perhaps because of his losses, Blackburn immersed himself in spiritualism. He financed several mediums; he invested in the *Spir-*

itualist newspaper; and Parkfield, his 'beautiful estate' in Didsbury, became a hub for the movement. According to eminent spiritualist Emma Hardinge Britten, almost all mediums of repute visited the house.

At Mrs Marshall's house, Blackburn was treated to the spectacle of, as one report had it, 'SPIRITS SPEAKING AUDIBLY AND FLUIDLY'. The said spirits were Katie King and her father John - believed to have been a Welsh pirate who lived during the 1600s. The pair grew popular during the following decades and were channelled by many mediums.

A less illustrious Mancunian than Blackburn who also visited Mrs Marshall was Mr J. Brown. In 1863, he witnessed a table 'tilt and oscillate until it became absolutely turbulent', and was informed by Marshall that his deceased mother and sister had appeared before him. Brown, who claimed to have 'considerable experience in investigating the phenomena of Mesmerism and Clairvoyance', was impressed by the séance. He felt the activity at Mrs Marshall's was 'but the dawning of further revelations from the spirit world'.

A Mancunian known only as 'T. B.', who attended a Marshall séance in 1862 with a married couple, claimed to have carried out stringent checks on the medium and her environment. The checks, though, did not stop the strange occurrences: the table turned and shook, and the female member of the party was 'violently lifted up in her chair and shaken as if by a shock of electricity'.

The group also received messages from the dead. T. B.'s friend heard from his late brother, whilst T. B. was contacted by his deceased son. 'It was strange', he wrote, 'that any one should know I had a son dead. Stranger still that his name was given, and yet more strange that the time of his death and the Christian and middle name of his mother should be given'.

As well as these successes, Marshall also gave out incorrect information, and after the séance, T. B. claimed he was 'not yet a spiritualist'.

Other Mancunians sat with another professional medium, Mr

Wallace, who began visiting the city in the late 1850s. Mostly, though, the Manchester scene consisted of 'private circles' of amateur mediums and enthusiasts. T. B., who was a veteran of such circles, informed the *Spiritualist* that his group initially struggled to get results, but then witnessed the 'convulsive heavings and tossings of a large square table, which were not much inferior in power to those seen at Mrs Marshalls'. T. B. also visited a circle to the south of the city at Alderley, which was centred around a 'well-to-do respectable farmer' called Mr Mayer. Although tables were moved, and the spirits revealed the 'personal histories of those present', Mayer claimed not to be a spiritualist and remained sceptical about the phenomena.

One of the most high-profile spiritualists in Manchester during this period was Edward Brotherton, who was a wealthy cotton merchant and educational campaigner. He was also the author of a pamphlet: *Spiritualism, Swedenborg, and the New Church*, and under the nom de plume 'Libra' he penned articles for the *Spiritualist* - most notably about the 'Spheres', where the spirits were said to dwell. Brotherton was also renowned for investigating the haunting of the Joller family, which occurred in Lucerne in the early 1860s. This was a particularly gothic affair involving knocking sounds; 'white formless shapes'; apparitions of small children; 'profoundly disturbing sobs'; the appearance of strange lights consisting of 'innumerable blue flames'; and much poltergeist phenomena.

Brotherton died just as spiritualism in Manchester was gaining momentum. An early sign of the movement's progress was the visit in autumn 1864 of the Davenport Brothers. As youngsters, William and Ira Davenport took their lead from the Fox sisters and produced knocking noises and table raps, but soon more impressive phenomena began to manifest around them: cutlery moved, voices were heard, and Ira flew through the air. The brothers were also said to have teleported sixty miles to the house of a relative, although sceptics claimed they simply travelled through the night.

The Davenport Brothers and the 'Box Trick'.

Soon after, they came to the attention of 'Dr' Jesse Babcock Ferguson: a Christian preacher who was sacked by the Nashville Church of Christ because of his spiritualist shenanigans. (The church later 'burned down in suspicious circumstances'). With Ferguson acting as a compère, the Davenports toured America in a show built around the 'Box Trick'. This involved the brothers being bound up, and hung upside down in a curtained box which contained musical instruments. After the curtains were closed, violins and trumpets were heard, which Ferguson attributed to the spirits, and when the curtains were opened the brothers were still bound and in their original positions.

Thirteen years later, under the title: AN UNEXPECTED VISITOR: A DEVIL, the *Spiritualist Magazine* printed a bizarre account of the Davenport's stay in Manchester. The piece was written by Samuel Guppy, who was part of a clique of mediums which included Frank Herne, who was backed by Charles Blackburn.

Guppy was friendly with the Davenports and was part of their entourage when they performed in Manchester. On one occasion, when they were due to leave their base in the city to do a show in Nottingham, Ira Davenport pulled out of the trip and Guppy kept him company. They spent some time at a restaurant, then enjoyed a few games of billiards, and eventually ended up at a photographers studio, where Ira made comical poses.

After collecting the photos, which had not yet hardened, the pair headed back to the hotel to conduct a spirit writing experiment. According to Guppy, all hell broke loose before they had a chance to begin: a book, a waistcoat, and a dress coat were flung about; a tumbler of water was pitched at them; a tea tray scooted across a table; a cigar box was smashed, and the 'nameless' content of a chamber pot was spilt across the floor.

When they asked the name of the spirit, it rapped out the reply: D-e-v-i-l; and when asked what it wanted, it replied: W-h-i-s-k-e-y. And whiskey, claimed Guppy, is what it was given. After Ira poured a shot and put it under the table, the drink disappeared. Furthermore, the photograph, which had been left to dry, was 'completely erased, the black varnish and face having been scraped off'.

The article was printed, claimed the editor of the magazine, to 'stay the foolish and unlearned thinkings of many who dislike the belief in personal devils - they approve of evil, mischieving spirits, but dislike that the letter 'd' be placed on the left hand side of evil'.

The Debunkers

The popularity of the Davenports and their ilk led to the emergence of various characters, such as stage magicians, conjurors, and even ex-mediums, who toured the country reproducing and the Box Trick and the various manifestations seen at séances.

In Manchester, the actor Henry Irving decided to form such an act for a brief run of shows. Irving, who found success playing Hamlet, was one of the first in England to see the Davenports perform: for he was at the London home of Dion Boucicault - who was an actor and dramatist - when they put on a private performance of the Box Trick. The act astonished Boucicault, but less impressed were the staff of a variety paper, the *Era*, who offered a prize of £100 to anybody who could reproduce the act.

Boucicault was outraged by this and fired off a letter to the paper in which he defended the brothers. Irving, though, was certainly not outraged and decided to win the money.

Henry Irving as Shylock

He later claimed that his religious beliefs - he was a practising Methodist - led him to 'destroy these universal spirit dealers'. But it was rumoured that he really wanted to gain revenge on Boucicault, who had been less than complimentary about his theatre company.

Yet another motive was attributed to Irving by Harry Houdini, who covered the affair in his 1924 book *Magician Among the Spirits*. Houdini was told by Ira Davenport that Irving put on the show because the brother's act lured away the actor's audience, leaving him with 'reduced receipts at the box office'.

Irving's show took place at the Athenaeum, before an audience of around 500, which the *Spiritualist* claimed consisted of 'Manchester tradesmen and merchants'. The brothers were played by two actors, Mr Maccabe and Mr Day, and Irving was said to have given a 'perfect imitation' of Ferguson.

Maccabe and Day were tied up by two members of the audience, as Mr Ogden, who was the chairman of the Athenaeum, looked on. The crowd was said to have been 'delighted' by the recreation of the Box Trick, and the *Manchester Guardian* requested a replay so that 'a large audience has the opportunity of enjoying such a treat'. Irving and company obliged a week later at the Free Trade Hall - and the audience, 'which included some of Manchester's most respected citizens', was once again delighted.

Irving and his colleagues were not Manchester's first debunkers: as noted, Dr Dunn targeted clairvoyants during the heyday of the mesmerists. Present in the town before Dunn, though, and more high profile than him, was the Scotsman John Henry Anderson, who was a legendary stage magician known as the Great Wizard of the North.

Anderson, who was said to have been the first magician to pull a rabbit from a hat, lived in Manchester during the 1840s and ran the Theatre Royal on Fountain Street. According to the *Manchester Courier*, he was popular in the town because of 'the extraordinary character of his grand 'soirees mysterieuses'', which illustrated 'the fallacy of magic, demonology, witchcraft, and necromancy'. During the following decades, with his daughter playing the role of a medium called 'Mademoiselle de la Cour', he debunked the spiritualists, especially the Davenport Brothers.

Other acts which passed through Manchester, reproducing supposedly supernatural feats, included Monsieur and Madame Robin. Their clairvoyance display, which they admitted was 'nothing beyond an ingenious trick', was so good that the *Manchester Times* claimed they would have been denounced as witches in previous ages.

Another high profile debunker, Herr Dobbler, along with his 'clever assistant' Peter Wernolf, appeared at the Free Trade Hall and the Mechanics Institute in the 1870s. Once again, the tricks of the Davenport Brothers were reproduced. Wernolf was tied up and placed inside a curtained box, and Dobbler sat amongst the audience to prove he was not meddling behind the scenes. A few minutes later, the hall was darkened and the audience witnessed the ghostly sight of a tambourine, which was smeared in phosphorous, moving behind the curtain. They also heard it jingle in what was said to be a 'desultory manner'.

In 1877, Mr Lees, who appeared at Hulme Town Hall, revealed to the audience that he spent four years as a medium and would demonstrate that spiritualism was predicated on 'trickery and deception'. There followed a variation on the Davenport's act, as well as a demonstration of table-turning and spirit rapping, and also a trick called the 'Spirit Bottle', which involved the answers to questions asked by audience members being found on a piece of paper sealed in a bottle.

Also in 1877, 'Monsieur Cagliostro', a character who paid homage to the eighteenth-century Italian mystic Count Alessandro di Cagliostro, appeared at the Free Trade Hall. The best part of his act was said to be the 'Mysterious Séance', which included a dancing skeleton.

During the 1880s, performers continued to reproduce the Davenport's routines. One such character was Irving Bishop, who was said by the *Manchester Times* to have 'pleasing manners, a fluent tongue, and the gift of humour'. As well as revealing the Davenport's secrets, he offered £91 000 to any spiritualist present at the Free Trade Hall who could produce phenomena which bamboozled him.

The most accomplished of the Davenport debunkers was John Nevil Maskelyne. He first saw the brothers in Cheltenham in 1865, and was so unimpressed by the Box Trick that he promised the audience he would reproduce it - which he did at a later date. Maskelyne enjoyed a successful career as a magician but never lost his desire to debunk, and in 1914 he founded the Occult Committee, which aimed to expose those who claimed to have supernatural powers. He also appeared at the Free Trade Hall, along with his partner George Cooke, in a show that included a sketch called Mrs Daffodil Downey's Séance.

Maskelyne's son, Nevil, later joined The Order of the Magi, a Manchester society of magicians which referenced the ancient Zoroastrian priests. The group grew from the informal Sunday evening meetings, known as 'Whiteley's Varieties', which were held at the Medlock Street house of the illusionist Harry Whiteley, and which welcomed touring magicians.

Business as Usual

Despite the success of debunkers such as Henry Irving, mediums continued to emerge in Manchester during the 1860s. There was Mr W. Hesketh, who was a trance speaker and clairvoyant; and Miss Barlow, who relayed messages from the dead through automatic writing, and also delivered improvised poetry whilst in a trance. Her new-found healing skills enabled her to alleviate any suffering caused by her verses. A few years later, Mr John Taylor discovered that 'miracles' occurred in his presence. Tables were said to: 'disobey the laws of gravitation when he placed his hands on them', and also to move when he didn't touch them. Even the weight of four gentlemen would not hold the tables still. Other characters from this era included Mr Jackson, who was a former policeman known for channelling the spirit of George Fox; and Miss Alston, who channelled spirits which spoke in broad dialects. Alston travelled to a London conference in 1867 to deliver a speech on *Spirit Guidance and cases of Providential Intercession*, and one southern gentleman could not believe that a young girl from the north could be so eloquent, and concluded, in an article for a periodical called *Human Nature*, that she must have been educated and guided by the spirits.

The most significant activist of this period was Mr R. Fitton, whose work laid the foundation for the Spiritualist Association of Manchester. Within its first six months, the association had promoted sixty circle meetings, and in 1869 it organised a conference which was attended by 250 people.

The first president of the association was John Page Hopps, a clergyman from Dukinfield who wrote articles under the name *Truthseeker*. One of his longer works, *Six Months Experience at home of Spirit-Communion*, described the usual table-turning antics and included transcripts of conversations with a spirit called 'Melly'. It was an uninspiring effort, but more influential was his 1868 monthly: *Daybreak*, which was marketed as: *A Journal of Facts and Thoughts in Relation to Spirit Communion*. After ten issues it was taken over by James Burns, a prominent spiritualist often found in

Manchester, who changed its name to *Medium and Daybreak* and converted it to a weekly circulation.

The initial success of *Daybreak* - demand was so high that a second edition of the first issue was printed - illustrates that spiritualism in Manchester, and indeed England, was in rude health at the end of the 1860s. During the following decade, the scene continued to grow; and for two of Manchester's most prominent spiritualist figures - Charles Blackburn and William Oxley - the 1870s delivered astounding manifestations. But the decade also dealt them severe blows, which must have led them to wonder if spiritualism was a sham.

William Oxley

The Angelic Order of Light

William Oxley, who was a wealthy factory-owner and a Liberal politician, fathered eleven children. One of his sons drowned in a river, and another, referred to by the family as 'the one who is not', disappeared. 'He was our third living son', Oxley wrote in 1885, 'a smart youth, a good French scholar, and a volunteer; but one fine autumn evening twelve years ago, while sitting at my front parlour window, I saw him take a book under his arm and go out, as I thought for an evening walk. We have never been able to get the slightest trace of him from that day to this'.

It would have been understandable if Oxley embraced spiritualism because of the loss of his sons, but this was not the case: for he had been a Swedenborgian, and believed in spirits long before his losses. After he converted to spiritualism, his Methodist father, who already disapproved of his son's allegiance to Swedenborg, was disappointed again and declared that: 'Spiritualism was the manifestation of the Wicked One, come to deceive the nations of the earth'. Even some of Oxley's old Swedenborgian pals were not impressed with his new faith, for they considered table rapping, levitations, and all the other antics, to be the work of 'disorderly spirits'.

One of Oxley's first acts as a spiritualist was to join a secret circle called the Angelic Order of Light, which has been referred to as both the Manchester Circle and the Oxley Circle. According to a few researchers, the Angelic Order was not his only secretive order - William Schroder, the author of *A Rosicrucian Notebook*, claimed that Oxley created the Society of the White Cross in Manchester during the early 1850s. It was said to have been an offshoot of an American group, and was thought to have focused on the 'sexual aspect of eternal affinities'. There was, though, no such group in the city during this period - although a society of that name was formed in London during the 1870s, and at least one medium with firm Manchester connections was a member. It is possible, of course, that Oxley also joined during this time, although details of his involvement are not available.

In contrast, his involvement with the Angelic Order of Light was well documented. As Oxley explained, the transcripts of the order's séances, which were called the *Angelic Revelations*, were 'printed for libraries, Masonic Societies, and for those who can appreciate the esoteric and spiritual philosophy therein'.

The cover illustration of the *Angelic Revelations* was said to have been produced by a spirit which was channelled by the Scottish medium David Duguid. The medium had asked Oxley to insert a blank piece of paper into an envelope and to hold it over a fire. When the envelope was opened a completed drawing was found. (Duguid was finally exposed in Manchester in 1905: at the age of

73, and after 2000 séances, he was caught passing off his paintings as the work of the spirits).

Despite the availability of its literature, the Angelic Order of Light retained an air of secrecy and refused to reveal the identities of its members. All that was known of them came from the eminent medium Emma Hardinge Britten, who revealed they were both 'ladies and gentlemen'; and that the chief medium, Mrs Lightfoot, was a non-professional 'lady in private life'.

Emma also noted that the séances 'were only participated in by such persons as the controlling intelligences elected to receive', and claimed that the 'favoured individuals were named by the presiding 'angels' according to the qualities of mind that distinguished them'. Thus the sitters were known by names such as 'Truth'.

Oxley described his first séance with the group:

The meeting was conducted outwardly upon the old evangelical lines, being opened by singing, prayer and the reading of the Word; after which the medium, who was a youngish lady of fine and delicate build, and evidently of a very refined nature, was entranced and the spiritual sphere which surrounded her gave a charm and power that I had never witnessed in the churches I had been involved with.

At one of the early meetings, Oxley was startled when the delicate medium channelled a masculine spirit. 'A deep rolling Scottish bass voice' issued from her, and Oxley felt she would not have been able to speak this way in her 'ordinary state'. The spirit identified himself as James Guthrie and told the circle of 'many incidents of his life', such as how he had been put on trial and then convicted and executed. None of the sitters had heard of Guthrie and so the spirit implored Oxley to check the facts: 'You are going to my native country', it said, 'and you shall prove the truth of every word I have uttered; give yourself no trouble, for the information will come in a way that will both surprise and convince you'.

'Suffice to say', wrote Oxley, 'it did come by ways and means that would take too long to detail, but I found every word he had told was true'. Guthrie, it transpired, had been a prominent protestant who was martyred in Edinburgh in 1661.

The spirits which contacted the circle were not limited to historical figures. Some of them claimed to be from other worlds, which reflected the interests of one of the sitters - who was said to 'clairvoyantly see objects and scenery not of this earth'.

The idea of other populated worlds was not original. Over a century before, Swedenborg claimed that God granted him the pleasure of speaking to humans who lived on other planets, including the moon. As well as describing their houses and livestock, he revealed that Lunarians carried air within their bodies because 'the moon is not surrounded with an atmosphere of the same kind as that of other earths'. The moon dwellers were also said to talk loudly, and 'from the abdomen'.

John Clowes reflected this preoccupation with extraterrestrials when he gave one of his translations of Swedenborg's work the following subtitle: *'Concerning the Earth's in Our Solar System, Which Are Called Planets; and Concerning the Earths in the Starry Heavens, together with an Account of Their Inhabitants, and also the Spirits and Angels There; From What Hath Been Seen and Heard'.*

Emma L. also professed to have seen the inhabitants of the moon in the late 1840s. She claimed they spoke from their bowels, and that they had large heads, vertical mouths, and were dwarf-like.

Other cosmic visionaries from the Manchester area included Daniel Newton - an apprentice grocer who spoke of 'visions of another world' in the 1780s; and Edward Gallagher, the city's foremost psychic healer, who claimed to 'visit other earths, see and converse with their inhabitants, and examine freely their mode of life and their mental and spiritual conditions'.

The Angelic Order of Light enjoyed an impressive scope of interplanetary contacts: cosmic entities called Orissa, Orissis, and Issis got in touch; as did Cenes, from the planet Cenes, who claimed not to be a 'departed spirit' and stressed that he had never visited Earth. The Queen of Egypt, who confused matters by being ambivalent about whether she had been an Egyptian Queen, revealed she had 'travelled throughout the mighty universe'. 'Forerunner' then popped by to inform the sitters that 'the universe has myriad forms of life'.

Other visitors had names that reflected the proto-new age ethos of the scene, such as Purity, Sympathy, and Mountain Flower. But not every visitor was an alien or a proto-hippy: Ralph, a regular Londoner, contacted the circle and revealed that he had been buried alive in 1664. Another regular character was an unnamed Mancunian clergyman, who had been critical of spiritualism whilst he was alive. He confessed to the circle that he had seen the error of his ways.

Although a few of these normal characters floated around Manchester's spiritual ether, they were vastly outnumbered by the exotics. One exotic spirit revealed that his kind: 'see symbols that surround people'. When discussing the sitter known as Truth, the spirit claimed to see: 'seven golden circles around the heart; four golden half-circles around the right of the head; seven golden full circles round the top of the head; three golden half-circles around the right arm, one golden circle around the right hand, and seven golden circles round the left arm'.

Spiritualists felt this kind of detail proved the veracity of the *Angelic Revelations*. One medium, they claimed, could not have created and sustained so many different characters over several years. And Sir Arthur Conan Doyle claimed the books contained authentic depictions of the spirit world and other dimensions. But even un-cynical modern readers would quickly conclude that they were full of abstruse and cryptic ramblings. The 'spirit' which saw the golden circles certainly enjoyed making baffling statements and refused to explain the meaning of the circles. After uttering something vague about the 'Seventh State', it excused itself by saying 'but I must pass on, the explanation will take what you call too long'.

Another spirit was equally vague when asked to reveal 'how long Earth has been inhabited by human beings'. 'This can only be answered', it replied, 'by what you call the mathematical science without, being helped by the exact science within'. When other spirits discussed magnetism they were also disappointing - merely stating that it was a mysterious force.

After seven séance-packed years, the Angelic Order of Light dissolved. It made a comeback, though, seven years later - and from the late 1880s until 1910, this new incarnation published further volumes which were collectively called: *Life and its Manifestations: Past, Present, and Future. A Series of Revelations from Angelic Sources, Containing a New System of Spiritual Science and Philosophy, Illustrated by Examples.* These new accounts were more straightforward than the original transcripts: or as the order put it - 'they offered truth of a more interior degree, disrobed, so far as possible, of the symbolic clothing which had characterised the Angelic utterances embodied in the first series . . .'

One of the spirits contacted during this phase was James White or 'Jezreel', who had claimed, when alive, to be the 'divinely appointed' successor to John Wroe. The Christian Israelites in Ashton, though, were not impressed, and so Jezreel founded the 'Later House of Israel', which was based in Kent. His followers were led to believe that they would become immortal - but then White ruined it all in 1885 by dying. His wife took the reins for a while, and like Ann Lee and Joanna Southcott and numerous others, she claimed to be the Woman Clothed with the Sun from *Revelation*.

Around 1910, after the original members of the Angelic Order had either died or called time on their séance days, a new group - The Psycho-Philosophical Society - took over the enterprise. This outfit remains obscure. All we know is that it was headquartered in Manchester and that two gentlemen from Higher Broughton -Thomas Powers and Robert Race - were members.

The Ghosts of Burlington Street

Oxley did not restrict himself to the Angelic Order - rather, he kept himself busy with several spiritualist projects and collaborated with many other 'truthseekers'. One of his main partners, especially during the mid-1870s, was Christian Reimers - a rotund German cellist who lived on Ducie Avenue, which was just off Oxford Road. Reimers arrived in Manchester in the early 1870s, after accepting a job with the Hallé Orchestra, and quickly established himself as a stalwart of the city's spiritualist scene. He formed several circles; he gave lectures and hosted events, and he wrote articles for *Medium and Daybreak* and the *Spiritualist* - detailing the 'extraordinary manifestations' which occurred in the city. He also spent much time at a gentleman's club which was off Great Ancoats Street - where he conducted long-running arguments with fellow members who were sceptical about spiritualism.

In January 1876, Reimers made his way to Oxley's house on Bury New Road and was shown to a study decorated with relics from various séances - bits of cloth, dried flowers, and other 'apports', as such things were called. Reimers explained that he needed help with an experiment which would secure a mould of a spirit's foot or hand - and Oxley, who perhaps imagined such an object taking pride of place in his study, agreed to assist.

One of the project's mediums was an American called Louise Firman, also known as 'Madame Louise', who relocated to Manchester, via London, sometime in 1873. She was accompanied by her son, who was a streetwise medium called Alfred, and by her sister. Two nieces, aged 16 and 14, were also in tow.

Also part of the project was an English ex-clergyman called Francis Ward Monck, who was the most high profile medium of the time. The press portrayed him as a man of endless integrity - as a tireless and selfless servant of spiritualism. He was also often praised for his uncanny ability to heal the sick. 'Monck has never failed', claimed one journalist, 'when treating those with gout and neuralgia . . . . his power over such ailments is something marvellous in the extreme'.

The simple truth was that Monck was a conman. In a spiritualist community littered with such characters, he stood out as an inveterate charlatan. He picked locks and let himself into his customer's houses; he shamelessly raised significant amounts of money through various 'benevolent funds' and other shady schemes; and he mercilessly exploited those who suffered from ill-health by selling them 'magnetized flannel' - bits of rag which he claimed were imbued with healing power, and which the user was supposed to rub on their body.

It was only natural, given that he was such a rogue, that Monck teamed up with Madame Louise - for she was also an audacious con-artist, who claimed to manifest the faces of historical figures. The faces were nothing but papier-mache masks, and the child-spirits which appeared at her Burlington Street séances were played by her nieces.

So it is clear that Reimers, and especially Oxley, who was the more credulous of the two, were sitting ducks.

Throughout the early months of 1876, and into the spring and summer, the mediums produced many 'wonders' for the pair. Spirits floated in the air; people levitated; strange music was heard, and furniture moved in the dark - and it all created a buzz in the city. In fact, Reimers claimed to have been inundated with requests for invites to sit with his circles.

Most impressive, at least for Oxley and Reimers, were the Burlington Street séances which yielded the wax moulds These artefacts were said to have been taken from the hands and feet of two child-spirits called Bertie and Lilly, and it was stressed that the moulds did not match the hands and feet of Mrs Firman and Monck. It was also noted that the mediums could not have smuggled in any props because they were rigorously searched before the séances.

For Oxley and Reimers, the moulds were of world-historical importance. They saw them as tangible proof of the after-life and were bullish in promoting them. Reimers loaned them to spiritualist friends in Leipzig; several articles were written about them; they were displayed in the Spiritualist Institution, and Oxley challenged 'scoffers' and 'men of science' to reproduce them.

But of course, Oxley and Reimers had been tricked. The security measures at the séances were not adequate - and Mrs Firman and Monck managed to smuggle her nieces into the room, and to take moulds of their hands and feet.

Towards the end of 1876, Oxley and Reimers should have realised they had been conned - for Monck was arrested in Huddersfield. He was charged with fraud after it was discovered that he had used a bunch of gizmos at a séance. During the trial, Monck was revealed to be a rogue and a scoundrel and was sentenced to six months.

Oxley and Reimers stood by him, wrote several articles in his defence, and never seemed to entertain the notion that the medium's arrest should have cast doubts over the authenticity of the spirit moulds.

Then, in 1882, *Confessions of a Medium* was published, which was written by an assistant of Alfred Firman's, and which revealed that all mediums were charlatans. Although the author changed the character's names, it was obvious that he was exposing Alfred Firman, and it was easy to identify other figures in the text - such as Monck and Mrs Firman's nieces.

Although the book didn't directly deal with the Manchester séances where the moulds were produced, it did reveal that Alfred Firman used plaster casts to produce moulds of spirit's heads; that Mrs Firman's nieces routinely masqueraded as spirits; and that Monck was a feckless character who, despite making large sums, was often in financial trouble. The book even featured a wealthy Manchester man, who was clearly Oxley, and who was shown to have been duped time and again by Alfred Firman.

But of course, it didn't change the minds of Reimers and Oxley. They were unwilling, or unable, to concede that the moulds were produced by trickery, and continued to write articles about the 'wondrous' artefacts.

The Haunting of Charles Blackburn

Confessions of a Medium also revealed that Charles Blackburn had been hoodwinked by Monck. The medium managed to secure a 'loan' from him by claiming that he needed money to develop a prototype of some strange device, which the spirits had impelled him to create.

Monck was not the first medium to target Blackburn - a few years before, Frank Herne, who was part of a clique which included Samuel Guppy and his wife, extracted money from the businessman.

Herne was an audacious character who was not scared of making far-fetched claims. He let it be known, for instance, that he disappeared whilst walking along a London street and woke up two miles away at Mrs Guppy's house. Herne's tall tale did not catch the public's imagination, but a few months later, when Mrs Guppy claimed to have made a similar strange journey, she caused a stir.

The affair began at a séance held in London by Herne, which was attended by a few Manchester spiritualists, including Mr Henry Morris, of Mount Trafford in Eccles. At some point, Morris suggested that they try to get the spirits to deliver Mrs Guppy to the room. A few minutes later, something hit the séance table, and when the gas lights were turned on the sitters witnessed a flustered Mrs Guppy lying there, wearing nightclothes. This episode was seized on by the press because of its comic value - for Mrs Guppy was upward of twenty stone and it would have taken powerful forces to move her.

The Guppy séance was a high point for Hearne, who was a mediocre medium. Despite his lack of skills, though, he managed to earn a place in the history of spiritualism by becoming involved, along with Mr and Mrs Guppy, in some of the earliest English spirit photographs, which were taken in 1872 by Frank A. Hudson.

Two years later, in October 1874, a spirit rapped on a table and spelt out that this form of photography had come to Manchester. Elizabeth Ann Williamson, a medium who was twelve years old and small for her age, was told by the dead that a spirit had appeared on a portrait of her which a Hyde Road photographer, Thomas M. Waters, took the previous week. Waters was said to have destroyed the plates because he considered them faulty, and so Elizabeth was instructed to sit again, to give the spirits a chance to appear once more. Although the face which manifested in the fresh photographs was partly shadowy, clear and defined features were discerned, and at later séances, it was revealed that the spirit was Dr Pearson, who had practised in Surrey during his 'earth-life'.

Mr F. Silkstone, of Hulme, believed the photograph indicated that Williamson would become a leading light of the movement. 'Great interest', he wrote, 'will now be attached (to her) . . and many warm hopes will be excited that this innocent guileless child will be the means of our obtaining in the future striking phenomena'. Silkstone, though, was to be disappointed because the young medium did not have a stellar career. Neither did Thomas M. Waters, who did not make a stir as a photographer of spirits.

William Hope was another photographer who claimed to catch Manchester's spirits on film. His adventure began when he developed a photograph of a workmate and noticed the form of a woman who was not present at the shoot standing next to his friend. Later, the friend claimed the woman was his dead sister. The following week, the process was repeated and the woman, along with an infant, appeared once more.

Hope went on to found the Crewe Circle and enjoyed a long and often successful career. Which is not to say that he wasn't exposed, because on numerous occasions he was shown to be a fraud and was called a 'common cheat' by the *Scientific American* magazine. Yet none of the mud seemed to stick - perhaps because followers such as Arthur Conan Doyle accused Hope's critics of conspiring against him. When he died, in Salford in 1933, Hope was still regarded by many to be genuine. It was not until the 1940s that he was comprehensibly shown to have been a charlatan.

Manchester would see other spirit photographers, most notably Edward Wyllie, who was famous for his work in California. Wyllie's party piece was to produce a photograph of the departed, after being sent an article which had belonged to them. This sounds impressive, but his performance in Manchester was poor. In 1910, he developed a photo of a spirit-boy who was stood behind the prominent spiritualist A.W. Orr. Initially, nobody could identify the boy, but it was later proved that this 'spirit' was very much alive.

Frank Herne also encountered problems when he helped Frank A. Hudson produce his spirit photographs in 1872. Hudson claimed that the presence of mediums such as Herne and Mrs Guppy helped him get results. William Harrison, who was the editor of the *Spiritualist* and a keen photographer, begged to differ. He looked at the images, detected signs of double exposure, and claimed that one of the ethereal figures was nothing more than Herne dressed up.

Such controversies meant that Herne lost his credibility. He did not, though, leave the scene, and instead began to mentor up and coming mediums. This was to prove unfortunate for Charles Blackburn - because one of the mediums advised by Herne, a young girl called Florence Cook, would be involved in relieving the Manchester businessman of almost all of his considerable fortune.

After meeting Florence, Blackburn was upset to hear that she intended to become a medium-for-hire. He believed that young ladies who marketed their psychic skills - such as the Fox sisters, who charged a dollar for messages from the dead - created an undignified spectacle. So he provided Florence with a regular income.

In 1872, Florence ensured that Blackburn got good value for his money when she materialized a spirit called Katie King, who was said to be the daughter of the pirate Henry Morgan. Katie appeared during several séances and wandered freely among the guests, whilst Florence was concealed in a cabinet with her head wrapped in a red turban.

After it was noted that the two girls looked the same, there was pressure for them to appear together. The pressure grew stronger when Katie announced she would stay in the material world for three years, but the Cook family, not surprisingly, refused to show Katie and Florence together.

For Mr John Volkman, a sitter at a Cook séance, this was all too much, and so he grabbed Katie when Florence was supposed to have been tied up, with wax-sealed ropes, inside a cabinet. Although Florence's supporters ensured that Katie escaped from Volkman's grasp, he revealed to the world that the two girls were one and the same. Her supporters hit back by claiming that witnesses saw Katie dissolve into thin air. They also claimed that Florence was found in the cabinet, still bound and with the wax seals undamaged.

Florence's reputation, though, was damaged, and it seemed that Blackburn would withdraw his support. But she played a masterstroke by requesting that an eminent scientist examine her. William Crookes, who was given the job, was certainly eminent. He had discovered a previously unknown element and named it Thallium; he was a pioneer in the construction of vacuum tubes, and he was a member of the Royal Society. But, for all this, he was no match for Florence Cook. She probably chose him because she knew he had spiritualist sympathies: she was probably well aware that he had investigated a prominent medium called Daniel Dunglass Home, and had claimed to see him levitate 'five to seven inches off the ground' on no fewer than 50 separate occasions. And she was probably confident that her true powers – she was young, attractive and flirtatious – would win over this middle-aged man.

For a while, Florence lived at Crooke's house. They justified this by claiming it would make it easier for him to observe her powers - but few were fooled, and it was soon rumoured that they were having an affair. By describing Katie in the following terms, Crookes seemed to confirm it:

> *Photography was inadequate to depict the perfect beauty of Katie's face, as words are powerless to describe her charm of manner. Photography may indeed give a map of her countenance, but how can*

it reproduce the brilliant purity of her complexion, the ever ranging expression on her most mobile features.

Throughout it all, Florence maintained that she was just an inexperienced girl who was embarrassed and anguished when Katie flirted with her sitters, and upstanding gentlemen like Blackburn and Crookes believed her. In 1874, Crookes claimed that 'it did violence to one's reason and common sense that an innocent schoolgirl of 15 should be able to conceive so gigantic an imposture as this'.

When Crookes published a report which vindicated Florence it provoked outrage. The scientific establishment mocked him and he was almost disowned by the Royal Society. Even Charles Blackburn, who dearly wanted to believe in Florence, concluded that they were having an affair and that he was paying for them, as he put it, 'to live under the rose'. Consequently, he withdrew his patronage; Florence withdrew her affections from Crookes, and the eminent scientist withdrew from spiritualism.

The Cook family, though, were to have a timely bit of good fortune. They discovered that Florence's sister, also called Katie, was another who was blessed with the power to see dead people. Blackburn was quickly informed of this astounding discovery and he began to fund the family once more. And to ensure that he did not lose faith in the Cooks, one of Katie's spirit guides, Lille Gordon, sent him a series of letters in which she heaped praise on the family.

In her first letter, written in 1877, she wished him and his daughter 'all the happiness they so well deserved'. Trevor Hall presumed that Blackburn received the letter whilst at a séance in Hackney: 'for it is difficult to believe that even Katie had the audacity to send a spirit letter from the spirit world to Manchester'.

Blackburn also received weekly reports on the manifestations in Hackney; and in February 1879, Katie Cook herself made the trip to Didsbury. 'It will be', wrote Blackburn, 'a little change from London'.

The séances at Didsbury were mostly attended by Blackburn's

friends, although his daughter Eliza was also present. Trevor Hall noted that transcriptions of these events provided: 'the last account available of Eliza whilst still sane'. He then floated the idea that the séances, and her father's other spiritualist adventures, might have contributed to her loss of sanity.

Charles Blackburn and Florence Cook with spirits

During the months following the Didsbury visit, Blackburn began to doubt Katie. It seems that on one occasion, when Lillie Gordon was 'floating' around the room, he checked Katie's chair and found it was empty. After he wrote demanding an explanation from the medium, Lillie replied: 'I can give you no explanation because Katie's chair was not empty. All I can say is that in the dark you must have mistaken your position . . . I am so sorry that you should doubt my word or Katies'.

Blackburn continued to have doubts, and so it was arranged

for a séance to be held under controlled conditions. The results, the businessman believed, vindicated Katie. He claimed she had produced a materialisation during an 'absolute test séance'. But when we consider that John Williams and the American Susan Willis Fletcher presided over the séance, then it seems much less like an 'absolute test': for both were mediums, and both would be exposed during later séances. In fact, Susan Willis Fletcher was later sentenced to a year's hard labour for fraud.

At some point during the next three years, Blackburn moved to London, and Eliza's health deteriorated so badly that she was confined to Brook House Asylum in Clapton. To make matters worse, Blackburn was also ailing, which caused him to worry about how Eliza would cope if he died. The ever-resourceful Cook Family came to the rescue by proposing that Eliza stay with them. 'This plan', wrote Trevor Hall, 'was to be furthered by all the means in their power . . . for the golden stream (of Blackburn's money) might become a torrent'. [2]

Soon after, Blackburn received the following letter from Lillie Gordon:

I hear you think of placing your daughter with Katie. If I may say so you could not do better. Katie will exercise a beneficial influence over her. I told Katie some years ago. From what I have seen I cannot believe the cause is a hopeless one. It might grieve you to be away from her and I am sure if you could see her frequently she would get reconciled to you, therefore do not despair for a brighter time is coming for you and her. I am so glad you and Katie are such good friends. She is a good intelligent girl and so deserves anyone's friendship. [3]

But Lillie's letter did not force Blackburn into action. Three months went by, Eliza remained in the asylum, and the Cook's feared their gilt-edged opportunity was slipping away. So another plan was hatched. Lillie Gordon, decided Katie, was to visit the Brook House Asylum, observe Eliza being mistreated by two members of staff, and then inform Blackburn in a letter.

The plan worked - for by the end of the year Katie was Eliza's official 'companion', and the whole Cook clan had moved into Blackburn's London house. Katie also wriggled her way into his will and was promised £750 and the whole contents of the London house. Blackburn also set aside £14 000 in a trust to ensure his daughter's well being.

Katie had obviously done well out of the will - £750 was a tidy sum in 1874, and the contents of the house must also have been of considerable worth, for it was a substantial building on West London's plush Elgin Crescent. But it was not enough for Katie, and by 1886 Blackburn's will was revised so that she was set to receive a further £1500.

By 1887, Blackburn was simply under the control of Katie. She decided that the Elgin Crescent house was too cramped, and in 1888 Blackburn and the Cook family moved into a large abode in Ladbroke Grove. From here, the Manchester businessman wrote a letter to Lillie Gordon in which he enquired about his daughter, Ellen, who had passed away 21 years previously. He noted that Lille had mentioned a signed card from Ellen and wondered if it was possible for his daughter to send him a letter.

Just over six months later, Blackburn revised his will again. The £14 000 which had been set aside for the well being of Eliza was now to be used to buy a house for Katie and her mother. Eliza was also to live there, along with servants, but would be removed and put in Brook House if her condition worsened.

Katie, though, did not want to hang around for Blackburn to die before the money was released. For although he was suffering from cancer, he seemed to be lingering on. So, with the help of faithful Lillie, she managed to get him to buy yet another house, this time in Monmouthshire. The house would belong to Eliza whilst she was alive, but after her death it would become the property of Katie. A further £15 000 was also awarded to the medium.

Four months later, William Holliday Cornforth, who was a trustee of the will - and who was set to receive £1000 for his services - asked to be relieved of his position and gave up his claim to the money. There is no evidence that Cornforth took this action because he could no longer watch Blackburn be so comprehensively exploited, but it seems to have been the case.

The new trustee had no qualms about making revisions, and in September 1890 a legacy of £1000, which was to have been paid to a woman called Catherine Messer, was removed. They also removed Harriett Elizabeth Blackburn, who had been married to Blackburn's son, from the will. The two women may have tried to make the businessman see sense. They may have earned the enmity of the Cook family by trying to expose them as gold diggers and charlatans.

Three months later, Katie was granted £2000 to acquire a 'winter residence' in the south of England. Once again it was owned by Blackburn's daughter but was to be left to Katie on Eliza's death. Furthermore, the furnishings for the house were to be paid for by Blackburn.

By now his health was seriously ailing and he began to feel desperate. As he lay dying he wrote a last letter to Lillie:

My own dearest spirit Lillie,
    You have written often to me for years and I want in my prostration a few lines of comfort from you....from your side can you see if the doctors are working correctly for my restoration, and if you don't know can't you see Pierpoint (presumably a dead friend) *or others to assist you in writing to me the best remedy - as I don't want to quit yet!*
    Of course we have had no séances of late as my condition has not been suitable for months. Still we know and feel you are about us and hope you will reply as usual. With my love and kisses, which I have so often received from you.

After writing the note, Blackburn placed it in his bedroom drawer and waited for an answer. The Cooks must have waited until he was out of the room, or asleep, before taking the letter and slipping in the following reply:

My Dearest Friend,
    Your letter gave me both pleasure and pain, pleasure in thinking

writing interests you, pain to think that I cannot give you comfort by telling you that you will recover. All is being done for you that is possible on your side and mine. Many are waiting to welcome you home I shall be with you always.

You must think you have had a long and useful life and have been just to all connected to you.

Will you look forward to our meeting not as we have done but in perfect unity and friendship and together we will watch.

I must not close this without thanking you once more for your great kindness to Katie, and those belonging to her, and she will endeavour to repay you by attending to your daughter, who will be happy with her . . . Please believe me that I am always with you and am your faithful Lillie.

This is not goodbye.

Just over a week after this correspondence, Blackburn lay on his deathbed and the Cook family worked hard to get their hands on the last of his money. With just hours to go, they secured one more revision to his will and gained thousands of shares in the Lancashire and Yorkshire Railway Company. Blackburn was too weak to sign the revision, but he managed to scribble an X before he died.

William Byant - in his biography of Alfred Russell Wallace, an associate of Blackburn's - made this tale even grimmer by claiming that the businessman 'and his feeble-minded daughter were found dead in mysterious circumstances'. But this was untrue: Blackburn died of natural causes, and Eliza, who lived for a time with the Cook family before she was relocated to an Eastbourne nursing home, passed away when she was seventy-three.

Spiritualist Royalty arrives in Manchester

One of the most renowned mediums to spend time at Blackburn's Parkfield estate was Emma Hardinge Britten, who moved to Manchester from the United States in 1881. A veteran of the movement, she had rubbed shoulders with many of its most notable figures and was considered to be part of the spiritualist aristocracy. According to *Medium and Daybreak*, many spiritualists considered Emma to be their 'spiritual mother' because it was through her 'eloquent and lucid teachings that they first obtained a knowledge of the new philosophy'.

Emma Hardinge Britten

Born in London in 1823, Emma was said to have been a supernaturally gifted child. She had visions, predicted people's futures, and talked of dead relatives who she should not have known had existed. In *Art Magic*, which was an account of her strange early life, she revealed that these powers brought her to the attention of a secret society which she referred to as the Orphic Circle, but which the members had called the Mercurii.[4] This bunch, she claimed, consisted of 'persons of noble rank' who were 'privy to knowledge about alchemy, freemasonry, and mediaeval Rosicrucianism', and were affiliated with 'many others then in existence in many countries'.

The Mercurii was, she stressed, the most secret of secret societies: 'the existence of the occultists, of whom I can only now allude, was undreamed of, and none of the members were known as such outside their circles'. To maintain secrecy, the identity of a member was not revealed until they had died, or as Emma put it: 'until they passed from Earth to the higher life'. So she left it until the 1880s before she revealed that the Mercurii's membership had included Lord Edward Bulwer-Lytton, the renowned author and occultist; Philip Henry Stanhope, who liked to introduce people to his crystal ball so they could observe the 'spirits of the sun'; and Richard Morrison, the most famous astrologer of the day, who the public knew as Zadkiel.

Fraternising with Zadkiel and the others were magnetic youths, including 'young ladies who conducted their experiments through the mirror and crystal', and who attracted 'pure and noble planetary spirits'.

The behaviour of the senior members of the society, though, may not have been pure and noble - for researchers have speculated that there was a sexual element connected to the Mercurii; and it has long been said that Emma, whose maiden name was Floyd, acquired the name Hardinge after taking part in a mystical marriage ceremony which may have included some form of sexual magic. Other researchers have dismissed this and maintain that Hardinge was simply a stage name - for Emma had spent time as an actress.

During the 1850s, she left England and the Orphic Circle for New York, where she was soon involved with another esoteric group known as the Order of the Patriarchs. This society, she claimed, 'embraced that of 'free love' in its most revolting form', and so she soon left and became a medium for a more respectable group. Whilst working with this outfit she got to know Kate Fox, who along with her sister had started the modern spiritualist movement.

During this period, Emma claimed to channel the spirit of a sailor who died after the steamship *Pacific* sank. This was controversial because the ship was not officially classed as missing, and its owners threatened to sue her. But when it became apparent that the ship *had* sunk they withdrew the threat, and Emma's reputation was established. Over the next few years, she became the most recognised trance medium in the United States.

Emma gained more recognition during the mid-1860s when campaigning for Abraham Lincoln. Her article in favour of him, *The Coming Man*, earned her much praise and she read it at over a hundred meetings in California. After her lecture engagements were over, she stayed in the state and claimed she wanted to 'deliver' it for Lincoln. It was a grandiose statement but some credited her with doing it.

Her profile was further enhanced during the 1870s when she claimed that the spirit of Robert Owen, the one-time Manchester mill owner and philanthropist who died in 1858, revealed to her the 'Seven Principles of Spiritualism'. The principles, which were along the lines of accepting the 'fatherhood of God', and believing in the 'brotherhood of man', were almost universally accepted by the movement, and stood the test of time.

Manchester: City of Esoteric Delights

Why did Emma - a Londoner who was fêted in the United States - choose to spend the rest of her life in Manchester? One explanation is that she wanted to join her sister, Margaret Wilkinson, who had lived in the city since she was packed off to a maternal aunt at the age of four. Despite growing up apart, the sisters managed to remain close, and Margaret accompanied Emma to the United States and became acquainted with the Fox family.

Manchester, though, offered Emma more than the chance to be close to Margaret: for it was now, more than ever, a city of esoteric delights. It was home to astrologers, homoeopaths, theosophists, mesmerists, occultists and freemasons. Vegetarians were also well catered for. Events such as 'Spiritualist Vegetarian Banquets' were held; a magazine called *Vegetarian Messenger* was published in the city; and as several writers have noted, Manchester in the 1880s had more meat-free restaurants than it did in the 1980s. One particularly lavish joint on Fountain Street included two dining halls, a lecture theatre, several rooms for billiards, smoking and reading, and was maintained by a staff of 21.

The dominant ingredient of the Manchester scene, though,

was spiritualism - which mushroomed throughout the 1870s. By the time Emma arrived, the city was home to many activists who organised book clubs and talking shops. One such enterprise was the Manchester Progressive Discussion Class, which aimed to *'bring forward . . . spiritualism, mesmerism, psychology, and kindred subjects'*; and which offered its members 'soirées', picnics, trips to the country, and visits to more local places such as Chorlton's Manley Hall. All who joined, stressed the secretary, George Dawson, of Back Quay Street, must be 'truthseekers'.

Serving the spiritualists were a new generation of home-grown mediums, and many of them were women. Miss Hall and Miss Shafto were both well known in the city and were mentioned in the papers. Also well known was a more experienced medium called Mrs Olive, of Brunswick Street, who channelled an Indian girl by the name of 'Sunshine'. On one occasion, Sunshine was nudged off the psychic line by Charles Dickens, which was a bit of mischief by Mrs Olive because the author had thought spiritualism was bunkum. Another female medium, who operated from Boston Street in Hulme, and who also made contact with Sunshine, was Miss Garbett. 'She spoke', claimed a colleague, 'in a state of exaltation and ecstasy, and poured forth sublime strains of eloquence, fraught with profound spiritual knowledge'.

Home-grown male mediums included Mr Johnson, a trance performer who was occasionally hyped by *Medium and Daybreak*, and who liked to hold forth on the spheres. There was also Mr Howell, who made a name for himself in London by breaking the news of Francis Ward Monck's arrest in Huddersfield before the press. Howell appeared unannounced at a meeting in Islington and claimed he was compelled to do so by the spirits, even though he was heading for a destination that was several miles in the opposite direction. After slipping into a trance, he dropped the Monck bombshell and earned considerable kudos.

Another busy medium in the Manchester area in the 1870s, who claimed to be able to 'see' a person's internal organs, was Edward Gallagher. According to Emma Hardinge Britten, he was a 'highly gifted seer who was permitted to describe hidden diseases and cure them by occult power'.

Gallagher professed to have had a life-long relationship with the dead:

> *I was born a seer and never underwent or needed any of the so-called occult training. From my earliest recollections to the present time, I am and have been clairvoyant and clairaudient. From my childhood to the present time, I have been seeing and conversing with the so-called dead as freely as if they were embodied friends I had known for years.*

Despite these experiences, Gallagher initially doubted that there was an afterlife. This was due to his 'intensely sceptical mind', and also because 'philosophical and scientific gentlemen' convinced him there was no life after death, and that his interaction with the spirit world was a sign of insanity. Gallagher took this to heart and began to suffer from a 'sad mental condition'. Even the intervention of a 'liberal minded Christian gentleman', who contradicted the scientific mob and proclaimed him to be a seer, failed to convince him he was really seeing spirits. Consequently, he decided that a study of anatomy would help him understand his experiences.

Eight years of studying failed to provide any enlightenment, though, and his mental state remained as fragile as ever. He also felt so 'physically prostrated' that he believed his life was in danger. All of which made his decision to sign up with the medical department of the 'Army of the Cumberland,' and to become involved with the American civil war, more than a little baffling.

He saw many supernatural events during the war. Men seemed to be 'carried a distance of forty yards without the aid of embodied human beings', and occasionally people suddenly appeared or disappeared. 'I saw as many as six materialised human beings', wrote Gallagher, 'two of them were full grown men, two were women, and two were children. I saw them materialise and dematerialise in the presence of about thirty gentlemen of honour and cultivated intelligence'.

All this other-worldly activity put his mind at rest. 'These manifestations of spirit power', he wrote, 'convinced me of the continuity of life after the death of the physical body'.

Yet the trip to America and Gallagher's involvement in the war may never have happened. In *Opiumopolis: Drugs and Crime in 19th Century Manchester*, the author revealed that the city was a magnet for quack doctors such as Gallagher and that many of them had an exotic tale to tell. One such character went by the name Professor Wills of Melbourne and peddled herbal medicine which he claimed was given to his father by aborigines. But he was neither a professor nor an Australian. Another quack, Sequah, claimed to be an American frontiersman but was really from Yorkshire. He peddled a 'secret concoction' which he claimed had been given to him by the Apaches after he won their trust. He became so popular that he franchised his scam and created several 'Sequahs'.

Edward Gallagher did not sell exotic potions and lotions, but he did market his ability to see auras. He claimed to have developed this gift after he returned from America and joined circles in Manchester which encouraged such supernatural phenomena. The auras, he explained, indicated the state of a person's health, and if an organ was diseased the aura was black.

Gallagher claimed this ability, along with his anatomical knowledge and the guidance of the spirits, enabled him to cure a multitude of the sick. 'Thousands', he wrote, 'today can bear out what I now declare, that through me sight has been given to the blind, the lame has been made to walk, the deaf to hear, and hundreds who were left to die by the old school were cured by me in a few days'.

Many mocked Gallagher and wondered if his patients were as healthy as his bank balance - but Emma Hardinge Britten noted that the doubters scorned him in public, then secretly sought him out for treatment on conditions which orthodox medicine failed to diagnose and cure. She also claimed that he attracted clergymen who consistently preached against spiritualism.

As well as producing home-grown characters like Gallagher, the city continued to draw in mediums and enthusiasts from far and wide - such as the secretary of the Marylebone Spiritualist Association, Mr C. White, who relocated to Higher Broughton and began holding 'domestic séances'.

A more high-profile incomer was Wilberforce Juvenal Colville, who was born on the South Coast, probably in 1857, although he claimed to be younger. He lost his mother when he was an infant, and his father was absent throughout his life, which left him in the arms of a grandmother who died when he was approximately twenty. All of which seems less than auspicious, and there has been speculation that he was left destitute. There was no chance, though, of him sinking without a trace: for he was blessed with huge self-confidence, and he reinvented himself as a public medium and claimed to have been American by birth. He also reinvented his family: his mother became a well-bred French woman called Marie Lavinia De Mourdan, and his father became an Italian who mysteriously vanished, or died, on a business trip.

Colville was an almost immediate success and he gained much coverage from *Medium and Daybreak*. The paper would have been confident in promoting him, for he was a trance performer rather than a manifestation medium - so there was no chance that he would be found masquerading as a spirit, or with gizmos and contraptions hidden in his clothing.

By August 1877, he had begun to visit Manchester, and during a performance at a private gathering on Bury New Road, he claimed to be controlled by St. Stephen. Mr R. Fitton, the long-time activist and president of the Manchester Association of Spiritualists, wrote a glowing review for *Medium and Daybreak*:

> *The intelligent control of our friend, in beautiful poetic language, depicted his earth life in the days and in the land of John the Baptist, with whom he was in close fellowship. He also told us of the life and labours of that great and loving brother Jesus Christ, telling us in a charming style of his first experience with Jesus. . . .*

Fitton also revealed that St. Stephen furnished them with details of *'being stoned to death for his allegiance to the truth'*.

After Colville visited the city several times, Clara Rowe, of Richmond Terrace in Hulme, claimed that the spirits campaigned for him to perform more often for the Manchester public. Soon after, the spirits were obeyed and Colville took up lodgings in the Strangeways area.

Wilberforce Juvenal Colville

He began his stint in the city by promoting his performances in the press. One advert revealed that an 'ancient Egyptian spirit' would most likely take possession of him, and would *'relate his experiences on earth and in the spirit-world'*. It was expected, the blurb continued, *'that information will be passed regarding the pyramids and other Egyptian antiquities'*.

At around this time, Colville was connected with the 'Star Circle', which was a fairly secretive group that operated under the aegis of Marie, Countess of Caithness, who was obsessed with Mary Queen of Scots. The medium published a pamphlet describing his work with the circle, *The Coming Kingdom of God . . . Teachings given at the residence of Lady Caithness,* which could be obtained from 4 Waterloo Rd, Manchester.

As his career progressed, Colville became more involved in the occult. In the late 1880s, after he relocated to San Francisco, he joined the mysterious Order of the White Cross, which was founded in London by Susan Willis Fletcher, who was part of Frank Herne's clique. It was a full-blown secret society which used passwords and was organised around a three-degree structure.

Colville was said to have been inspired to become a medium by Cora L.V. Scott, who he saw perform on the South Coast. Cora, who was born in New York State, began her career when she was eleven years old. After a fainting spell, she started to pass on messages from dead friends and relatives, sometimes in a low and guttural voice; and when she was twelve, she was ordered by the spirits to stop attending school.

During the 1870s, she spent much time in England and often worked in Manchester. A writer for *Medium and Daybreak* speculated that her guides on the 'other side' were empowered by the city's spiritualist ethos. In contrast, another writer claimed that the psychic atmosphere of the Temperance Hall, where Cora performed, was so tainted by a plethora of Manchester's previous sects and mystics that she could not operate properly. She decided, it was claimed, never to return to the venue.

Another visitor from the United States in the 1870s was Frederick Evans, who was the head of the Shakers. It was almost a century since Mother Ann left for America, and now, for a short time at least, the sect once again had a presence in the city.

The Shakers had left Manchester because of its indifference to them. They were just another sect in a town full of sects and they struggled to be noticed. Evans, though, had no such problems and easily filled the Free Trade Hall. His popularity was the result of the sect being seen as a precursor to spiritualism, which Evans encouraged by claiming: 'all Shakers are in a greater or lesser degree, mediums', and by stating that 'manifestations, visions, revelations, prophecies and all sorts of gifts of various kinds are as common to us as gold in California'. He also let it be known that he considered Emma Hardinge Britten to be a 'wonderful medium'. Only her married status, he claimed, prevented him from inviting her to join the Shakers.

The success of Evans' tour of England was not, though, entirely due to the spiritualistic aspects of the Shakers: he was also popular because the sect's communalistic principles offered an alternative to the relentless grind of capitalism. Two men who attended Evan's Manchester meetings to hear about the Shaker's communalistic ethos were David Brown, who was from Yorkshire, and Robert Stephens, a Mancunian weaver who managed a co-operative store in London. Both agreed to follow Evans back to the United States to join a Shaker commune. In Brown's case, though, it ended badly and he was soon back in England, complaining that 'Shakerism was unquestionably slavery modified'.

Not all of Manchester's spiritualists were progressives. In fact, the scene that Emma Hardinge Britten found in the early 1880s was largely organised by conservative characters and was marked by a little class tension.

Fighting the capitalist corner was a member of the Manchester Spiritualist Association who used the nom de plume 'Fairplay'. In a report delivered to the association, he attacked those who argued against professional mediums. They were 'so spiritual in their wants and desires', he claimed, that they overlooked the 'inherent love of riches' which was 'part of man's nature'. 'It was the promise of riches', he continued, 'that urged man to seek fresh fields of conquest'.

Higher rates of pay, he argued, would deliver better educated and more eloquent mediums; and he claimed that such characters were required because some mediums, such as a young Mancunian boy he recently witnessed, were giving substandard performances.

W. T. Braham, of Stretford Road, who was also a significant member of the association, was outraged by the comments. He defended the boy medium - 'out of the mouths of babes and sucklings cometh wisdom' - and criticised Fairplay's materialist views. Although Braham was a businessman, he stressed that making money, or 'filthy lucre' as he put it, was not the only factor which compelled mankind; and he illustrated the point by asking: 'Is money the chief object that impels the fireman to rush into the midst of the flames to rescue the child from the burning mess?'

Braham also complained that since Fairplay and his cronies

had assumed power within Manchester's Spiritualist Association, the price of hiring a medium had risen from 5 to 35 shillings; and consequently, he stressed, it was more difficult for 'the facts of spirit-communion' to reach all 'truthful enquirers'.

Mr J. Campion, who was the president of the Manchester and Salford Spiritualist Society, was also concerned that the movement was forgetting its roots. In 1881, he met five friends for a discussion at the Trinity Coffee Tavern, and they decided that the way forward was to eschew large scale gatherings for 'cottage meetings or home circles in every local district'. This would, they hoped, encourage the development of new mediums, and enable all 'to know more of the mysteries of the spirit-land and our future abode'.

But itinerant mediums, such as Cora L.V. Scott and W. J. Colville, would not have been keen on returning the movement to its roots. They were professionals who needed to address large meetings and to attract a constant stream of clients at private séances.

Emma Hardinge Britten also needed Manchester to be a hotbed of commercial spiritualism - for she used the city as a base for a publishing business called the 'Two Worlds of Manchester'. This enterprise was formed in partnership with several of the area's most prominent spiritualists - including J. B. Tetlow, who was a psychometric medium; W. T. Braham, the watchmaker who was Fairplay's sparring partner; an influential Rochdale writer called P. Lee; and R. Fitton, who was the secretary of the city's spiritualists association. William Oxley was also an early director of the company.

The Two Worlds occasionally produced occult paraphernalia, such as a planchette called the 'Telepathic Spirit Communicator'. This device, which was manufactured by W. T. Braham, and marketed as 'a marvellous and successful means of spelling out names and messages by spirit people', was merely an alphabet printed on a board with a pointer attached which could be moved along the letters. A more advanced version, called the 'Wonderful Spirit Communicator', came with blurb which promised that 'messages can be obtained from spirit people in every home'.

The company's most important venture, though, was a weekly spiritualist paper, which was also called the *Two Worlds*.

The Two Worlds

In the first issue, which was produced at a house on Petworth Street in Cheetham Hill, Emma cited the 'vast demand in the northern section of England' as the reason for founding the paper. She also claimed to have been 'stimulated by the counsel of our beloved allies in the higher spheres', who had 'suggested to us the modus operandi by which our enterprise should be conducted'. It was not the first time a publisher claimed to be advised by spirits: James Burns, who took over John Page Hopps' monthly *Daybreak* in the late 1860s, let it be known that they told him to convert it to a weekly paper.

During the *Two World's* first few years, several stories were published which indicated that Manchester's appetite for spirit manifestation was as strong as ever. Despite the exposure of several manifestation mediums who worked in the city, such as Francis Ward Monck and Alfred Firman, séances were still held with the aim of producing visible spirits. In fact, this quest for sensational results earned the city a rebuke from a writer who covered a conference in Oldham for *Medium and Daybreak*: 'The Manchester delegation', he claimed, 'made the common mistake of running after novelty and excitement'.

Excitement was definitely found at a Pendleton séance given by a medium called Henry Turner in July 1888. The *Two Worlds* revealed that the circle, which consisted of six people who sat in a room that was dimly lit by gas, was entertained by 'lights that shone most brilliantly'; by 'knockings from all parts of the room'; and by the appearance of a little boy which one of the sitters identified as his son. Also on the bill were a little boy and girl, who appeared simultaneously and carried spirit lights, and the spirit of a black man who 'lifted a picture from the wall' and handed it to a member of the circle. Then came ten figures, 'all clothed in fine drapery', who 'walked about the room and shook hands with the sitters'. The reporter, Thomas Beaman, was not clear on whether the forms appeared simultaneously or in smaller numbers, but either way, Henry Turner obviously intended to produce a spectacle, and his sitters were deeply moved: 'Words are inadequate', wrote Beaman, 'to express the feelings we entertained in the presence of those strange and mysterious forms from another world'.

A few years later, the *Two Worlds* revealed that other manifestation had occurred at the Brooks Bar home of T. W. Braham, one of the paper's directors. Braham was not present at the séance, but his wife was - along with a medium called Mrs Mellor and 22 spiritualists from across the city. After the usual preambles - the setting up of a cabinet, and the singing of hymns - lights appeared and a little black spirit girl, 'Cissy', materialised. Later came an adult male spirit, 'Geordie', and a female form recognised by one of the sitters as her sister. Another two forms were said to have failed to fully materialise because the magnetic power in the room was exhausted.

Another story involving a director of the *Two Worlds*, this time J. B. Tetlow, appeared in 1889. He was reported to have lost consciousness for twenty minutes after he touched the belongings of James Smith, a Manchester man who had been missing since he took 'a day's pleasure in the country'. When Tetlow came round, he gave 'an accurate description of Mr Smith'; described him walking down a lane to a river and a landing stage for boats, and then revealed that the man had drowned. His body, believed Tetlow, was caught up in the mud of the river bank; and approximately two weeks later, Smith was found floating in the River Mersey at Northenden. Mr Edwin Else of Salford, a friend of Smith's who put Tetlow on the case, paid testament to the medium's 'wonderful accuracy', and revealed he had alerted the paper to the story because he wished the details to be 'part of the marvels of present day revelations'.

Despite running such stories, the *Two Worlds* was not particularly focused on hyping the supernatural talents of its directors - and did not especially promote any other Manchester mediums. Rather, it sought to be national and international in scope and often reported on the scene in the United States. Another issue included a feature on: 'Spiritualism amongst New Zealand's Maoris'.

Several articles sought to establish that spiritualism was an ancient phenomenon. This was a movement-wide obsession, with all the other publications seeking to prove that it was not a vulgar modern craze. They all published pieces which linked spiritualism to many epochs and historical characters. The *Two Worlds*, for instance, argued that the Druids and various biblical figures had been spiritualists.

Also in common with its counterparts, the paper was taken with the notion that ancient civilisations had been superior to their modern successors. One writer, J. H. Fletcher, argued that they had mainly been superior in terms of language and architecture. Mr Fred Amesbury, though, upped the ante when he claimed that India possessed a telephone system which was two thousand years old, and was found in temples in Panj, 200 miles from Madras. The local priests were said 'to have laughed when they were told that (telephones) had only been invented in England and America within the last dozen years'.

Occasionally, news from outside the spiritualist bubble found its way into the paper: such as a story about the squalid conditions of Salford's lodging houses, which was lifted from *City News* and ran under the headline: ASTOUNDING REVELATIONS CONCERNING THE DENS WHERE THE POOR OF MANCHESTER HERD TOGETHER.

Another mainstream issue, which caused such a furore that it could not be ignored, concerned the murders in Whitechapel. An editorial revealed that correspondents had asked: 'why the spirits hadn't disclosed the name and whereabouts of the wretch' who perpetrated the 'shocking and inhuman acts of murder and mutilation?' Although Emma dismissed the notion of detectives from beyond the grave, or as she put it: 'a spiritual Scotland Yard', others did not reject the idea and several psychics attempted to assist with the investigation.

Robert James Lees was the most renowned of these characters. Lees, who lived in Manchester from 1875 - 78, when he worked for the *Manchester Guardian*, claimed to have been a visionary medium since he was an infant - when he was often visited by the spirit of a Highlander who sang him to sleep. At the age of thirteen, he was said to have become Queen Victoria's favourite medium. This tale, which was almost certainly a myth, had Lees installed in Buckingham Palace, consoling the bereaved queen with messages from Prince Albert.

It might have been thought, given his mystical gifts, that Lees would have enjoyed Manchester's spiritualist scene, but this was not the case: for he claimed that fraudulent activity by mediums caused him to leave the movement in 1868. Consequently, he spent his time in Manchester debunking spiritualists. His partner in this enterprise was the Reverend Thomas Ashcroft, who worked as a minister in Bury and other Lancashire towns.

Robert James Lees

Ashcroft was not the first cleric in the Manchester area to denounce spiritualism, and he certainly wasn't the last. During the first decade of the 20th century, the Reverend McKenna of the Catholic Truth Society claimed that séances were part of the 'black arts'. Around the same time, the Reverend Day, of the Holy Name on Oxford Road, condemned the 'popular modern cults of spiritualism and occultism', which he claimed were 'identical with devil worship, black magic, and with the necromancy of the past'. They should be regarded, he continued, 'as the continuation of Satan's revolt against God'. More measured was the Rev. G. N. Williams, of the McLaren Memorial Baptist Church, Chorlton-cum-Hardy, who criticised occultists for chasing 'secret things which belong only to God'.

None of the anti-spiritualist preachers who followed Ashcroft, though, were as committed as him to the campaign against the movement. Nor were they as high profile: for he was often mentioned by both the spiritualist and mainstream press.

The recruitment of Lees was a coup for Ashcroft: for the young man entertained audiences by demonstrating how mediums produced supposedly supernatural effects during séances. (As noted, he appeared at Hulme Town Hall in 1877, in a show which replicated the Davenport brother's act). But Ashcroft did not have it all his own way, because Lees maintained that if he was ever confronted with compelling evidence of true communication from the afterlife, then he would return to spiritualism.

In November 1884, he claimed to have been presented with such evidence. At a séance which he attended with two American men, a spirit revealed that it would be worthwhile for one of them to reopen a mine which he had abandoned. Sometime later, information from the United States proved that the spirit's advice had been correct, and this was enough for Lees.

Ashcroft did not take the news well and criticised Lees. The medium responded by sending a letter to *Light*, which detailed the séance with the two Americans, and which was used by the paper as part of a general attack on Ashcroft. The editor concluded his piece by predicting that 'Mr Ashcroft, now that his bubble has been pricked will be silenced'. This was, of course, wishful thinking, and Ashcroft continued with his campaign. September 1888 found him in Ardwick, where he delivered two lectures at the Co-operative Hall on Downing Street, which the *Manchester Courier* reported under the headline: SPIRITUALISM: A FARCE AND A FRAUD.

The letter which Lees sent to *Light* formed the basis of a spurious article that appeared in the *Chicago Sunday Times Herald* on 28th

April 1895, and which set in motion the myth of the medium's involvement in the Jack the Ripper case. The journalist claimed that Lees was dining with the two Americans when he suddenly proclaimed: 'Great God! Jack the Ripper has committed another murder'. The three gentlemen were said to have immediately made their way to Scotland Yard, where news of the new murder was received by an inspector, just as Lees was relating his story.

The article also claimed that during the killing spree, Lees travelled on an omnibus and became convinced that a fellow passenger was the Ripper. When the suspect alighted at Marble Arch, the medium followed him and tried to get a policeman to help. But Lees was dismissed as a lunatic, and the man disappeared in a Hansom cab.

More visions followed, including one which involved a postcard. The police admitted to receiving such a card and decided to take Lees seriously. Finally, after more murders, Lees led the police to a fashionable address where they arrested a physician who was said to have treated members of the royal family. The man was placed in an asylum and a mock funeral was held to explain his disappearance. Or so the story went.

Lees was forgotten for much of the twentieth century, but in the 1970s interest was renewed when a piece on him appeared in the *Criminologist*. The author, Dr Thomas Stowell, claimed that the daughter of William Gull, who was a physician to the royal family, had told a story which partially matched the Lees account. A medium and a police inspector, she maintained, had visited her parents' home in Mayfair.

Richard Patterson, the author of *The Story of Jack the Ripper: A Paradox*, didn't entertain the notion that Gull had been the killer. He did, though, have faith in Robert James Lee's psychic powers, and he claimed the medium had indeed seen the murderer on the omnibus on Edgware Road. The Ripper was, he believed, Francis Thompson: a poet, mystic, and occultist who grew up in the Manchester area, and who haunted Edgware Road after he relocated to London.

Patterson reckoned that Thompson was scarred by a brutal

Ashton childhood, which included being held under siege in a Catholic church during the Murphy Riots. As an adult, the poet was said to have been further unhinged by opium addiction and years of homelessness. Also significant, believed Patterson, was his fascination with esoteric texts and the works of Edward Bulwer-Lytton. 'Thompson was particularly interested', he wrote, 'in volumes on Black Masses and necromancy'.

The occult motives which Patterson attributed to Thompson were, to say the least, unconvincing. They included a desire to resurrect a favoured prostitute, in the form of some all-encompassing spirit, by murdering five other street girls. Five was, Patterson explained, a supremely mystical number for Thompson.

Another psychic, who claimed to have dreamt about the killer, was Charles Barber of Ardwick. The Ripper was, he claimed, 'about 5 feet 7 inches, rather stout, a little round shouldered or short necked, not much hair on his face, aged 40 or over', and was a sailor from Liverpool. His ship, the *Alaska*, was said to have been docked in London at the time of each murder.

Barber's letters were ignored by the Vigilance Society and the police, but *Spy* magazine published a few of them - until the editors became tired of him and stated that they would 'allow his convictions to lie dormant for a while'. Soon after, Barber claimed to have been vindicated by a news story about Fredrick Bailey Deeming, who was arrested in Australia after killing his wife. This triggered a search of Deeming's old house in Rainhill, and the bodies of his previous wife and four children were found. All had their throats cut, which led to speculation that the murderer was the Ripper. Barber wrote to the Home Secretary, claiming that the arrest proved his 'information was right', and requested a reward.

The fact that no psychics or mediums were effective in assisting the police meant that awkward questions were asked of spiritualists. To the critics, it seemed that mediums received trivial details about departed relatives but failed to secure useful information that could lead to the apprehension of murderers. And when Emma Hardinge Britten attempted to answer these charges in the *Two Worlds,* she floundered. First, she argued that the spirits should not directly intervene in the case, or in any earthly affairs, because it reduced humans to 'automata'; then she maintained that it would not be fair to expect the deceased to 'spend their eternity in doing for man what man ought to do for himself'; and next, she floated the notion that the spirits might be hindered by criminal elements in the afterlife who were protecting the murderer. Criminals, she explained, remained nefarious after dying. Furthermore, they were said to take up positions nearer to earth than the 'purer and more sublimated inhabitants of higher spheres', and this was thought to give then them an advantage over their benevolent counterparts when dealing with mankind. Finally, entering into some distasteful speculation, she wondered if 'the angels in heaven, who love, pity, and care for the suffering ones', had permitted the Whitechapel women to be martyrs, in order to hasten moral, political and social reform.

The Jack the Ripper case was not the only difficult issue that spiritualists had to deal with in 1888: for in November, two of the Fox sisters admitted they were charlatans. Before a crowd at the New York Academy of Music, the sisters demonstrated how they produced rapping sounds by clicking or cracking their joints.

The movement had, of course, weathered many storms, but this latest controversy had the potential to truly damage it: for the Fox sisters had launched spiritualism, and what made it worse was the fact that the movement's 40th anniversary had been extensively celebrated just eight months previously. In a March issue of the *Two Worlds*, Emma wrote: 'On Saturday night, the 31st of this present month, will be commemorated as one of the most striking and unprecedented evidences of Divine influence exercised upon and through the human race that has ever yet been recorded on the page of history'. She went on to claim that the sisters, 'those humble children', had created a 'cable that anchors millions upon millions' around the globe.

But there were no more mentions of 'humble children' in the *Two Worlds* after the Fox's confessions: rather, the sisters were described as 'degraded', and Margaret Fox was singled out as a 'dissolute woman'. Along with other spiritualist publications, the

Manchester paper claimed the confessions were false and argued that the sisters had been manipulated by 'Jesuitical conspirators' who were the sworn enemies of spiritualism.

The editorial ended on a bullish note by claiming that the 'jubilation' felt by enemies of the movement would not last; that séances and meetings would continue; and that 'genuine mediums' would redouble their efforts to communicate with the 'spirit presence'.

The Unseen Universe

It transpired that the confessions made little impact on the movement. Just two years later, the scene was vibrant as Manchester hosted the largest gathering of believers that Britain had witnessed. The conference, which Emma organised with the help of 'spiritual guides and friends in the higher life', was held at the Co-op Assembly Rooms in Ardwick. The *Two Worlds* detailed the interminable speeches given by delegates from around the country and noted that many of them stayed on and visited the Ship Canal works.

So Emma was riding high: her conference was such a success that it became an annual event, and eventually coalesced into the National Union of Spiritualists, and the *Two Worlds* was on its way to becoming the most popular publication of its type in the country. But in 1892, she had to deal with a crisis when the board of the company accused her husband of financial impropriety and stripped her of the editorship of the paper.

The following year, she attempted to bounce back with a monthly magazine dedicated to: *'Spiritualism, Occultism, Ancient Magic, Modern Mediumship, and every subject that pertains to the Whence, What, and Whitherward of Humanity'*. Its title, *The Unseen Universe*, had already been used by the Manchester-based physicist Balfour Stewart for a book that stressed the ether was full of intelligence and life. Emma, though, was not overly concerned with original titles - the *Two Worlds* had been used at least twice before.

The Unseen Universe was touted as a departure from the other papers. It would not, promised Emma, 'trench upon the ground already occupied by the London Spiritual papers'. In ended up, though, as similar to other spiritualist publications - with the usual mix of spiritualism throughout history; stories about sundry strange phenomena; reviews of spiritualism around the world (and precious little about the Manchester scene); much pseudo-scientific theorizing; and articles by guest mediums, such as W. J. Colville.

What made the paper worse than the others was its over-reliance on material by Emma and her sister Margaret. There were many excerpts from *Ghostland*, her 1876 book, and pieces from an unfinished novel - *The Mystery of 9 Stanhope Street*. There was also an abundance of ropey poetry.

The paper folded after 12 issues, probably because of poor sales - although Emma insisted that she ended the project so she could concentrate on her autobiography, which she claimed she was urged to write by 'those who know in fragments something of my past wonderful life'. She maintained that she simply could not disappoint these people, and described them as: 'good friends who have still found me out, even in the midnight obscurity of Manchester spiritualism'.

Emma's dig at the city was as a sign of her frustration - for although she still made public appearances, and was still fawned over as one of the movement's grande dames, she was no longer central to spiritualism. The damp squib that was *Unseen Universe* effectively marked the end of her career.

In truth, there was nothing obscure about the city's spiritualist scene, and it was just two years after she made the remark that Harrison D. Barrett, the president of the American National Spiritualists Association, declared that: 'The orbit of British Spiritualism, to use an astronomical simile, may be described as an ellipse, of which London and Manchester are the foci'.

A photographic memoir of the scene of this era can be found in the *Two Worlds* portrait album, which was published the same year that Barrett visited the city. It was printed by the Manchester Labour Press Society, which was based on Tib Street, and which had been invested in by Edward Carpenter, who was an early gay rights pioneer and a proponent of a kind of mystical radicalness.

There was nothing radical, though, about the album. In fact, it was an indulgence which flattered the more affluent and prominent spiritualists. Emma was certainly flattered - her portrait was placed near the beginning of the book, along with a fawning description of her as a 'medium, seer and prophetess . . . who was peerless and incomparable'. Further into the album was Florence Cook, who was also flattered, and also included were most of the gentlemen from the board of the *Two Worlds*, who looked as sombre as any of the 'spirits' ever caught on film.

Although the album gave the impression that the city's spiritualists were uniformly earnest and respectable, the police did not always agree. They bracketed mediums with fortune-tellers and crystal ball gazers and occasionally made arrests. Harrison D. Barrett compared the attitude of Manchester's police with the force in Philadelphia, which tended to target mediums. 'The fortune telling cry', he wrote, 'was the peg the authorities based their action on'.

Spiritualism and Fortune-Telling

The police were not alone in linking spiritualism with fortune-telling, for spiritualists did the same. Their press regularly published articles about wise-folk, astrologers, and all manner of characters who divined the future; and the *Two Worlds* went as far as to produce a range of 'magic crystal skrying balls' in the late 1880s. Also indicative of the link between the two pursuits was the fact that Emma Hardinge Britten started her career as a skryer in the Orphic Circle, under the instruction of the legendary astrologer Zadkiel.

Characters who made a living from the telling of destinies had been present in the Manchester area for centuries. Most of them are forgotten, but a few are mentioned in the records. John Booker, as already noted, began his career in Manchester; and before him, there was Edmund Hartley, who probably practised some form of fortune-telling.

Another notable figure was Richard Morris, who was also known as Dick Spot because of a mark on his face. Ronald Hutton, in *The Triumph of the Moon*, claimed that Spot was a Mancunian, although this does not appear to have been the case. Rather, he was born in Bakewell in 1710 and took up the trade because he was raised by a fortune-telling aunt. According to the *Astrologers' Magazine*, which was published in the 1790s, 'he was thought by most country people to excel most astrologers'. Furthermore, his reputation at recovering lost property was so formidable that thieves were said to voluntarily return the loot when they heard that he had been consulted. After working in Buxton and other towns, Morris settled in Shrewsbury. But he may have also spent time in the Manchester area, for the fact that he left his money to hospitals in the town indicates there was some connection.

One wise-man-cum-astrologer who definitely hailed from the Manchester area was Old Rollinson, whose heyday was probably the 1820s and 30s. He lived in a cottage in Roe Green and had a day job as a 'gaffer' at the Bridgewater Trust, but at night he told fortunes and cast healing spells. According to John Harland, the *Manchester Guardian* reporter, 'people from the villages and hamlets for miles around' consulted him. One patient who was successfully treated was the uncle of an acquaintance of Harland's. The uncle suffered from a 'very severe haemorrhage', and was believed to be bleeding to death. His nephew contacted Rollinson on his behalf and received 'a small piece of parchment with sundry unintelligible characters upon it, which was sewed up in a small bag'. The uncle wore this near his heart and soon, it was claimed, the bleeding stopped and he recovered.

At some point, Harland was allowed to inspect Rollinson's occult library - which included William Lilly's *The Christian Astrologer* and Zadkiel's *The Grammar of Astrology* - but the reporter was not impressed and called the wise-man a 'tyro'. Rollinson's peers, though, were more respectful and joined him for regular meetings of a secret magical society. Harland was informed by a confidant of Rollinson that: 'these meetings took place in the upper chamber of a quiet public house in Manchester, where the posse locked the door behind them and remained for hours in deliberation'. The confidant never made it into the chamber. Instead, explained Harland, 'he had the honour of remaining outside the door as a watchman, guard, or sentinel, to prevent any prying listeners from approaching. He never knew what was discussed but presumed they dealt with 'magic and such like".

Another wise-man-cum-astrologer from this period was Clayton Chaffer, who decorated his consulting room in Dukinfield with occult books, brass instruments such as horologues, and pictures such as 'Raphael's *Witch or Oracle of the Future*. [5] There was also Matthew Halliwell, a Middleton weaver and self-taught astrologer, who was said to have lived 'in a small house that was surrounded by rumour and mystery'. [6]

During the early 1840s, fortune-telling was particularly popular in villages such as Middleton, Tonge, Alkrington, and Chadderton. The *Manchester Courier* described the scene this way: 'The mania of the populations of the villages and their vicinities, for obtaining glimpses into futurity, by consulting several arch impostors, bearing the name of fortune-tellers, or conjurors, is becoming of greater extent every day'. The 'mania' was said to be partly the consequence of the disappearance of a Middleton man, 61-year-old Archibald Hilton. He went missing after attending a funeral at Tonge, and after a search of all the pits and rivers in the district, his friends and relatives turned to a fortune-teller from Collyhurst Bridge, who was said to attract 'hundreds' of customers every day. After she revealed that Hilton drowned in the river near Rhodes Print Works, the water was searched in vain by hundreds. Another fortune teller, from Street Bridge, Chadderton, revealed that Hilton had been murdered and was buried within one hundred yards of a certain house in Alkrington. He claimed to know the name of the murderer but would not divulge it because he did not want to get involved with the police.

In January 1842, the *Manchester Courier* dispatched a journalist to the area. Along with 'two trusty friends', he 'traversed several paths, which wound by fertile knolls and agreeable pastures', and finally came to the 'neat' house of a 'conjuror'. Once inside they were ushered into a cramped study, which was said to be 'fit for melancholic reflection and hermit-like meditation', and which was stocked with books by the likes of Roger Bacon and William

Lilly. The fortune-teller then 'gazed through a glass of wondrous power' and claimed to see that Hilton had been killed at a colliery in Alkrington and that his body would be found at 11 o'clock the following day. The journalist, though, wasn't convinced - for he looked in the glass and saw that the 'particles' which were said to represent the colliery were nothing but 'atoms of water'. After the 'conjuror' gave the journalist's companions information they knew to be false, they travelled back to Manchester and professed to be 'more deeply impressed than ever with the gullibility of the lower orders of the district'.

It is understandable that one of the fortune-tellers in the Hilton case mentioned his fear of the authorities, for during the 1840s there was a police crackdown on the trade. One of the most notable to be arrested was James Bradshaw, who made a living from carpentry but was referred to as a 'prophet' and a 'soothsayer' by the *Manchester Courier*. Bradshaw, though, preferred to call himself a 'professor of prognostic astrology', and distributed cards and bills which revealed that through the study of the 'sublime influence of the heavenly bodies' he could foretell 'all accidents in the life of an individual'. He also promised to 'philosophically demonstrate, from the positions amid configurations of the planets, at the time of birth, the influence each configuration geometrically formed will have upon the fortunes, conduct, and health, of the individual'. In November 1842, Chief Superintendent Beswick and Inspector M'Mullin posed as customers and arrested Bradshaw, who was sentenced to a month in jail.

The following year, Inspector M'Mullin arrested another fortune teller, Isabella Moody, who the *Manchester Times* called 'a wily old creature'. She was later acquitted.

The prosecution of astrologers, particularly the imprisonment of James Bradshaw, inspired Zadkiel to found the British Association for the Advancement of Astral Science and the Protection of Astrologers in 1844. The association, though, proved to be ineffectual and the arrests continued.

Many of those who appeared in court were characters who played at being wise elders, or as the *Manchester Times* put it: they were 'old people pretending to the gift of witchcraft'. One elderly man called James Reynolds, who was an ex-weaver with a taste for Zadkiel's almanacks, was said to have used his fortune-telling skills to exploit a 'gentleman of considerable wealth', and was imprisoned for a month in 1845.

Another elderly character, who was acquitted in 1853, was Mr Brownhill from Eccles. Brownhill was trapped by an undercover policeman who asked for information on a young woman who he pretended to be 'very concerned for'. The astrologer, the court heard, then consulted a book - *The Prognostic Astronomer, or Horory's Astrologer, containing an improved method of solving 10,000 inquiries relating to futurity: by Dr W. J. Simmonite* - and informed the officer that the young woman would eventually marry him, although her relatives would disapprove. After the defence lawyer argued that: 'Some of the greatest philosophers had believed in astrology', and after the judge heard that the old man truly believed in the art, Brownhill was acquitted. He had to promise, though, to give up astrology.

Dr William Joseph Simmonite, the author of the book that Brownhill consulted, was one of the most renowned astrologers of the age. Born in Sheffield in 1810, he first achieved fame as a 'weather prophet' in the late 1830s and then published *The Quarterly Celestial Philosopher* and several almanacks. By the mid-1850s, he was such a prominent figure that a charlatan began to imitate him, or at least to capitalise on his name. The bogus Simmonite appeared in Manchester in 1856 and handed out the following bill:

> Dr. Simmonite, from America, professor of astronomy phrenology, and astrology', begs leave to inform his friends and the public, that it hath pleased God to give him superior gift of knowledge and understanding in future events. He has been deaf and dumb from his birth, and has already given that satisfaction which has astonished every one who has witnessed the wonderful gift God has given him. Numbers can sound forth his praise, and bear testimony that, although deprived of speech and utterance, his maker has endowed him with that wise gift that will enable him to obtain support from those who may wish to have a knowledge of future events. His gifts are from Heaven, and far sur-

pass all that has ever been witnessed on England's shores. His terms are moderate, and he respectfully solicits those who may feel disposed, to witness what God has given, &c. &c.

In a house on Mangle Street, off Piccadilly, 'Simmonite' peered into crystal balls and communicated with his customers by writing on slates. He was arrested after he informed one customer that her husband was in Crimea when the man was dead, and after another customer complained that he gave wholly inaccurate information about her daughter. The judge proved to be fairly lenient and gave him a three-month sentence which was to be suspended if he left town. To add to the mystery of it all, the *Manchester Courier* reported that this 'humbug' was 'escorted from court by two very fashionably-attired young females'.

Soon after, an outraged Dr W. J. Simmonite informed the *Manchester Guardian* that the charlatan 'was never in America', and was not the 'author of several books on mathamatics etc'. Rather, he was 'a native of Lancashire called Woods . . . who was a comb-maker by trade'. 'I wish', Simmonite stressed, 'to get hold of him to make a proper example of him'.

Less fortunate than the bogus Simmonite was Mary Montgomery, who was said by the *Manchester Courier* to have 'practised the arts and unholy rites of fortune telling'. She was imprisoned for two months for deceiving two young servant girls. Also sentenced during this era was John Rhoads of Salford, who was called a 'weird man' in the papers, and was said to possess 'magic glasses of most portentous appearance'; 'curiously written charms'; 'manuscript books which were unintelligible to any one save the writer'; and other occult books, including Zadkiel's almanacks. He was imprisoned for 'invoking evil destinies', although only for a week.

Indicative of how characters such as Rhodes fascinated many spiritualists was the decision by the editor of the *Spiritualist* to run a lengthy article in 1860, under the title *Crystal Seeing in Lancashire,* which promised to reveal the 'curious particulars connected with the occult powers possessed by the lower classes in busy Lancashire'. The piece, which mainly dealt with Manchester and its hinterlands, was far-fetched but entertaining. It was inspired by a Manchester skryer called 'Mr P', who recollected a wise-woman from his childhood. She was said to have 'greatly astonished' a female neighbour by allowing her to view her son, who was away with the army, in a crystal; and she was also reported to have enabled another female neighbour to keep watch on her salesman husband as he worked in Stalybridge. Mr P, who was a teacher in the suburbs, became acquainted with many skryers, including a school sexton, and an 'extraordinarily good seeress' called Marsha. He estimated that Stockport had a population of 300 of these characters, and he noted that demand for crystal balls was so high in Manchester that 'overflowing baskets' of them could be found in the city's shops.

Mr P also revealed that Manchester's 'seers' often operated clandestinely, and 'kept their secret from the uninitiated'. This was a consequence of the police continuing to arrest fortune-tellers during the 1860s. For instance, in 1862, Alice Vickers, who had made a living from telling fortunes for several years, received a month-long sentence. It was surprising, though, that the judge was so lenient: for Vicars had told Mary Ann Leek, of Pollard Street, that her marriage had been damaged by witchcraft, then she demanded money for quicksilver, which she claimed would help her magically redeem the relationship. Finally, she told Mrs Leek that she should kill her husband before he killed her.

A year later, Alphonso Gazelle, also known as Stephen Scott, escaped a prison sentence because he charged his customers for astrological charts, rather than the reading that accompanied them. After his lawyer argued that he was no more breaking the law than any others who sold almanacks or books on astrology, he was cautioned and discharged.

Another who was discharged was George Demlord, a 70-year old from Quebec. He came to the attention of the authorities in 1868 after he brazenly circulated flyers and gave readings at his lodgings on King Street. The judge claimed that he would have served three months if not for his age.

During the 1890s, as the *Manchester Courier* noted, 'the art of palmistry came into vogue' in the city. The police, though, were not impressed by the practice being fashionable and treated palmists like they treated other fortune-tellers. And so in 1895, Andrew Pearson of Salford was charged with 'unlawfully pretending to tell fortunes by means of palmistry'. He argued that palmistry was 'an acknowledged science' which enabled him to 'read character by the head and hand'. The judge, although he did not accept the argument, let Pearson off with a small fine.

'Madame' Sarah Gordon was another palmist who appeared in court. She arrived in Manchester in early January 1901 and began reading palms from her room at 73 Ford Street. One of the palms she read belonged to an undercover police constable. She told him that he would become a mechanic; that he would sail around the world before he was thirty; and that women would bring him to ruin. He, in turn, told her that she was under arrest. The judge fined her 40 shillings.

The police campaign against palmists and other fortune-tellers during the 1890s inspired Joseph Dobson, who was a Halifax solicitor and astrologer, to found the Occultists' Defence League. This organisation, which proved to be more effective than Zadkiel's 1840s Astrologer's Association, provided members with the services of a solicitor who was well versed in legal cases against occultists. In 1901, the league provided a solicitor to defend three Manchester characters who were part of a trial of seven palmists. The *Manchester Courier* reported that the seven were 'well-known exponents of the ancient and occult art of palmistry', and that the trial caused a 'flutter of excitement' in the court. The hearing, though, turned out to be fairly mundane and ended with the palmists receiving fines.

This purge of the city's fortune-tellers, and the fact that the police targeted such characters for decades, might suggest that the law's attitude towards them was clear cut: this was not, though, the case. There were situations - village fêtes, garden parties, church bazaars, and charitable events - where fortune tellers could operate with impunity. 'No such gathering was complete', revealed a lawyer in 1896, 'without a lady who practiced palmistry'.

That fortunes could be told in some situations without fear of prosecution, and not in others, was a case of class discrimination. Fortune telling was deemed to be acceptable if it was used to raise funds for some respectable middle-class cause or organisation, but it certainly wasn't if the palmist was operating out of a slum district and using the trade to subsist. Thus in 1853, the organisers of a fair at Knott Mill felt free to reveal in the *Manchester Times* that 'several conjurors and astrologers' would be present; and in 1898, the management of Old Trafford's Botanical gardens unabashedly trumpeted in the *Manchester Courier* that Palmistry, along with 'Children's Dances, Cinematograph, Dramatic and Variety Entertainments', would be one of the activities at a fun day. And yet Madame Roscoe of Hulme, described by the *Manchester Courier* as being 'poorly dressed', and Madame Ernest of Salford were respectively fined in 1904, and bound over in 1908 because they read palms to make a living.

The police, though, were not alone in viewing fortune-tellers through the filter of class: many middle-class astrologers also had a snobbish attitude towards practitioners who were considered to be socially inferior. They claimed their own 'scientific' astrology had little to do with the kind that was peddled on the street.

No group was more indignant when linked to 'common' fortune tellers than the spiritualists. Manchester's spiritualists were certainly indignant in 1895, after Emma Smith, a medium from Dunham Street in Hulme, was targeted by the police. A policeman's wife, who was sent to trap Smith, pretended to be engaged to a young man who worked at the Post Office and asked the medium if a marriage would ever occur. Smith said it would, but warned her that she 'would have to coax' the young man. After another witness claimed that Smith warned her about a 'dark young man', the medium was arrested.

Her case, which became something of a cause celebre, was covered by both the spiritualist and the mainstream press. High profile figures from the city's spiritualist community, such as Mr

Wallace, who was an editor at the *Two Worlds*, and William A. Wesley Orr, who was a close friend of Emma Hardinge Britten, testified that Smith's powers were genuine. Professor Ross, who was a mesmerist, also spoke up for her; and Mr William Robertson, who was a spiritualist and a miner, claimed that Smith saved his life by foretelling that an accident would happen at Bradford pit.

The court was not impressed. The prosecution inferred that the *Two Worlds* editor might have been biased because Smith advertised in the paper, and much was made of the medium referring to a 'dark young man', which was likened to the 'tall dark stranger' cliché used by fortune-tellers.

After Smith was found guilty and fined £5, the spiritualist press defended her. The *Two Worlds* claimed that the city's spiritualists had been 'startled' to hear that a 'psychometric medium could be arrested as a common fortune-teller', and *Light* called the trial 'an absurdity'. It also claimed that the prosecution's witnesses 'were capable of deception and lying', and accused the magistrate of 'palpably speaking through a cloud of ignorance and prejudice'.

The *Manchester Courier* hit back at *Light*, claiming that it was 'flippant' and unable to take criticism. The *Courier* also took a general swipe at spiritualism by arguing that any true revelations by spirits would not take the form of 'table rapping and manifestations in darkened rooms'. What was the use, the paper asked, of Smith being familiar with spirits: 'If such spirits could not, in a friendly way, warn her of the impending court proceedings'.

The spiritualists were also unhappy with the *Manchester Times*: for it conflated a report of Smith's case with that of Margaret Hartley, who was not only a fortune teller but was also alleged to be involved in the distribution of drugs.

The *Two Worlds* attempted to have the last word on the Smith case by including her in their album of Manchester's spiritualist worthies, and by claiming that. 'her powers have considerably developed since her trial'.

Three years after Smith's prosecution, in May 1899, came another notable case, which involved eighteen-year-old John

Moray Stewart-Young. Although he was arrested for embezzling from his employers, the court also heard that he was a bogus medium.

Young, who was called a 'mysterious youth' by the *Manchester Courier*, appeared in the dock wearing a velvet jacket and a bowler hat, and visible on one of his fingers was a large amethyst ring. These dapper clothes belied the fact that he was from a humble 'one-up one-down', which was situated on Ardwick's Back Kay Street.

To escape from Ardwick had been Young's rasion d'être: it was why he forged his employer's signature on a bunch of cheques, and why he took elocution lessons. With the stolen money he rented a house on Nelson Street, which was a fashionable middle-class area that was home to the Pankhursts, and furnished it lavishly. He created a library, a music room, and called the largest chamber the 'Christian Spiritualist Hall'. The table in the middle of the 'hall' was rigged with what was described in court as 'a small trap and cord', which was presumably used to produce rapping sounds.

After Young served six months of hard labour, he continued to reinvent himself. He claimed, in a memoir called *Osrac, the Self Sufficient*, which he wrote after emigrating to Nigeria, to have had an affair with Oscar Wilde whilst a teenager. Although he used his forging skills to fabricate letters from the writer, not many were fooled.

After a successful career as a merchant in Africa, during which he was given an honorary title by the Igbo people, Young died in 1939. His funeral was said to have been attended by ten thousand people.

A School for Prophets

The year before Young's trial had been spiritualism's jubilee, and Manchester decided to celebrate the occasion by holding a 'four day bazaar and international fair'. Of course, this would have been made difficult by the Fox sister's admission that spiritualism was bunkum, but Margaret Fox withdrew her confession in 1891, and that was good enough for many - in fact, the organisers paid tribute to the sisters by commissioning a reproduction of their wooden Hydesville house, where the first spirit communications were said to have taken place.

The festivities were opened by Emma Hardinge Britten, who was suffering from severe rheumatism and was confined to a wheelchair. At a meeting attended by three thousand, she revealed that Victor Hugo had said to her, 'again and again, that there is no more death; that which is called so is a splendid success'. *The Lancet* claimed this was a 'typically French comment'.

Emma died the year after the jubilee, and her followers decided to honour her by founding a 'School for Prophets'. She long dreamt of establishing such a school and first mentioned the idea in *Art Magic,* when she proposed it would 'provide a class of duly qualified magnetic Physicians, Prophets, Mediums, Clear Seers and Spiritualist persons'. She hoped that after graduation the students would serve the country as the 'mystics of antiquity' had served their civilisations.

Emma described how the place should look:

The floors of the (séance) room should be intersected with plateaus of glass to prevent the escape of magnetic fluid. The air should be purified with streams of ozone; and the walls surrounded with graceful forms of art and well selected colours.

The teaching staff would consist of 'holy women and scientific men', along with 'good, pure-minded, and healthy magnetics'; and the pupils, or 'young fresh susceptible organisms', would be chosen from applicants with the greatest gifts. Their talents would be finely honed. Clairvoyants would 'practice gazing steadily into the crystal or mirror'; and mediums would be taught how to handle electromagnetic batteries, which were thought to enhance the chances of communing with the dead. (Mediums who used this method were often referred to as 'electricians').

For Mr Charles H. Dennis this was too much. In a letter published in the *Two Worlds*, he stressed that the 'tingling jarring sensations produced by the batteries' would agitate the medium and make him or her less receptive to the dead. He also objected to the general idea of the prophet school and believed that formal training would turn mediums into little more than priests, and turn spiritualism into just another orthodox religion.

On the whole, though, the response to the school was positive. 'Imri', in the *Two Worlds*, claimed to have experienced 'genuine pleasure when reading the paragraph under the title: *A Modern School of Prophets*', and stressed the need for the 'establishment of an institution where those most suited to be 'interpreters' of heaven-born instructions could be prepared physically, mentally and spiritually'. Imri then revealed that the 'angel world' would support the venture, because it encouraged a 'spirit of inquiry and research' which would help to unite the spiritual and material worlds.

The 1890s saw constant support for the school, and after Emma died the aspiration was kept alive. Finally, in 1900, the Emma Hardinge Britten Memorial Institute and Library opened on Bridge St. It cost £5000 and included an impressive library stocked with over 3000 books about spiritualism, most of which were from the collection of Sir Arthur Conan Doyle.

A few years after Emma's death, W. J. Colville claimed that 'since her passing to spirit life, this earnest worker has occasionally made herself known to me'. Initially, he was puzzled because Emma, who was dark-haired, appeared as a 'radiant maiden with light golden curls'. However, when he visited her sister in Manchester, Colville was shown:

> *A picture taken many years ago, representing Emma Hardinge in youthful costume as Queen of the Fairies. This picture represented the young lady, who afterwards became Mrs. Britten, in flaxen ringlets, and in every way was precisely as she showed herself to me on the occasion of my vision.*

In 1907, John Lobb published: *In Talks with the Dead: Lumi-*

nous Rays from the Unseen World, Illustrated with Spirit Photographs. It contained a photograph of Emma which was said to have been taken three years after she died. The caption read: 'Miss Emma Hardinge Britten, the eloquent speaker and talented writer, being 'dead' yet speaketh. Her name will ever be fresh and fragrant in the history of spiritualism'.

The Wars and the Last Witch

In the *History of Spiritualism*, Sir Arthur Conan Doyle revealed that several mediums foresaw the First World War. A few of the predictions were made as the war loomed and were not particularly impressive, but one was striking because it was issued 39 years before the conflict began. 'The general fact,' Conan Doyle wrote, 'of a great world catastrophe, and England's share in it, is thus spoken of in a spirit communication received by the Oxley Circle in Manchester and published in 1875'.

He then quoted a section from the *Angelic Revelations* which warned of: 'a mighty struggle, a terrible bloodshed according to human modes of expression, a dethronement of kings, an overthrow of powers, great riot and disturbance; and still greater commotion amongst the masses concerning wealth and its possession'

This can, of course, be seen as just another vague prophecy of doom. But it is understandable, given that doom and destruction were unfolding before people's eyes, that such prophecies were viewed with interest.

It is also understandable, given the horrific loss of young lives, that spiritualism flourished during the war. In Manchester, a new generation of mediums - such as Mr and Mrs Hunter, who ran a popular operation out of 363 Oxford Road - emerged to meet the demand.

Reports of supernatural events also emerged during the war. Perhaps the most famous was the tale of the Angels of Mons - which posited that spiritual entities had protected British soldiers on the battlefield. The yarn originated from the fantasy writer Arthur Machen, who was inspired by tales of the fighting at Mons to write a story called *The Bowmen* - which had the spirits of archers from the Battle of Agincourt returning to help the modern forces. Machen stressed on several occasions that the piece was fictional, but the story took on a life of its own as parish magazines reprinted it, and as soldiers began to claim they had seen the spirits. The *Manchester Guardian* then boosted the myth when it published a sermon by the popular preacher Reverend R. F. Horton, in which he claimed that 'no thoroughly modern man should be foolish enough to disbelieve the statements' of the soldiers - or to 'pooh pooh the experience as hallucination'.

A less celebrated story of a wartime spirit was promoted by the Manchester spiritualist A. W Orr, who revealed in a newspaper that he had been contacted by a young Bolton medium who had a premonition of her brother's death on the battlefield. She claimed she began to write a letter but only managed 'Dear' before falling asleep. When she woke, though, the following letter, which was not in her handwriting, was before her:

> *Mother - I was left to die on the battlefield at quarter to three in the afternoon, on Thursday, shot through the stomach by a sniper. Tell Annie (his wife) 5s is in my inner pocket, and photos and a wallet. Ask for my things from the War Office, and leave rest to God. Albert.*

Orr, who vouched for the medium's 'respectability and credibility', revealed that Albert's death was not officially confirmed until weeks later.

The police, though, maintained their belief that mediums were neither respectable or credible and continued to make arrests. In 1915, for instance, they nabbed Mr and Mrs Hunter. The couple told the magistrates that they were genuine psychic mediums and herbalists, but the court dished out a £5 fine.

Another medium, Mary Barnes of Gorton, found trouble in 1916 after she predicted, during a session at the Longsight Spiritualist Church, that a woman whose husband was in the army would receive a 'letter from abroad'. The police considered this to be 'preying on a soldiers wife' and charged Barnes.

For Manchester's spiritualists, this was a prosecution too far - so they hit back by establishing the 'United Spiritualists Defence Fund'. As well as assisting mediums who had incurred legal costs, the fund backed a campaign - headed by a trance medium from Bristol called Earnest Oaten - to amend the Witchcraft and Vagrants act. Oaten had no luck with the campaign, but his profile was boosted and in 1919 he was installed as the editor of the *Two Worlds*. He claimed to have been told by the spirit of Emma Hardinge Britten that he would land the job.

Oaten proved to be a dynamic editor and made history by becoming the first spiritualist to appear on the BBC in 1934.

During the 1930s, Manchester continued to attract high-profile mediums - such as Lillian Bailey, who travelled from Crewe to Manchester twice a week during the 1930s to give public and private séances at the 'School for Prophets'. Later, she developed an exclusive clientele which was said to include Mae West, Mary Pickford, and senior members of the British royal family.

Another frequent visitor during this period was Helen Duncan - who became infamous during World War II as the last British person convicted under the Witchcraft Act of 1735. Her reputation, though, was poor long before the trial. In 1928, photographs of her materializations had shown they were nothing but crude papier-mâché dolls; and in 1931, the famous researcher Harry Price was so frustrated after he attempted to examine her under controlled conditions that he wrote: 'Could anything be more infantile than a group of grown-up men wasting their time, money, and energy on the antics of a fat female crook'.

When attempting to restore her reputation, Duncan agreed to hold further séances under test conditions. One was held in Manchester in April 1932 and was attended by Ernest Oaten and a 'committee of ladies' who ensured that the medium had nothing secreted in her clothes by dressing her in a special gown. After further checks were made on the cabinet the séance got underway. According to a report in the *National Spiritualist*, Duncan pulled out all the stops: strange lights appeared behind the curtains; spirit voices barked orders; ectoplasm swirled around; and the sitters were treated to a roll call of their lost school friends, husbands, parents, and other loved ones. There was also a drama when Duncan screamed for no apparent reason and the sitters were forced to: 'sing softly to restore harmony and to build up vibrations'.

Those who were impressed by the séance may have changed their opinion the following year when she was convicted of fraudulent mediumship in Edinburgh and fined £10.

In 1944 came the witchcraft trial, which was the result of Duncan announcing, during a séance in Portsmouth, that the spirit of a soldier had informed her of the sinking of HMS Barham. This was not supposed to be public knowledge, and so the Navy took notice and Duncan was put on trial. Her legal fees were covered by the Defence Fund which was established after the arrest of the Gorton medium Mary Barnes.

Many witnesses were called to attest to Duncan's authenticity as a trance medium. One man from Blackpool explained that she had materialised his mother-in-law, who had recently died from injuries sustained in the Manchester blitz; and another claimed his dead grandfather appeared at a Manchester séance:

> *He was a very corpulent man . . . he looked around the room very quizzically until his eyes met mine . . . his face was brown and bronzed in the same way . . . the same look was in his eye . . . (he spoke with) the same expression and tones.*

Despite such testimonies, and despite claims that the proceeds of her séances often went to charity, Duncan was sentenced to nine months. Ever since there have been two main misconceptions about the case: one of them has it that she was the last woman to be convicted of witchcraft, whereas she was actually found guilty of obtaining money by fraudulently claiming to have magical powers; and the other maintains that she imparted information at the séance which she should not have known because it was strictly classified. Yet, as Graeme Donald has stressed, the government's attempts to suppress the news of HMS Barham's fate failed and rumours 'spread like wildfire'. Thus Duncan 'simply picked up the gossip and decided to turn it into profit'. *1*

After she was released, Duncan promised not to give further séances, but she soon lapsed. At a gathering in Manchester, she once more produced manifestations and her supporters were thrilled. Mavis Smethurst, who attended the event, recalled that Duncan addressed her past: 'Helen showed us the clothes she would wear, all black both outer and underwear, the reason being, she had been unjustly prosecuted and sent to prison in the 1940s for fraud, so she was anxious to let us see that everything was above board'.

Smethurst also claimed that Duncan's performance was 'conducted in good red light', and described the following manifestation:

> *The entities appeared just as if they were still in the flesh. The clothes were quite normal and in good colours. There were ten sitters and we all sat in a row about six feet from where the spirit forms built up. There was nothing in front of us so we all had a good view. After the spirit entities had finished speaking to their loved ones I was astonished to see them collapse on the floor and quickly disappear.* 2

During the mid-1950s, Duncan was arrested whilst she was holding a séance. She died soon after, which led her supporters to claim that the police were responsible for her death because they wrenched her from a trance. Others, though, noted that she had been overweight and in poor health for years.

Electronic Communication for the Spiritual Emancipation of the People

A more modern take on spiritualism was attempted in Manchester by the Electronic Voice Communication Society in 1949. The society, as the name suggests, sought to use technology - such as specially adapted cameras, tape recorders and radios - to reach the spirit world. This was not, though, a fresh aspiration: in 1871, the *Manchester Evening News* ran an article which prophesized the invention of a 'psychographic camera' that would record spirits; in 1920, Thomas Edison speculated about creating 'an instrument so delicate as to be affected or moved or manipulated by our personality as it survives in the next life'; and during the next two decades, several experimenters claimed to have picked up strange voices on electronic equipment.

At the International Spiritualist Federation in 1948, a Dutchman called Mr N. Zwaana demonstrated the 'Super-ray', which he claimed facilitated direct communication with spirits; and the following year, after an electrical engineer called Mark Dyne arranged for the machine to be brought to Manchester, the Electronic Voice Communication Society was born. Their manifesto, *Electronic Communication for the Spiritual Emancipation of the People*, which cost sixpence, was published in 1954.

The spiritual emancipation of the people did not occur in the 1950s, but in 1962 the *Manchester Evening Chronicle* revealed that the spirits had informed Mark Dyne that 'a new age was commenced'. The machine which delivered the message, explained Dyne, utilised 'a Morse buzzer and a lamp', and communications came through as a series of flashing lights. He also informed the Chronicle that he sought to augment the contraption by setting up a 'highly sensitive camera' and a 'radio receiver', which would deliver images of the spirits and amplify the sounds they made.

Dyne explained how such devices would work:

> *Just as ordinary radio and TV signals are unseen vibrations through the air, so I believe there are disturbances in the ether caused by the spirit world. All we have to do is to find the wave length and frequency and we shall be able to pick them up.*

CHAPTER EIGHT

The Occultist of Burton Road, and other True Tales

Manchester's occultists and spiritualists had much in common. They shared a belief in the spirit world, and both groups attempted to communicate with the dead. There were also many individuals with a foot in both camps - mediums such as W. J. Colville and Emma Hardinge Britten were deeply interested in the occult, and a few of the city's foremost occultists closely followed spiritualism.

There were, though, notable differences between the two movements. Spiritualism was a popular movement, whereas occultism was more elitist. Occultists were also more preoccupied with arcane knowledge and the mysteries of Egypt and the east than the spiritualists. Which is not to say that the spiritualists didn't dabble in such topics - their periodicals often carried articles on ancient India and Tibet. Eastern mysticism, though, was largely the domain of the occultists. Characters such as John Yarker liked nothing better than to pore over arcane eastern texts, whilst others were more than happy to don faux-oriental gear when participating in ceremonial magic.

Introducing Mr John Yarker - Occultist Extraordinaire

Yarker, who was Manchester's most prominent occultist during this era, was a scion of the Leybourne family from North Yorkshire. After an early childhood in the village of Swindale, the family moved to various places in Lancashire and eventually arrived in Manchester in 1849, when he was sixteen years old.

John Yarker

The city at this point was taken with mesmerism, whilst the advent of spiritualism was just around the corner - and Yarker developed an interest in both. In later years, he used his skills as a mesmerist on a 'good clairvoyant', who then filled in the gaps in a family history that he was working on. His interest in spiritualism, meanwhile, earned him the scorn of a fellow occultist, the Reverend W. A. Ayton, who claimed that Yarker, although 'learned and intelligent', was too much taken with 'ordinary spiritualism'. (It was not that Ayton didn't believe in spirits - for he claimed that a long-dead girl, who he had been in love with, appeared in his alchemical laboratory and tried to entice him to kiss her.)

Yarker's real passion, though, was not mesmerism or spiritualism but Freemasonry. He joined his first Masonic outfit, Manchester's Lodge of Integrity, in 1854, when he was just twenty-one. Two years later, he entered the Jerusalem Encampment, which was the town's Knights Templar organisation, and from then on he sought out lodge after lodge, and society after society, with the passion of a boy scout collecting badges. To list them all would be tiresome - even Yarker, when noting them for the introduction pages of his books, cut short the list with 'etc, etc'.

Several of his societies, though, were influential and deserve to be mentioned. The Societas Rosicruciana In Anglia, for instance, was devoted to the study of the original Rosicrucian manifestos and was established in London around the mid-1860s. The Manchester branch - referred to as the 'Manchester College' - was headed by Yarker. It is not to be confused with another organisation, the Order of Rosicrucians, also known as the Brotherhood of the Holy Cross, which was founded in Manchester in 1852. This group was restricted to twelve members and their identities were kept secret, which was strange because the order was more of a supper club than a serious occult enterprise. On the first Monday of each month, the group met over dinner and heard a speech on antiquarian and literary matters relating to the Manchester area. One such lecture concerned *The Origins and Derivations of local street names within the Hundred of Salford*. After a while, the secrecy was dropped and it became known that the group included several prominent characters called John, such as John Harland, the reporter who spent time with the wise-man Old Rollinson; John Just, who was a master at Bury Grammar School; and John Leigh, who was the city's first Medical Officer of Health. And as if to prove that it was definitely not an esoteric secret society, Harland began to publish their transactions in the *Manchester Guardian*. By 1869, the group was defunct, and would soon be forgotten. In contrast, Societas Rosicruciana In Anglia acquired legendary status because of its influence on later occult groups.

Several of Yarker's orders boasted that they were 'ancient brotherhoods'. L'ordre du Temple, which he joined in Paris in

1869, claimed to have an unbroken lineage that stretched back to Jacques de Molay. This was easily trumped, though, by another of his outfits: The Ancient Order of Zuzimites, which let it be known that it was 6000 years old. All of which was, of course, nonsense - but Yarker believed the claims. As we will see, establishing the ancient pedigree of Freemasonry was his life's work.

THE KNEPH

Official Journal of the Antient and Primitive Rite of Masonry.

Vol. 1, No. 1.]   JANUARY 1st, 1881.   [MONTHLY

During this period, he lived at 43 Chorlton Road, but in 1876 he moved with his family to the 'Poplars' on Burton Road, where he would stay for the rest of his life. It was a short walk from Parkfield, the Didsbury estate of Charles Blackburn. It is not clear, though, if Blackburn and Yarker were acquainted: but it seems unlikely, given Yarker's interest in spiritualism, that he would not have occasionally associated with such a stalwart of the scene - the financial backer of the *Spiritualist* nonetheless.

From the Poplars, Yarker expanded his occult enterprises, and in 1881 he became the driving force behind a publication called the *Kneph* - which took its name from the ancient Egyptian symbol of the winged egg, and which was edited by Kenneth MacKenzie, who was one of Yarker's Societas Rosicrusias In Anglia colleagues. The journal promoted Yarker's various societies: such as the Ancient Order of Zuzmites, and also the Swedenborg Rite, which he imported from Canada, where it was administered by

Samuel Beswick - the Stockport native who had been raised in the New Church during the 1820s and 30s. Most of all, though, the *Kneph* covered the business of the Antient and Primitive Rite, which was Yarker's most cherished outfit. This mishmash of alchemical and Egyptian occult references was an amalgamation of the Rites of Memphis and Misrain and had been knocking around Europe since the first two decades of the 1800s. By the 1880s, Yarker had become the Sovereign Grand Master and was administering it from Manchester. Strangely, the *Manchester Courier* deemed the business of the rite newsworthy in 1883 and reported that 'a great number of nationalities, including Greeks, Syrians, Egyptians, Indians and Jews', met at the Grosvenor Hotel on Deansgate to attend a general meeting.

The Antient and Primitive Rite may have been cherished by Yarker, but it certainly wasn't loved by the ruling body of English Freemasonry, and neither was the Swedenborg Rite. Both outfits were considered to be outside of the official Masonic cannon. They were, it was deemed, 'irregular' and 'clandestine'. And Yarker, who was unwilling to kowtow to the authorities, was also considered irregular and was expelled from various official bodies. Henceforth, he was lumbered with a reputation - which was reinforced by generations of Freemason historians - as a 'rogue-Mason', a 'degree-monger', and a charlatan. Consequently, much of the *Kneph* was taken up with articles which defended Yarker's reputation and attacked the Grand Lodge.

The Celestial Brotherhood

Three years after he founded the *Kneph*, Yarker became a member of the Celestial Brotherhood. This outfit was run by John Thomas: a Welshman, born in 1826, who wound up living on Earl Street in Longsight in the 1890s. He was almost as much a part of the occult zeitgeist as Yarker - but whereas Yarker was a student and promoter of the occult, rather than one who claimed to have powers, Charubel was a full-on psychic and mystic. He was, wrote the astronomer Kim Farnell, 'a seer, prophet, and healer, who also had the ability to see elemental spirits'. (According to W. A. Ayton, Charubel became 'subject to the will of the Elementaries, and lost control of himself').

Charubel

Yarker was not the only notable member of Charubel's Brotherhood: for Gustav Meyrink, who became famous for his novel *The Golem*, joined in 1895 and was given the name 'Theaverel' - 'I go, I seek, I find'.

Alan Leo, who was born in London in 1860, was another notable member and was named 'Agorel' by the Brotherhood. He has routinely been referred to as the 'father of modern astrology', largely because he established the practice of giving psychological or character-based readings, which to a great extent replaced the old habit of predictions and prophecies. He also infused the practice with an eastern-flavour, due to his interest in Theosophy and Indian astrology.

Leo was not, though, such a mystic when he arrived in Manchester. Rather, he was a greengrocer called William Frederick Alan. Manchester, though, soon transformed him from an ordinary shopkeeper into an obsessive astrologer. The process began when he developed a stress-based illness and consulted Dr Richardson, who was one of the city's herbalist-cum-astrologers. Richardson not only improved the grocer's health, but also instructed him in the art of constructing horoscopes, and introduced him to the city's occult subculture.

Another of Charubel's outfits was the British and Foreign Society of Occultists, which published a periodical, the *Seer and Celestial Reformer*, in the 1880s. The editor was J. J. Morse, who went on to run the *Two Worlds*, and Charubel contributed articles and administered the subscriptions. It is likely, though, that not many people did subscribe because the paper was light-weight and lacked quality. It carried few articles, but for some reason ran several lengthy pieces on the composer Handel. The standard improved, though, after new owners re-launched it as the *Occult Magazine*. They promised to deliver a paper devoted to: *'Ancient wisdom, philosophy, folklore, magic, crystalmancy, astrology, mesmerism, occult spiritualism, and other branches of a kindred nature'*; and they increased the number of contributors. The three main writers - Zanoni, Mejnour, and Glyndon - took their names from characters in Edward Bulwer-Lytton's 1842 novel Zanoni, which dealt with Rosicrucian themes. William Oxley also chipped in with a piece about a 'Fossilized Giant' that was found in a bed of 'hematite clay' near the Giant's Causeway in Ireland, and which was displayed in Manchester in 1876. (The next issue carried a letter from an Irishman who revealed that it was a hoax).

The *Occult Magazine* also carried many mentions of the Hermetic Brotherhood of Luxor - a society administered by the new owners, which specialised in practical occultism and is thought to have been influenced by Emma Hardinge Britten.

Charubel's involvement with the magazine ended after the takeover. He did, though, place an advert in the first issue of the revamped publication, aimed at 'people suffering from chronic complaints' - which indicates that he was not above a bit of charlatanism, for he claimed he could help the chronic sufferers by utilizing 'magnetic healing from a distance'.

That Charubel could indulge in a little bunkum would not

have surprised Gustav Meyrink - for when he joined the Celestial brotherhood he received details of a 'mystical rite' which the Welshman comically hyped by claiming it brought the user: 'face to face with terrible realities'.

The realities that Charubel himself faced just before moving to Manchester may not have been terrible, but they were definitely grim. He suffered from such financial woes, explained W. A. Ayton in a note to a fellow mystic, that he was forced 'to send begging letters to everyone'. And whilst in Manchester, as Kim Farnell has stated: 'He became less and less active and by the time he was 82 years old he no longer left his room'. At the age of 80, though, he was active enough to publish a book, which as Ellic Howe noted, was 'unreadable but fascinating'. The extended title gave indicated what was in store for the reader: *Psychology of Botany: A Treatise on Trees, Shrubs, and Plants, etc, for the cure of diseases and ailments, of the human system, (without medicine) by Sympathy (Positive and Negative) on the Soul Plane, by "Charubel" (The Great Seer), a Collegian who trained for the Gospel 60 years ago, gave his whole life up for the love of Nature and the Study of the Supernatural Elements, &c., &c.*

As well as continuing to write and publish, Charubel, as Kim Farnell noted, also remained very much in touch with the occult scene:

> *The world came to his door, and he received many visitors from all over the globe. . . . Esotericists, astrologers, healers and spiritualists all travelled to study at the feet of a man who they regarded as a great teacher'.*

Whether John Yarker was such a visitor is not known. But it is probable, as a member of the Celestial Brotherhood, that he made the short journey from Burton Road to Longsight, to sample Charubel's occult philosophy.

The Hermetic Order of the Golden Dawn

During this period, Yarker also became one of the Society of Eight - which mainly focused on alchemy, although one meeting was dedicated to the tarot. That Yarker was one of the eight illustrates just how much of a heavyweight he was in the world of English occultism: for whilst some of his brethren from other groups and lodges were solely interested in making business and social contacts, the Society of Eight, like the Societas Rosicruciana In Anglia, consisted of the country's most serious occultists.

According to the historian Jocelyn Godwin, the group was a link to England's occult past - because Frederick Hockley, who was one of the eight, associated during the 1820s with the Mercurri, which was the secret society that Emma Hardinge Britten worked for as a girl. Hockley was also reputed to have studied with Francis Barrett, who in 1801 published *The Magus* - a primer on magic and esotericism that was to become legendary. Also one of the eight was W. A Ayton, who was said by the poet Yeats to be akin to the 'great adepts of the past'.

As well as being a bridge to the past, the society also shaped the future of the occult in Britain - for in 1888 two of its members, William Wynn Westcott and Samuel Liddell MacGregor Mathers, founded the most iconic Victorian magic outfit of them all: the Hermetic Order of the Golden Dawn.

When it came to dressing up in exotic garb and adopting arcane names or 'magical mottos', the members of the Golden Dawn reigned supreme. They chose Latin names, such as W. A. Ayton's 'Frater Virtute Orta Occident Rarius', which translates as 'those that rise by virtue rarely fall', and they loved to don robes and Egyptian headdresses. One of the most famous photographs of MacGregor Mathers has him dressed as an ancient Egyptian, and looking like a precursor to the Wilson, Keppel and Betty variety act.

Despite the exotic trimmings, the order's meetings often resembled social get-togethers. In fact, Alex Owen, in her excellent account of the order, likened it to a 'gentleman's club': and George Cecil Jones, or 'Frater Volo Noscere', claimed it was: 'a club, like any other club, a place to pass the time and meet one's friends'.

A less critical appraisal would note that Westcott and MacGregor Mathers assembled a large and varied array of occult traditions and moulded them into a coherent system. First Order initiates - the Golden Dawn consisted of three orders - were taught astrology, geomancy, cabalism, and alchemy. They were also introduced to the writings of Hermes Trismegistus, Rosicrucian thought, John Dee's Enochian system, and the magic of ancient Egypt.

It seems strange, given Yarker's enthusiasm for such enterprises, and given that he knew several of its most influential members, that he never joined the Golden Dawn. W. A. Ayton may have revealed the reason: 'Yarker', he wrote, 'quarrels with everybody'. It's possible, then, that Yarker avoided the order because of a fractious relationship with Westcott or Mathers, or both.

There were, though, others with links to Manchester who did join. Thomas W. Wilson, known as 'Sub Rosa', had a druggists on Cross Street and was described by Ayton as 'a chemist with occult proclivities'. He proved useful to Ayton when he concocted some incense for him, which was made from Verbena: a herb said to have magical qualities.

A more influential Golden Dawn magician was Annie Horniman, who often stayed at the Midland Hotel, where she caught the attention of other guests by wearing exotic clothing and 'openly smoking cigarettes'. Her family owned Horniman's Tea, which operated out of the city, and Annie owned the Gaiety Theatre - and got involved in all aspects of the business: she set ticket prices, chose the plays, and even ensured that occult symbols were incorporated into the programme designs.

She was a popular figure in the city - mainly because she promoted the 'Manchester School' of writers: a group which included Harold Brighouse and Stanley Houghton, and also Alan Monkhouse, who satirized the Gaiety scene in *Nothing Like Leather*. Annie played herself in that production and received a standing ovation.

> GAIETY THEATRE, MANCHESTER
>
> Sole Proprietor and Licensee: Miss A. E. F. Horniman
>
> General Manager   B. Iden Payne
> Acting Manager   Edwin T. Heys
>
> The following is a description of the well-known Symbol that appears on all announcements of Miss Horniman's Company

As for the Golden Dawn, her unofficial role in the order was to financially support MacGregor Mathers, which she did generously, and for which she received little gratitude. Her official role, though, was to instruct second-order initiates in the art of astral travel, of which she had extensive experience. If she wasn't running the Gaiety in Manchester, she might be found on Saturn, Jupiter, Mars, Venus, Mercury, or even the Sun.

One of the astral techniques she used was known as 'Travelling in the Spirit Vision', and involved concentrating on a symbol of the desired destination. If Horniman wanted to reach Saturn, she stared at a circle of indigo, which represented the planet, until she felt herself pass into it. On one occasion, after reaching Saturn, she used a magical procedure to summon a guide, who turned out to be male, winged, tall, and clad in half-armour. He claimed his fellow beings had psychic abilities, and also that his civilisation was in decline. Three weeks later, Horniman and a friend journeyed to Jupiter and met a tall and beautiful woman who was clad in classical robes. This lady revealed she had 'seen much of Earth', which she referred to as 'your miserable world', and claimed it 'made her sad'.

Alex Owen, in *The Place of Enchantment*, argued that: 'It is unlikely that the two magicians believed that they were visiting the actual planets'. Rather, she claimed, 'it is almost certain that

Annie Horniman

Horniman conceived of these journeys as explorations of the states or energies associated with each planet, and thought of their planetary experiences as real in the purely magical sense'. And yet Horniman's accounts of her astral travels were not vague descriptions of 'energies'. As noted, she claimed to meet and converse with living entities, and she gave potted histories of the civilisations of different planets. It seems clear, then, that she either believed she had visited the planets in an astral sense, or that it was just a flight of fancy which may have been concocted to aggrandise her status as a magician.

Horniman's time in the Golden Dawn was fraught with conflict. She was dismissed from the order after a dispute with the autocratic MacGregor Mathers, and after being reinstated she was dismayed to discover that the organisation had become infected with sub-groups. Florence Farr, who was an actress and a leading member of the order, headed such a group, known as 'The Sphere'. The members every Sunday at noon, but not exclusively on earth. According to one member, Dr Robert William Felkin, they congregated on the Astral Plane, where they communed with an Egyptian master.

Other issues which dismayed Horniman included the lack of

meticulousness concerning written records, and the increasing influence of Dr Edward Berridge, who was allowed to champion sexual magic - particularly the notion of intercourse between the magicians and elemental spirits. It was not just Horniman, though, who experienced difficulties - for the whole order was riven by political disputes. One bone of contention came in the shape of Aleister Crowley - who quickly passed through the first-order, and with MacGregor's blessing was initiated into the second-order in Paris in 1900. This caused the London lodge to object on the grounds that Crowley was 'morally depraved'.

As the dispute rumbled on, a sex scandal occurred involving another occult group, but which dammed the Golden Dawn by association, and by 1902 the order had dissolved. A new incarnation, the Hermetic Order of the Morgenroth, was formed but lasted only a year.

During the twentieth century, several occult orders appeared which were influenced by the Golden Dawn. They were mostly uninspiring, but there was one intriguing outfit, known as the Brotherhood of the Path, which was active during the 1930s and 40s. It published a journal called the *Golden Dawn*, and claimed to be an 'Occult Fraternity that aimed to promote the study of ancient wisdom teachings'. Although mostly based in East Yorkshire, it had a Manchester outpost which was made up of students from the university.

The Palladian Order

During the 1890s, John Yarker was caught up in a controversy when several French writers claimed he was one of the leaders of a diabolical secret society which had a presence in Manchester.

This affair - which popularised the terms 'Black Mass' and 'Satanism' - was largely the work of Marie Joseph Gabriel Antoine Jogand-Pages, who used the pen name Léo Taxil. In a series of pamphlets and articles, he claimed that Freemasonry had been infiltrated by the 'Palladian Order', which worshipped the devil.

Soon after, a character called Dr Bataille emerged and confirmed that Taxil's tale was true. In another series of articles, which became the book *The Devil in the Nineteenth Century*, he claimed to have infiltrated the order and to have discovered that it worshipped Baphomet - the goat-headed human figure which was associated with the Knights Templars. He also claimed to have met the Palladian leaders, including John Yarker.

Bataille explained that his adventure began in 1880 - when he was working as a surgeon aboard the *Anadyr*, which was returning to Europe from China. Signor Carbuccia, a regular passenger who was a silk merchant and a 'dealer in curiosities', climbed onboard at Ceylon. Bataille knew him to be virulent and cocksure, and so he was shocked to find that the merchant was suddenly a timid old man.

Carbuccia was reluctant to talk about his transformation, but Bataille pressed him until the merchant unburdened himself. He explained that after joining a lodge in Naples he developed a taste for esoteric organisations. A. E. Waite put it this way: *Carbuccia fell upon occult Masons like the Samaritan among thieves . . . he became a Sublime Hermetic Philosopher, he fraternized with the Brethren of the New Reformed Palladian, and optimated with the Society of Re-Theurgists'*. And whilst in Manchester, Waite continued, the merchant was *'allured by Memphis initiates into Kabbalistic rites'*.

In Calcutta, eight days before his conversation with Bataille, Carbuccia found that the Palladists were feverishly excited. They had purchased the skulls of three missionaries from a source in China and were preparing to use them during a new magical rite. A séance was held, and as Waite claimed: 'Christ was cursed impressively and Lucifer was solemnly blessed at the altar of Baphomet'. Soon, a human figure appeared. He was 'tall, bearded, distinguished and infinitely melancholy', and the Palladists accepted him as Lucifer. As he paced around, he looked deep into the eyes of the Masons, and Carbuccia later claimed he would have given ten years of his life to have avoided his gaze. Finally, the figure shook hands with the cabal's Grand Master and then there was darkness. After torches were lit, the Masons found the figure had disappeared and that the Grand Master was dead. During the following days, Carbuccia became convinced he was damned.

After hearing this tale, Bataille decided to infiltrate the order. Like Carbuccia, he travelled the world and witnessed fantastic sights: in Ceylon, he met an ape with a good grasp of Tamil; elsewhere he witnessed the Palladian order carrying out human sacrifices, and at a séance, he saw a crocodile manifest and play the piano.

Another character who confirmed Taxil's claims was Domenico Margiotta, who was an Italian ex-Mason. Margiotta's story was not as fantastical as Bataille's, but he did agree that Freemasonry was under the sway of the Palladian Order, and he also implicated Yarker - who was said to be the head of a 'triangular province' in Manchester.

The tales of Taxil and company caused a sensation in France. Their books were particularly popular with Catholics and were taken seriously by the church. But how did Yarker's neighbours on the Withington and West Didsbury border react? Did they believe that Yarker was a Satanist and a leader of the sinister 'Palladian Order'? Or were they oblivious to the claims of Taxil and his colleagues?

If any Burton Road residents *had* been worried, they may have been reassured in 1896 when A. E. Waite refuted Taxil in a book called *Devil Worship in France*. Waite demonstrated that the order was a fantasy, and dismissed the claims against Yarker as 'categorically untrue'. It was stressed that Yarker had never met Dr Bataille;

that he had no idea what a 'triangular province' was; and that the first he had heard of the order was when the scandal began in France.

Yarker was also defended by the *Manchester Courier*, in an article which claimed that the affair amounted to an attack on Freemasonry - or as the paper lyrically put it: 'it was a crusade against the brethren of the mystic trowel'.

A year after Waite's book and the *Courier* article were published, Taxil admitted that the whole affair was a hoax. He revealed that Dr Bataille was created by himself and Dr Charles Hacks, and he claimed to have been motivated by a desire to highlight the irrational and gullible nature of the Catholic Church.

The Arcane Schools

In 1896, three years after the Palladian affair, Yarker published his masterwork, *The Arcane Schools*, in which he tried to establish continuous links between the ancient Aryans and the Freemasons. As noted, this was a familiar Yarker theme, which he had touched on in several other books, such as *Notes on the Scientific and Religious Mysteries of Antiquity; the Gnosis and Secret Schools of the Middle Ages*.

He began *The Arcane Schools* by arguing that the Aryans had sprung from Atlantis. This was, he conceded, a questionable notion - for the existence of the ancient civilisation was 'not absolutely accepted of history'. He claimed, though, that its existence was 'too probable to be passed over in silence', and in arguing his case he referred not only to Plato's famous references to the place but also to mentions of it in Tibetan and Egyptian legends. He also quoted contemporary authors such as Augustus Le Plongeon, who suggested that ancient Maya had been linked to Atlantis; and Yarker noted that many Theosophists took its existence as a matter of fact and believed it had possessed advanced technology.

Although Yarker's take on Atlantis was not as far-fetched as some, he still referred to outré theories which maintained that it had been destroyed by both a great deluge and a civil war between white magicians and those who indulged in black magic, or as he put it: those who journeyed down the 'left-hand path'.

After the deluge and the war, he explained, the Aryans took to highland and mountainous regions, including Tibet; and later they migrated to various other nations, all the while taking their mysteries and rituals with them. Yarker traced them through historic civilisations, including Celtic or 'Druidic' Britain, where they 'superintended the erection of religious structures', such as the henges; and he found evidence of them in ancient Assyria, Babylonia, Mycenaean Greece, and China.

He also found many references to the Craft in the culture of ancient Egypt. In a manuscript which was '3 - 4 000 years old', he noticed the 'sign of a fellow freemason' incorporated into a picture of Isis and Nepthys; on statues of Isis and Osiris at the Rosetta-gate he found 'Masonic marks'; and on artefacts from the 12th dynasty he saw: 'the swastika, the equal limbed cross, a five pointed star, and an open crossed like square and compass'. (When dealing with Freemasonry in North Africa, Yarker quoted from William Oxley's 1884 book *Egypt and the Wonders of the Land of the Pharaohs*, which the Manchester spiritualist wrote after touring the country).

After dealing with the ancients, Yarker outlined the history of the Craft in medieval and early modern Britain and mentioned several characters from Manchester's occult history, including John Dee, John Booker and John Byrom. He also noted that guild men had worked on the 'Collegiate Church in Manchester', and that they met at the adjacent 'Seven Stars, a very ancient hostelry'.

He then dealt with modern Freemasonry, and mentioned Manchester's 'Euphrates Lodge, or Chapter of the Garden of Eden', which was granted a charter in 1769, and which Yarker 'tried to save from erasure in 1854', only to be met with indifference by the 'old members'. He also referred to the Templar Lodge or 'Jerusalem Conclave', which was 'remade' in the Manchester Royal Encampment in 1786. And finally, he brought proceedings up to date by mentioning the restoration in the city of the 'old degrees of Red Cross, Heredom, Kadosh', and he also described his own cherished projects: the Antient and Primitive Rite and the Swedenborgian Rite.

Yarker and the Great Beast

A. E. Waite called *The Arcane Schools* a 'chaotic volume', but others were complimentary. The *Universal Freemason* claimed it was 'monumental' and 'epoch making', and reckoned that Yarker 'instilled conviction in every line'. More praise came from Aleister Crowley, who reviewed it in the *Equinox*, which was the journal of his various societies. He noted that it was eruditely written, and asserted that Yarker 'abundantly proved' the ancient lineage of Freemasonry.

Crowley had already been called the 'Great Beast' by his mother, but he had not yet been dubbed the 'wickedest man in Britain' by the tabloids, and he was years away from being the country's number one bogeyman. But as noted, his reputation amongst fellow occultists was already poor, and he had upset many of the magicians in the Hermetic Order of the Golden Dawn. Yarker, though, was not concerned about Crowley's reputation, and soon after the *Equinox* review, he sent him a note of thanks. The pair began to correspond, and Crowley became an initiate of the Antient and Primitive Rite. This constituted a change of heart by Crowley because he had considered Freemasonry to be: 'either vain pretence, tomfoolery, an excuse for drunken rowdiness, or a sinister organisation for political intrigues and commercial pirates'.

After Yarker's death in March 1913, there was a battle for the ownership of the Antient and Primitive Rite between leading Theosophists and Crowley, who intended to subsume the rite into his Masonic-style occult society: Ordo Templi Orientis.

The OTO's case for ownership was a strong one - for as early as 1902, before Crowley became involved with the order, Yarker had given it license to use both the Antient and Primitive Rite and the Swedenborg Rite. In contrast, the Theosophical Society had few solid links to the rite - other than a certain overlap of members. It wanted to assume control, though, in order to incorporate it into a new society, the Star of the East, which was part of a madcap plan to introduce a new messiah to the world. (See the following chapter for the involvement of Alan Leo and another Manchester mystic in this scheme.)

Crowley was on holiday in France in March 1913, and for several weeks he was unaware that Yarker had died. In his *Confessions,* he claimed he was alerted to Yarker's passing by the supernatural adepts known as the 'Masters'. They warned him that something was wrong, he explained, by sending two lizards across his path. Initially, Crowley took this to mean that 'treachery was at work in London', but later realised it was also a sign of Yarker's death, and an indication of the Theosophist's plan to gain control of the Antient and Primitive Rite.

Crowley claimed to have discovered, when back in England, that Yarker's death had been 'concealed from his colleagues by the machinations of Theosophists'. Furthermore, he learnt that the Theosophists intended to 'convey a secret council at Manchester to select a successor to Yarker' - which he believed was 'illegal' because the members were not given sufficient notice. Crowley, however, managed to wing it to Manchester, where he gave a protest speech. He did not intend, he proclaimed, to complain about the breaking of the rules, and he was not about to quibble at the presence in the meeting of those who were not authorised to be there. Rather, he claimed, the issue that prompted him to 'come to this Valley of Manchester from my peaceful encampment in the Valley of Paris', was the Theosophical society's plan to attach the rite to their new messiah project. This would, he said, 'drag our holy Rite into the mire'. And he urged the Brothers not to let down 'generation upon generation of ancestors, even beyond the ages of history', who had passed the rite on.

Finally, the meeting was abandoned and Crowley arranged for a new gathering at his London studio, where he was installed as one of the leaders of the rite.

Euphemia and Norman

Before doing business with Yarker, Crowley associated with two other characters from Manchester: Norman Mudd, and later, Euphemia Lamb. Both had lived in Moss Side, although it is not known if they ever met.

Norman Mudd

Euphemia was, according to Crowley, so 'incomparably beautiful' that Augustus John was compelled to paint her 'again and again'. Mudd, in contrast, was said to resemble: 'a clammy poultice of sour war bread . . . (and was considered to be) a nearly liquid mass of loathsome detestable putrescence'. This was more than a little unfair, although in truth Mudd was not a handsome man. He had a weak chin and a pouty mouth, and to make matters worse he lost an eye after becoming infected with gonorrhoea. Playing on his unprepossessing appearance, he introduced himself with: 'My name's Mudd, you won't remember me'. Yet some did remember him: Jane Wolfe, one of Crowley's 'Scarlet Women', recalled that he was 'a fussy man, set in his ways, and lacking in social position'.

Mudd, though, was the son of a headmaster, so it was not as

if he was from the lowest of the lower orders. After he was born in Prestwich in 1889, his family moved about the city, living in either Chorlton or Chorlton-on-Medlock and at various addresses in Moss Side. Mudd attended Ducie Avenue school and Manchester Grammar, and then studied mathematics at Cambridge, where he fell in with a set centred around the Pan Association and the Free Thought Association. Both of these groups were founded by Victor Neuberg, who was a poet, vegetarian, mystic, and a protégé of Crowley's. Neuberg introduced Mudd to Crowley, and the pair spent much time talking. When looking back on this period, Mudd wrote: 'I then understood for the first time what life was like or might be; and the spark of that understanding has been in me ever since, apparently unquenchable, always working'.

Firmly under Crowley's spell, Mudd agreed to distribute his literature on the campus. This brought him into conflict with the college Dean, Reginald St. John Parry, who had received a letter which revealed that Crowley was a paederast and under investigation by the police. Parry summoned Mudd and ordered him to desist from distributing copies of Crowley's book. Mudd refused, called a meeting of the Free Thought group, and sent a defiant note to Parry. The Dean responded by giving him an ultimatum: if he resigned as secretary of the Free Thought group, wrote a letter of apology, and promised to cut his ties with Crowley, then he could stay at the college. If he refused he would be rusticated. Meanwhile, Crowley sent a letter to Mudd's father in which he claimed that Norman's tutors were 'indulging in things so abominable that among decent people they have not even a name'. Mudd's parents, though, were not impressed with Crowley. They considered him to be an 'evil genius' and felt that he could blight their son's entire life. There is little doubt, then, that they would have been delighted when Mudd caved in and agreed to the Dean's demands.

Although he secretly maintained his correspondence with Crowley for a while, this was to be the end of Mudd's first stint with the magician.

The year after the Cambridge dispute, Crowley relocated to

Montparnasse and met Euphemia Lamb, who was just as bohemian and promiscuous as he was.

Euphemia, otherwise known as Nina Forest, claimed to have been 'born on a boat to Bombay'. She grew up, though, in Moss Side, and later met the medical student Henry Lamb, who was born in Australia but spent his childhood in Manchester. Together they headed for London, where he became a successful painter, and she became Euphemia Lamb, a much sought after artist's model. The 'Euphemia' tag was given to her by Lamb because he felt she resembled the Saint of that name in Mantegna's painting.

Euphemia Lamb

In London, and later Paris, she cultivated a wild girl image. She mixed with the Cafe Royale crowd; she went on road trips which she financed by dancing in bars; she dressed, for a time, as a 'young man' - which made her irresistible to Augustus John; and she had a fling with Crowley.

In his biography of Crowley, Richard Kaczynski claimed the affair faltered because of the magician's indifference. Yet in his *Confessions*, Crowley gave a different impression. He eulogized her beauty, then praised her intelligence: 'She could hold her own in any conversation about art, literature or music'; and he also noted that she was funny: 'She was the very soul of gaiety, and an incomparable comedienne'. Finally, he lamented that she would 'have been a grande passion' - had he been able to get under her skin.

After a while, Crowley began to feel 'somewhat insulted' by her detached nature. But he got over this and concluded that her temperament was due to her being a natural adept or magician.

After a while, the Great Beast and the great beauty were joined in Paris by Victor Neuburg - Norman Mudd's friend from Cambridge. At the time, Neuburg was sexually inexperienced and tended to romanticise and idealise women; and now here he was, in the company of two jaundiced wind-up merchants: a lamb for Euphemia and Crowley to slaughter.

After Neuburg got drunk on absinthe and lewdly propositioned Euphemia - causing her to remark: 'You would not say such things to your don's wives at Cambridge' - Crowley decided to teach him a lesson. He cast Euphemia as a 'morbidly modest young woman' who had fallen for Neuburg but was 'wounded to the heart' by his 'gross wooing' - and she played the part to perfection. Before long she was 'engaged' to Neuburg. 'She had a husband round the corner', wrote Crowley, 'but one ignored such flim flam in Montparnasse'.

Meanwhile, Crowley arranged for another friend to help rid Neuburg of his virginity by taking him to a brothel. When Euphemia found out about this infidelity, she claimed she would never forgive Neuburg, and that she would never speak to Crowley again. The young poet was said to be heartbroken at losing a 'woman of purity', and spent days moping about. Finally, Crowley revealed that Euphemia was a sexually liberated woman and that the engagement was a sham.

The magician no doubt found it hilarious that Euphemia acted coy and inexperienced, for her sexual shenanigans were legendary. She slept with numerous artists and was said to have worked her way through six partners during a particularly energetic night. This would have pleased Crowley, who approved of such 'Scarlet Women' and utilised them as the embodiment of the female sexual spirit in his magical system of Thelema.

Neuburg, though, could not relinquish his pure Euphemia,

and accused Crowley of telling 'outrageous lies'. Finally, the magician took him to a hotel room where Euphemia lay naked on a bed as she smoked a cigarette, and the poet's image of the pure and ideal woman was shattered.

It was cruel and tawdry, but Crowley insisted he had done Neuburg a good service by purging him of his 'romantic idealism'. 'Had I not', claimed Crowley, ' he would have been the prey of one vampire after another as long as he lived'. The magician also claimed the lesson helped the young man's magical powers to evolve.

The affair between Crowley and Euphemia did not last long. She was too canny to be sucked into the role of the Scarlet Woman and soon moved on. Crowley and Neuburg also moved on, and in November and December 1909 they found themselves in Algiers. The Great Beast believed he could look after himself in North Africa, but he felt his young protégé looked a bit wet behind the ears and required a change of image. And so Neuburg shaved his head and left two tufts on his temples which were twisted to form horns. 'He was now', wrote Crowley, 'a demon that I had tamed and trained to serve me as a familiar spirit'.

As they traipsed through the desert, Crowley experimented with John Dee's Enochian magic and carried out numerous magical rituals. During one conjuring attempt, which involved Neuburg sitting within a magic circle, many strange entities manifested - including a holy man, a serpent, and a 'naked savage with froth-covered fangs'. Euphemia also made an appearance. Ever the femme fatale, she tried to lure Neuburg from the safety of the circle, but he resisted.

Soon after, the magicians called time on their experiments and headed back to England. They were said to have been marked for life by their experiences in the desert.

After a period in the United States, where he met Leah Hirsig, who became his most significant Scarlet Woman, Crowley established a villa in Cefalu which he called the Abbey of Thelema. It was there that his reputation as the 'wickedest man in the world' was cemented, as the popular press printed rumours of depraved sexual ceremonies and ritual murders.

The tales of murder circulated after the death of Raoul Loveday, who was a 23-year-old Oxford student and Crowley devotee. According to the *Daily Express*, Loveday died after taking part in a ceremony which involved drinking cat's blood. This was just tabloid nonsense - the truth was that he had been taken ill after drinking water from a polluted spring. The tales of depraved sex rituals, though, were more accurate - for Crowley had begun to experiment with the use of sexual fluids and excrement.

Norman Mudd became involved in this scene when he arrived as a replacement for Loveday. After graduating from Cambridge, he returned to Moss Side and then left for Bloemfontein University in South Africa. He spent around a decade at the institution, where he ran the Applied Mathematics department and wrote several papers, including a critique of Einstein, and a work called *The Gravitational Potential and Energy of Harmonic Deformations of Order*. Like John Dee, who wrote a *Mathematicall Preface to Euclid*, and Henry Cornelius Agrippa, who stated that 'maths have such an affinity with Magick', Mudd considered the study of numbers and investigations into the occult to be part of the same 'Great Work'.

At the university, though, he was starved of magic. He dreamt of his Cambridge days with Crowley, when he had enjoyed a glimpse of 'what life could be', and in 1920 he decided to track the magus down. He arranged a year's sabbatical - although he never returned to South Africa - and sailed to England. Once there, he learnt that Crowley was in the United States and so he crossed the Atlantic, only to discover the magician had returned to England. The trip, though, was not a complete waste of time because Mudd was initiated into the Argentium Astrum, which was Crowley's mystical order. When back in England, he learnt that Crowley had returned to the Abbey in Cefalu and followed him there.

Mudd may have hoped for a serene and idyllic retreat, where he could pursue the Great Work and sit at the feet of a master magician, but he found chaos. Crowley was financially broke, his reputation had been torn to shreds by the popular press, and Mussolini had decided to expel him from Italy. To make matters worse, Mudd fell in love with Leah Hirsig - Crowley's main Scarlet Woman.

After the Abbey broke up, Mudd became impoverished and began drifting. He stayed for a while with Hirsig in Paris, where she wrote in her diary that she had slept with 'a man who does not know who he is but is commonly called Norman Mudd'. A month or so later he signed himself into a London homeless shelter.

In 1925, Mudd was banished from the Argentium Astrum, probably because he clashed with Crowley over his interpretation of the *Book of Law*, which was Thelema's sacred text, and also because of his affair with Leah Hirsig. By 1927 he had lost interest in magic.

We don't know the details of his remaining years, although his path can be traced through the Isle of Man, Spain, and London. In 1934, he spent some time at the Manor Hotel in Guernsey. It is unclear if he had any connection with the island. Perhaps he was there for work or family reasons, or perhaps he was drifting through. What is clear is that he was deeply depressed, for on the evening of Friday 15th June he put on a pair of bicycle clips, filled his trousers with stones, and waded into the sea. His body was found the day after at Portlet Bay.

Crowley, who outlived Mudd by 13 years, significantly influenced England's occultists for the rest of the century. His ideas were incorporated into Wicca - a movement which found a home in Manchester. One particular Mancunian Wiccan, Alex Sanders, emulated Crowley by studying the Enochian system; by indulging in gay magick rituals; and by claiming to have travelled down the left-hand path. Also like Crowley, he was denounced as evil and satanic by the tabloids.

Before we explore Wicca, we will visit Crowley's old enemy - the Theosophical Society, which had a significant presence in late Victorian Manchester.

CHAPTER NINE

The Mysterious Masters

One of the strange things about living in the world is that it is only now and then one is quite sure one is going to live forever and ever and ever. One knows it sometimes when one gets up at the tender solemn dawn-time and goes out and stands alone and throws one's head far back and looks up and up and watches the pale sky slowly changing and flushing out marvellous unknown things happening until the East almost makes one cry out and one's heart stands still at the strange unchanging majesty of the sun – which has been happening every morning for thousands and thousands of years. One knows it then for a moment or so.

Frances Hodgson Burnett, *The Secret Garden*

Given its mystical leanings, Manchester was always going to be a happy hunting ground for the Theosophical Society. It was always going to be seduced by tales of supernatural entities, known as the 'Masters' or 'Mahatmas', who were said to dwell both on earth and the astral plane. William Oxley was certainly seduced, and Emma Hardinge Britten and John Yarker also worked with the society in the 1870s. During the following decades, Manchester produced other figures, such as Ernest Wood and Alice Bailey, who became prominent in the global movement.

Helena Petrova Blavatsky, the aristocratic Russian who was Theosophy's leading light, believed she was primed by the Masters to create the society; and she claimed to have first seen one of these characters, known as Morya, in a childhood vision. Other strange occurrences in her early years included hallucinations; conversations with invisible friends which she called 'little hunchbacks'; and what seemed to be waking nightmares, which led to her being exorcised several times.

At seventeen, Blavatsky was briefly married to an older man, and then she embarked on years of travel. Her accounts of her time on the road, although highly embellished and fantastical, were mostly entertaining: they included tales of smoking opium and hash; of seeking out Coptic magicians in Cairo; and of mingling with mesmerists in Paris. Blavatsky also claimed to have met the mysterious Morya in England in 1851. He revealed she would travel to Tibet, where she would prepare for the 'most important task' of founding the Theosophical Society.

But Blavatsky did not immediately head for the Himalayas. Rather, she passed through North and South America, India, Kashmir, and Burma, before reaching Tibet in 1856. She was not, though, primed for her 'most important task' whilst there, and later headed back to Russia. Serious illness followed, as did a spell of giving piano recitals in Transylvania, and a stint fighting for Garibaldi whilst disguised as a man - or so she claimed. Then, in 1868, whilst in Florence, she received a message to meet Morya in Constantinople. From there they travelled to Tibet, where she was introduced to another master, Koot Hoomi, and her latent superhuman powers were developed. Finally, she was ready to educate the west in the ways of Theosophy.

In New York, she teamed up with a journalist and lawyer called Colonel Henry Olcott, and they mixed with the crème of the city's occultists. The Theosophical Society was officially created after members of this crowd gathered at Blavatsky's apartment to hear a speech on Egyptian cabalism by an architect called George Henry Felt. A prominent presence at the meeting was Emma Hardinge Britten, and also in attendance was another occultist with links to Manchester, who we will meet later.

The three main objectives of the society, which Olcott codified in 1877, were the creation of a global brotherhood; the promotion of a comparative study of all religions; and the development of man's latent powers. The movement's philosophy was further elucidated by Blavatsky in her book *Isis Unveiled*, and also by a series of letters which were said to have materialised from nothing and to have been penned by the Masters. The book and the letters contained complex tales of reincarnation, and of ancient 'root races' which had lived on the lost continents. Later leaders of the society made these notions even more fantastical. The Stockport-born C.W. Leadbeater claimed that Atlantis had produced flying machines that were powered by 'Vril': a force which was first mentioned by Edward Bulwer Lytton in his novel *The Coming Race*.

Such tales meant that many felt the Theosophical Society lacked credibility. It was not, though, just the notions of Vril and lost continents which were questioned, but also the veracity of Blavatsky's claim to have crisscrossed the globe: for it was often pointed out that Tibet, at the time she claimed to have visited, was not open to Europeans. Also questioned was the notion of Himalayan Masters. They were said by a writer for the *Two Worlds* to have simply sprung from 'the founder's vivid imagination' during the latter half of the 1870s.

However, one occult master who inspired Blavatsky definitely existed. But rather than residing in a Himalayan retreat or on the astral plane, he lived on Burton Road.

Yarker and Blavatsky

John Yarker's book, *Notes on the Scientific and Religious Mysteries of Antiquity; The Gnosis and Secret Schools of the Middle Ages; Modern Rosicrucianism; and the various Rites and Degrees of Free and Accepted*

Masonry, influenced Blavatsky when she wrote *Isis Unveiled*. 'Whilst engaged on (the book)', she wrote, 'we have received most unexpectedly, through the kindness of a friend, a copy of Yarker's volume ... it is brimful of learning and, what is more, of knowledge, as it seems to us'.

The kind friend was Charles Sotheran: a Freemason, socialist, writer, and protégé of Yarker's, who was present at the first meeting in Blavatsky's apartment. In fact, it was Sotheran who suggested the name 'Theosophical Society'. Although a Londoner by birth, he had several connections to Manchester: he was a member of Yarker's Swedenborg and Memphis and Mizraim lodges; his uncle, Henry Sotheran, was a renowned book dealer with business interests in the city; and he married his first wife in Manchester in 1869. He also contributed articles on the esoteric foundations of Freemasonry to the *Manchester Freelance,* which was edited by a high-ranking Mason called John Beresford.

The articles brought Sotheran to the attention of James Fraser, the Bishop of Manchester, who offered him a job as the editor of his *Annual Calendar*, which was a report on the Manchester Diocese. His work with Fraser led to a stint in New York in 1874, as an editor of a monthly magazine. Yarker eased Sotheran's way into the city's occult and Masonic circles with a letter of introduction.

Sotheran was soon busy in those circles and became close to Madame Blavatsky. Not only did he recommend Yarker's book to her, but he also arranged for the Manchester man to award her several Masonic degrees, including the Royal Oriental Order of Sikha and the Sat B'hai, which was an order devoted to 'the study and development of Indian philosophy'.

This outfit has had a few critics - Ellic Howe, for instance, called it 'an exercise in human folly', and 'by far the most ludicrous promotion of the period'. Yet it is of interest because it may have pushed Blavatsky a little further towards eastern esotericism at a time when she had not yet fully developed her ideas in this field. Yarker certainly believed that the order influenced Blavatsky, and claimed the Theosophical Society stole the Sat B'hai's thunder.

A further indication of Yarker's influence on Theosophy was Blavatsky's desire for him to be significantly involved with the society. She intended, as the scholars Katharina Brandt and Olav Hammer have noted, 'to create a distinct ritual for the Theosophical Society together with Yarker'. But there was to be no such collaboration, and the society did not develop along Masonic lines - although it did incorporate a secretive higher level which was not accessible to the rank and file.

Theosophy versus Spiritualism

The original New York Theosophical Society was short-lived. Charles Sotheran left when he discovered that Blavatsky was a strident critic of socialism; and others, such as Emma Hardinge Britten, cut their ties when Theosophists began to criticise spiritualism.

According to Blavatsky, spiritualists were 'lost', 'ruined', and 'degraded', and their 'irresponsible mediumship' was 'one step away from black magic'. She also argued that spiritualists were mistaken in believing that the manifestations they observed were the spirits of the dead. Rather, she claimed, the 'spirits' were destructive astral forms which exploited the gullible by 'assuming the garb of angelic visitors and professing to give revelations from God'.

Her partner, Colonel Olcott, also dismissed the idea that manifestations were spirits and attributed them to the psychic powers of mediums. Spirits were a consequence, he claimed, 'of thought transference and hypnotism'.

Many spiritualists, not surprisingly, hit back. W. H. Wheeler, who was an activist from Oldham, gave a speech, *The Fallacies of Theosophy,* at the Vegetarian Restaurant on Fountain Street; on the same night, E. W. Wallis, who was Emma Hardinge Britten's colleague, also laid into Theosophy.

For the next few years, the *Two Worlds* ran articles which were critical of the society. One writer asked: 'Where are these Mahatmas?' - then he challenged the Theosophists to 'show us one'. Another piece rubbished the idea that Blavatsky possessed 'occult powers', and claimed that Theosophical theories were 'vague and shadowy', 'contradictory trash', or simply 'gibberish'.

But not all of Manchester's spiritualists opposed Theosophy, and several lobbied for the unification of the two movements. This caused consternation at the *Two Worlds*, and the editors argued that because Blavatsky 'denied every item of our faith', it would not be possible for such 'opposing doctrines to unite'. 'Spiritualism and Theosophy', they maintained, 'are as wide apart as the poles of the earth'.

William Oxley agreed with this and joined in with the attacks. He had once, though, been a keen Theosophist. He wrote articles for the society's journals; he attempted to join a secretive branch of the movement which was not open to regular members; he sent a long letter to Koot Hoomi, in which he explained his mystical philosophy; and he claimed the master had visited him three times in astral form.

But leading Theosophists were not impressed with Oxley. They refused to admit him to the secretive branch; they did not respond to his long letter, and they denied that the master had paid him an astral visit.

Koot Hoomi, in a letter to Alfred Percy Sinnett, an English writer who was one of the founders of the movement, tried to sugar-coat this rejection:

> *Kindly write to (Oxley) to say that he must not feel vexed at my denial. I know he is thoroughly sincere and as incapable of deception or even exaggeration as you are. But he trusts too much to his subjects. Let him be cautious and very guarded; . . . He is a valuable man, and indeed, more worthy of sincere respect than any other Spiritualist mystic I know of. And although I have never approached him astrally or conversed with, I have often examined him in thought.* 1

Oxley, though, was not placated: for unless he truly was a believer and had swallowed the whole Theosophical line, he would have realised that he had not been rejected by a wise and spectral adept, but by the very flesh and blood form of Alfred Percy Sinnett. He would have realised that he had been slapped down by a fellow occultist who had no intention of letting him join the party.

So he hit back. He used the spiritualist press to denounce the society, claiming there was a 'yawning chasm between the promises of the Theosophists and the substantiation thereof'. Then it got petty - as Blavatsky claimed that Oxley was 'not a philosopher, and still less a sage' and that he was simply miffed because 'one of our Masters had rejected to notice him'. And later, Oxley's book, *Philosophy of Spirit*, was given a negative review in the *Theosophist* by Djual Khool, who was said to be a 'chala', or servant, of Koot Hoomi.

A more effective critic of Theosophy was Emma Hardinge Britten. The fact that she was present at the inception of the society gave her the authority to strip away the mythology which had grown around it.

In a *Two Worlds* article, she noted that in the early days there was no talk of spirits being mischievous astral entities, and no claims that spiritualists were 'degraded' or 'ruined'. Rather, she stressed that the society had been spiritualist in essence - for not only were many of the early members spiritualists, but Blavatsky herself had claimed to be one.

Furthermore, Emma did not recall any mentions of the 'Masters' during the New York days. These mysterious characters were said to have arrived after Blavatsky and Olcott relocated to India. It was only then, Emma claimed, that these chaps with 'unpronounceable names' appeared.

Emma also highlighted, on several occasions, the various controversies around the society. She directed readers of the *Two Worlds* to a series of scathing articles which appeared in the *New York Sun*, one of which was headlined: THE FRAUDS OF MADAME BLAVATSKY; and she noted the so-called 'Coulamb Affair', which involved ex-members of the society who had been close to Blavatsky labelling her a charlatan.

The most damaging issue, which Emma also drew attention to, was the investigation of Theosophy by the Society for Psychical Research, which was formed to scientifically investigate paranormal events.

The Hodgson Report

The Society for Psychical Research, although based in London, was national in scope and several eminent Manchester gentlemen were founder members - such as Professor Alfred Hopkinson, who was a lawyer and a lecturer at Owens College; Dr Angus Smith, of Oxford Road, who was an associate of the scientist William Crookes; the Irishman Richard Hooke, of Higher Broughton, who was a renowned portrait painter; Henry H. Howorth, who was the MP for Salford South; and Gervase Marson, of Birk Crag on Great Clowes Street. What Gervase did for a living is a mystery, but we do know that he had the odd mystical experience. For instance, on the morning of December 6th 1879 by shouting 'Portland . . . Portland'; and then discovered the next day that the Duke of Portland died at the exact time he was shouting his name. who claimed to have the odd supernatural experience.

The most significant Manchester-based founder member was the physicist Balfour Stewart - who, as noted in the last chapter, was the author of *Unseen Universe*. Stewart began as a vice-president of the society and then became its second full president.

Early in his SPR career, he was involved in the investigation of the Creery girls, who claimed they could telepathically communicate. They were the daughters of A. M. Creery - a clergyman from the Manchester area who was also a founding member of the society. After the Reverend Creery delivered a speech about his daughter's talents in 1881, the SPR despatched Stewart and Alfred Hopkinson to visit them at home, which for the moment was in Buxton. The gentlemen were delighted with the results. It seemed that the sisters, as well as a servant girl, could indeed transfer their thoughts, and a statement was made to the public.

The girls were rumbled, though, in October 1887, when the researchers realised they communicated by coughing. For one researcher this was too much to take, and he maintained well into the 1920s that the girls were telepathic. As for the Reverend Creery - he was initially considered to have been an innocent dupe, but modern researchers question this. They highlight his undistinguished career - he seemed to have been shunted around parishes in Cheetham Hill, Heaton Moor, and Buxton - and speculate that he may have been planning to take his girls on a lucrative tour.

Richard Hodgson, the SPR member who was despatched to India in 1885 to investigate Blavatsky, was not as gullible as Stewart and Hopkinson and concluded that the Theosophist was an 'imposter', albeit an 'accomplished, ingenious and interesting imposter'. In his report, he revealed that the mysterious 'Mahatma letters', which were said to have materialised in a closed cabinet, were placed there by Blavatsky, via a secret opening. Furthermore, after noting that Koot Hommi's prose style was the same as Blavatsky's, he concluded that the latter wrote the letters.

Alice Bailey

Although the Theosophical Society was damaged by the report, it was far from finished and continued to attract members after Blavatsky's death in 1891. One such recruit was Frances Hodgson Burnett, who spent her early years in Cheetham Hill and Burnage. She turned to Theosophy after her son died of consumption, and her most famous book, *The Secret Garden*, which she worked on whilst visiting Buile Hill Park, was concerned with the latent powers of the mind and was influenced by the movement.

Alice Bailey was another writer and Theosophist who spent her childhood in Manchester. Born in 1880, she seemed to have been a member of a military regiment rather than a family. She was up at 6 am, 'regardless of the season or the weather'; piano lessons commenced at 7:00; breakfast was served at 8:00, which she ate 'alone in a large room'; prayers with her family and servants followed at 9:00; school lessons with the governess commenced at 9:30; and then, after a walk, lunch was taken with the adults. 'But we were not,' stressed Bailey, 'permitted to speak and our good behaviour and silence were under the anxious eyes of our governess'. After lunch, the good times rolled as she 'rested for an hour on a flat sloping board whilst the governess read aloud from some improving book'. Another walk followed and there were more lessons until 5 pm - when a nurse and maid got her in formal dress so she could greet the guests: 'There we stood in the doorway and made our curtsies and thus endured the misery of being talked to and inspected until our governess came to fetch us'. Further lessons followed until 8 pm, and then it was time for bed.

Alice's mother died of tuberculosis at the age of 29, and the disease took her father two years later. Consequently, Alice was a deeply miserable child: *'I was morbid, full of self-pity, lonely, exceedingly introspective . . . and convinced that no one liked me. I was the unhappy, self-dramatised centre of my little world'*.

She attempted suicide when she was five, by throwing herself down some kitchen steps; she tried to smother herself with sand when she was eleven, and she tried to drown herself in a river when she was fourteen. She survived, she explained, because 'the instinct for self-preservation was too strong'.

Things improved after a mysterious stranger appeared when Alice was visiting relatives. Her family were at church and she was alone reading when a man, who she believed to be Jesus, entered the room. He gave her, she claimed, a pep talk:

> *He told me there was some work that it was planned that I could do in the world but that it would entail changing my disposition considerably; I would have to give up being such an unpleasant little girl and must try to get some measure of self-control'. My future usefulness to Him and to the world was dependent on how I handled myself and the changes I could manage to make. He said that if I could achieve real self-control I could then be trusted and that I would travel all over the world and visit many countries, "doing your masters work all the time" . . . He added that He would be in touch with me at intervals of seven years apart.* [2]

For a while, Alice led a fairly normal life: she married, had three children, and relocated to the USA. After her marriage collapsed, she joined the Theosophical Society and began working at a branch in Hollywood. Soon after, something strange happened:

whilst walking through the 'Shrine Room' she saw a portrait of a man and recognised him as the visitor from years before. He wasn't Jesus Christ but Koot Hoomi.

In 1919, another Master contacted her:

> *I had sent the children off to school and thought I would snatch a few minutes to myself and went out onto the hill close to the house. I sat down and began thinking and then suddenly I sat straight and attentive. I heard what I thought was a clear note of music which sounded from the sky, through the hill and in me. Then I heard a voice which said 'There are some books which it is decided should be written for the public . . . will you do so?* [4]

The voice belonged to Djwal Khul, who was also known as 'the Tibetan'. He was first mentioned by Blavatsky, and was said to 'preside over a large group of Tibetan Lamas'. To have been psychically instructed by this particular master, though, may not have always been a pleasant experience: for sprinkled throughout the works of Bailey were indications that Djwal Khul had a darker, all-too-human side. In fact, he could seem more like a fascist than a benign spiritual leader. 'The Jews', wrote Bailey/Khul, 'are a reincarnation of spiritual failures from another planet'. This can be seen as a new, cosmic kind of prejudice, but more traditional racial slights soon followed as Jewish people were said to 'love the possessions of the world more than the service of the light'. Bailey also indulged in scapegoating when she claimed that the Jews allowed their 'great wealth and influence' to 'cause dissension among the nations.'

When not indulging in racial stereotyping, Bailey developed more typical new age themes and filled her books with musings on the occult, yoga, white magic, telepathy, healing, and art. Millenarianism was also part of the mix - for Bailey believed her era was special, and that He would soon reappear. 'The present', she claimed, 'is unique, Christ is presented with a unique opportunity brought about by certain world conditions'.

Bailey's Jesus, though, was very different from the messiah that Ann Lee and John Clowes encountered. He would not be, she warned, 'the *Christ who left His disciples centuries ago'*, but a 20th century Christ; and she predicted that:

> *The radio, the press and the dissemination of news will make His coming different to that of any messenger; the swift modes of transportation will make Him available to countless millions, and by boat, rail and plane they can reach Him: through television, His face can be made familiar to all, and verily 'every eye shall see Him'.* [4]

Ernest Wood and Geoffrey Hodson

Ernest Wood and Geoffrey Hodson, born in 1883 and 1886 respectively, became active members of Manchester's Theosophical Society. Both men also gained prominence within the international movement, and both spent time in the Madras suburb of Adyar, where Blavatsky and Colonel Olcott located the society's headquarters.

As children, they both had supernatural experiences. One of Hodson's first strange occurrences happened in Lincolnshire when he was five or six years old.

> *I was in a half-dreaming, half-waking state,* he wrote, *when it seemed that, from within the sun itself, a huge birdlike figure of fire, with a long tail shaped like that of a lyre bird, descended and entered my whole body through the crown of my head, almost setting up a blazing fire within me.*

Most people would have dismissed this as simply a vivid or lucid dream but Hodson felt it was something more, and noted that he had a similar experience as an adult in Ceylon. On that occasion, he identified the entity as a 'kind of solar intelligence'.

Hodson claimed to have been visited by spirits throughout his early childhood. They appeared as 'ugly elemental faces' which 'grinned and grimaced' by his bedside. When they became too disturbing, he sobbed and his mother came to his rescue. He knew, though, that not all supernatural entities belonged to the dark side - for even as a child, long before he heard of the Theosophical Society, he was aware - or so he claimed - of the existence of the Masters.

> *I was convinced, he wrote, that there existed somewhere a secret Brotherhood of perfected Beings with a hidden headquarters from which the Members went out into the world to teach and perform deeds of mercy. I knew that when They met each other, They used certain signs for mutual recognition; and when They became fatigued by Their efforts to bring wisdom to human beings, They could return to Their secret headquarters for rest and refreshment.*

Ernest Wood's early mystical experiences were more modest. One of the more notable happenings, which hinted that he had lived past lives, happened in Manchester when he was sixteen. He was walking home from school when a disembodied voice asked if he would be tall or short 'this time'. Due to Wood being in a 'mood of humility', which incorporated a 'dislike of anything in the world in the shape of pomp or display', he chose to be short. For the next few years he 'scarcely grew', until a spurt at sixteen saw him reach five foot six.

Wood's parents were progressive sorts - his mother was creative and liked to make the family's clothes, and his father, who ran the family-owned stationery warehouse, liked to dine in the city's vegetarian restaurants and was interested in esoteric subjects. It was no surprise, then, that Wood began to explore Manchester's occult scene.

When he was approximately seventeen, he attended a lecture given by Annie Besant which changed his life. (A decade later Geoffrey Hodson also attend one of Besant's Manchester lectures, and also found the experience to be life-changing). Besant had risen to prominence in the Theosophical Society after the death of Blavatsky in 1891 - which irked the *Two Worlds* because the editors respected her work as a campaigner for worker's rights and felt she had made the wrong choice by becoming involved with a society which possessed 'vague and shadowy occult beliefs'. One writer even commented on rumours that she had been 'enchanted, hypnotised, or psychologised' by Blavatsky.

Ernest Wood

Wood was certainly enchanted by Beasant - he believed she had 'a sort of superhuman halo or atmosphere about her', and he claimed that the audience at her lecture 'seemed to believe that she walked as easily in the worlds of the dead as in those of the living'. Soon after the talk, he became a Theosophist.

He met several interesting characters during his time in the society. One old gentleman 'lived in the Mill area' and made his living as a 'knocker-up', which meant he wandered through the streets rattling bedroom windows with a long stick. 'This occupation', wrote Wood, 'gave him plenty of time to indulge in his hobby - the study of Greek and Neo-Platonic philosophy, in which he had read profoundly'.

Another notable figure was the wife of the society's president. She was a missionary by nature and invited waifs and strays to her house. 'One such character', wrote Wood, 'was a boot and shoe repairer from a back street, who was half-crazed with incoherent visions and would talk on all occasions'. This eccentric, who was said to be 'indifferent to soap and water', often 'inadvertently insulted people'.

There was also a 'literary young lady' who used to bore Wood with her 'excessive enthusiasm for Plato'; and a senior lady who had been a 'manageress in some sort of factory where many girls were employed', and who studied yoga, meditation, and Eastern Philosophy.

Wood soon became the vice-president of the Manchester society and began a group which tried to realise the third object of the movement - which was to develop mankind's latent supernatural powers.

The group indulged in tests similar to those Balfour Stewart conducted for the SPR. 'The first experiment', explained Woods, 'was the 'battery of minds'. It involved a woman sat before a semi-circle of people who all tried to telepathically send her a word. 'After a short time', claimed Wood, 'the lady who took the first turn as subject said: 'I am afraid I do not see anything at all. All that has happened is that I seemed to hear someone calling 'puss, puss, puss'. We were quite satisfied, Wood stated, 'for the word which I had written on the paper was 'cat''.

Soon, a star performer emerged. He was a gentleman who 'received the messages with about fifty per cent correctness'. He also proved remarkably good at identifying who was stood near him when he was blindfolded.

But it was not all good fun, for Wood was irritated by the presence of a separate cabal which operated within Theosophy. This was the group which Oxley had tried to join, and according to Wood it exuded a 'slight atmosphere of superiority and sacerdotalism'.

An editorial in the *Two Worlds* claimed the cabal was a sinister secret society which corrupted 'innocents' by offering them 'hidden knowledge - the wisdom of the Gods and the way of attainment of superior powers'. But there was, stressed the editor, a price: 'Before being permitted to enter the mystic interior brotherhood', the initiate 'must sign away his independence'. The piece concluded with a general attack on such groups: 'the day for secret doctrines and secret societies, with their passwords, signs, symbols and other mystic mummery has gone. The time has passed for esoteric compacts, and the hour of uncovering and making manifest has been heeded. Mystery, magic, authority, doctrine and dogma have too long held sway over humanity'.

This was, of course, just a petty point-scoring: for the *Two Worlds* had not attacked secret societies when they were connected to spiritualism. Rather, Emma Hardinge Britten praised the Angelic Order of Light, and the paper carried advertisements for its literature. The editorial was also comically overblown: for Wood, when he finally entered this inner sanctum, was not offered divine wisdom. Rather, he was underwhelmed by the experience.

In 1907, Wood was irked when another secret society, which was in direct competition with his group, emerged in Manchester. Based on something called the 'Pharma Ritual', the society was inspired by Annie Besant and had a pronounced feminist ethos.

Women in leadership roles were often found in spiritualist and occult circles, Emma Hardinge Britten being a good example. The Theosophical Society reinforced this trait by connecting with the women's movement. In Manchester, the connection was made by the likes of the Rusholme-based Irish poet, Eva Gore-Booth, who was deeply interested in Theosophy and mysticism and was the secretary of the North of England Society for Women.

Charlotte Despard, who was a novelist, suffragette, and Theosophist, believed the two movements would ultimately combine. At a 1913 lecture in Market Street, for the Manchester branch of the Woman's Freedom League, Despard explained that a merger was inevitable because both the women's movement and Theosophy were essentially spiritual.

The Pharma Ritual secret society seemed to indicate this was indeed happening: for eight of the twelve founding members were women.

Initially, the new order proved to be popular with Manchester's Theosophists and lured away several members of Ernest Wood's group - by making several outrageous claims and promises. 'They not only boasted', Wood wrote, 'that the masters were keenly anxious to have the new movement promoted', but also promised their members they would receive the 'power and force of the hidden adepts'. Furthermore, they let it be known that a master would 'manifest himself visibly to the members' of the new group.

Shortly after this schism, Wood was elected president of his lodge. His time in charge, though, was short because he experienced several visions involving Madame Blavatsky, Colonel Olcott, and an unspecified Master, which convinced him he should travel to India. The first happened as he was meditating with a group of friends: 'I suddenly became aware of a Master standing opposite me across the table, and speaking to me'. After the Master put him through a kind of catechism, Blavatsky declared to Olcott: 'he's ripe, we'll send him to India'.

But Wood did not immediately pack his bags, because he claimed not to trust visions and believed they could be 'unconsciously embellished' by the desires of the beholder. He decided to leave, though, after the following psychic episode:

> *One night as I was going home alone on top of a tramcar, I seemed to see Mrs. Besant in front of me, asking me to come to her. Still, I took no notice. In my opinion there was nothing decisive enough to call for any action. Then another vision came. I was going down some steps from a railway station at night. The steps were roofed in and only dimly lighted. Suddenly the whole cavern-like place was brightly illuminated, and I saw Mrs. Besant standing before me in a golden radiance. She spoke to me: 'I want you to come and help me'.*

When he reached home, Wood told his parents that he was going to take a trip to India for three months. He did not return, though, for thirteen years, and lived in India until just after World War II.

Away with the Fairies

Four years after Wood left, Geoffrey Hodson arrived in Manchester. He was not in a positive state of mind because his mystical worldview had been 'completely shattered' by an atheist. His faith was restored, though, after he read Annie Besant's *Esoteric Christianity*.

When he got to hear Besant speak, Hodson found the experience as mystical as Ernest Wood had a decade before. He described it this way:

> *I was privileged to hear her lecture and to have, in that connection, a profoundly moving experience. This was in March of 1912, shortly after I had moved to Manchester. I was delighted when I saw advertised the fact that Dr Annie Besant was to lecture in the famous Free Trade Hall there, and of course I attended. Not only was I enthralled by the philosophy she expounded but, as I watched her, I saw what I later came to know was her aura, shining out from her far beyond the walls of the building, filled with rich and wonderful colours and radiating streams of benediction to the world. So great was the impact of this experience that I immediately joined the Theosophical Society.*

Hodson was soon assigned to a group which travelled from Manchester to the surrounding towns, spreading the society's occult message. In Wigan, after giving a talk on life after death, Hodson was approached by a woman who claimed that he had visited her dying son, and had reassured the whole family by convincing them that the boy 'would only be leaving his physical body'. Hodson had no recollection of the visit and was sure he had never met the woman. After some pondering, he concluded that he must have made an astral visit to the family.

Soon after, Hodson claimed that he too was visited by astral entities. The first to come calling was none other than Koot Hoomi, who appeared before him at a meeting of the Theosophical Society's secret inner sanctum. The next entity appeared after

World War I broke out - he was an unnamed 'very great Master', who wore a robe, radiated a 'white light', and carried an 'upward-turned shining sword'. The Master did not say anything, but he didn't need to because the message was clear: Hodson, who had refrained from going to war because of his peaceful instincts, was to enlist in the army. (Meanwhile, in India, Ernest Wood considered returning to England to become involved in the war, but took the advice of high-ranking Theosophists who implored him not to).

Geoffrey Hodson

Hodson's war was, needless to say, peppered with mystical experiences. The first occurred in Dorset when he was undergoing basic training and was 'superphysically' visited by his brother, who was fighting in France and appeared to have his head bandaged. Hodson guessed that his brother had died, and it was quickly confirmed that he was mortally wounded during the Battle of Lens.

Soon after, Hodson found himself in France, where he was apprehensive because he was required to go behind the German lines. He tried to find peace by meditating before a stained-glass depiction of Saint Martin, which was in a church in the village of Colombey-les-Deux-Eglises, and then a strange thing occurred.

Hodson described it this way:

> *I became aware that the Saint "moved from the window" and had come to stand directly above and behind me. I felt a great stream of healing grace and spiritual power descend upon me; and then, almost as though he spoke in words, I received the absolute assurance that, in whatever actions I might be engaged in the future, I would be quite safe and would return home unharmed when the war was over. I could scarcely believe that such a thing had happened to me, but the conviction became so strong that my fear completely vanished.*

As the war raged on, Hodson was in danger on several occasions but came through unscathed. One notable incident involved a 'huge shell', which he believed was 'aimed directly' at him, and which landed and exploded a few yards behind him. 'I was forced to lie flat in the ground', he wrote, 'by pressure, as of a hand, between my shoulders. . . . and all the power of the explosion passed over me'. He escaped with a mild concussion.

After the war, Hodson returned to Manchester and re-established himself in the Theosophical Society. He also resumed his old job, which was in the sales department of a large interior design firm. It was difficult, though, for him to settle back into his old routines, for the war had changed him. He no longer cared about selling household decorations, and constantly felt the urge to 'give everything away'. But soon, things became a lot less humdrum - for Hodson became involved in a 'fairy scare'.

The girls responsible for the scare, nine-year-old Elsie Wright and sixteen-year-old Frances Griffiths, were the successors to the Creery Sisters - for they were also middle class and respectable, and they also managed to make fools of many eminent gentlemen. The hoax began when the girls made little cardboard creatures and photographed them in the woods behind their houses in Cottingley. Elsie's father, who was a keen photographer, immediately knew the photographs were fakes, but her mother, Polly, believed they were genuine. After listening to a lecture about 'fairy life', which was hosted by the Bradford Theosophical Society,

Polly showed the photographs to the speaker and news of them spread through occult circles.

Hodson with Elsie and Francis

Arthur Conan Doyle, who heard of them just after he was commissioned by *The Strand Magazine* to write a feature on fairies for its Christmas 1920 edition, decided to begin an investigation. First, he roped in photography experts, who did not believe the photos were of genuine fairies but conceded that they were not double exposures; then he searched for sent a psychic who was willing to look for the fairies, and Hodson was recommended for the job. If anyone could see the little creatures, the thinking went, then the super psychically sensitive Hodson would.

Conan Doyle may have thought that Hodson would charm the girls - for the psychic was handsome, youngish, and liked to talk. The girls, though, were not impressed. They felt that Hodson was a 'fake' and a 'phoney', and they later called him 'preposterous'. After a few hours spent in his company, near the stream at the back of the houses, the girls began to 'see' fairies out of sheer boredom. Elsie said she had noticed a six-foot-tall specimen stood near a tree and was surprised when Hodson revealed that he could also see it. The girls were also surprised in 1925 when Hodson published a book, *Fairies at Work and at Play*, which extensively detailed the fairies that he saw at Cottingley.

Hodson's psychic routine may not have been good enough for Elsie and Frances, but the Theosophists lapped it up and his career took off. Many books followed, including 1927's *The Kingdom of Faerie*, and by 1933 he had established himself as the 'Director of Studies for the School of Wisdom', at the society's Adyar headquarters.

The New Messiah

By this point, Ernest Wood had been in Adyar for over two decades - and like Hodson, he spent a lot of his time writing. In 1933, he published *Is This Theosophy?*, which detailed his early life in Manchester and his travels through India and the east. It was a good time to promote such a book, because just a few years earlier James Hilton, a writer who was born in Leigh, enjoyed great success with *Lost Horizon* - a novel which included several Theosophical tropes. The story was based in 'Shangri-la', which was a version of 'Shambhala' - a mystical and utopian place from ancient eastern mythology that was mentioned by the likes of Blavatsky and Alice Bailey; and one of Hilton's central characters, who was several hundred years old, resembled a Master.

Wood did not profess to have found Shambhala, or Shangri-la, but he did claim to have met mystical Indian men who possessed 'extraordinary powers': quiet men who 'hid their lights under the bushels of simple religiosity and under the pretence of madness'. Mostly, though, he spent his time with English mystics who were drawn to Adyar, such as Alan Leo, the ex-Manchester grocer turned astrologer. (When recalling his time in India, Leo claimed 'unquestionable sources' informed him that reincarnation and karma were 'part of the ancient mysteries of astrology'. This led to speculation that he had been contacted by the Masters).

Wood spent the most time with C. W. Leadbeater, who was one

of the leaders of the worldwide society. Leadbeater trained as an Anglican priest and then became a spiritualist after being inspired by the medium Daniel Dunglas Home. In 1884, he joined Blavatsky in India, after being advised to go by Koot Hoomi. Whilst there, he claimed to have met both Hoomi, who showed him how to achieve astral consciousness, and Djwal Kul, who was another Master. In later years, Leadbeater, who had obviously acquired a taste for meeting fantastical characters, announced that he had spent time with the Comte Saint de Germaine. The Comte, who was arrested in 1743 as a Jacobite spy, intrigued London society by maintaining he was 500 years old. He died in 1784, but that didn't stop Leadbeater from claiming to have met him, and to have discovered that he lived in a castle in Transylvania, where he practised magic whilst wearing a 'suit of golden chainmail which had once belonged to a Roman emperor'.

Whilst in Adyar, Ernest Wood was kept busy as a kind of personal assistant to Leadbeater. When he had spare time, he often swam in the Bay of Bengal - and it was there that he met Krishnamurti, the boy who was to be groomed as the 'World Teacher'.

Wood occasionally helped Krishnamurti and his friends with homework problems, and he discovered that the boy who was to teach the world was not the brightest of the bunch. In fact, Wood recalled that he was 'particularly dim-witted'. So it was a surprise when Leadbetter declared that the boy had a 'remarkable aura'; that he was destined to become a 'great spiritual leader'; and that in a past existence he had inspired Jesus.

The formal name for this leader was 'Lord Maitreya', and he was first mentioned by A. P. Sinnett - the English journalist who had clashed with William Oxley. Blavatsky embellished the Maitreya idea in the *Secret Doctrine*, then Leadbeater developed it further - explaining that this being had not only known Jesus, but had also been present in Atlantis, ancient India, and ancient Egypt.

That his son had such an illustrious past must have been a surprise to Krishnamurti senior, who was a retired government worker. But he seemed to have accepted the idea - probably because he was a devoted Theosophist - and he signed Krishnamurti into the care of Mrs Besant.

Aleister Crowley, as we have noted, was a vehement critic of the scheme, but more worrying for Besant and Leadbeater was the disapproval of fellow Theosophists. Rudolph Steiner, the head of the German society, opposed the project because his outlook was broadly Christological, and so he could not accept the premise that He had returned in the form of this Indian boy. Consequently, Steiner demanded the resignation of Besant. She retaliated by stripping him of his office, and he left the society soon after. Krishnamurti's father also came to doubt the World Teacher project and launched an unsuccessful law-suit against Besant for the return of his son.

The opponents of the scheme did not object merely because it was blasphemous, and had the potential to ruin a young life - they were also repulsed by Leadbeater's murky past. Rumours of paederasty had dogged him since 1906 when he was forced to retire from the society because of a scandal in America. And later, an eleven-year-old boy called Herbert Van Hook, who was also said to have been groomed for the World Teacher role, emerged with accusations against Leadbeater. The aftermath of this affair saw approximately 700 British Theosophists revoke their memberships. Amongst them was George Robert Mead, who went on to found the Quest Society, which Annie Horniman joined after her stint in the Hermetic Order of the Golden Dawn. The affair was also used by Aleister Crowley, who told those who attended the Manchester meeting of the Antient and Primitive Rite after John Yarker died, that they should reject the advances of the Theosophists because Leadbeater was a 'senile sex-maniac'.

Despite these significant setbacks, the project carried on, and the Order of the Rising Sun, and later the Order of the Star in the East, were formed to support the boy. Over the next few years, he was given standard school lessons and also a grounding in Theosophical thought and mysticism. Leadbeater claimed that he waited until the boy was asleep, and then took him on an astral journey to meet Koot Hoomi. The Master was said to have put Krishnamurti on probation before accepting him as his pupil.

The first appearance of Lord Maitreya in the boy was said to have occurred as he presented recruits to the Star in the East with certificates. According to Leadbeater, a 'tremendous power flowed through' Krishnamurti, and his audience either cried or fell to their feet.

For the next few years, Krishnamurti travelled extensively in Europe and was welcomed in England by occultists such as Alan Leo. Eventually, he settled in California and underwent a physical and spiritual experience, involving pain and then a feeling of 'immense peace', which he called 'The Process'.

This phenomenon happened at regular intervals, and it excited the Theosophists. Ultimately, though, they were to be disappointed - because Krishnamurti became so disillusioned that he renounced the World Teacher project, left the society in the late 1920s, and encouraged his followers to express themselves as they felt fit.

Leadbetter took this badly and denounced Krishnamurti. Geoffrey Hodson was also annoyed and wrote a book, *The Search for Light*, in which he was highly critical of the former World Teacher. He claimed Krishnamurti had 'led people into darkness'; and that his promotion of self-expression turned those who were once 'refined of speech', vegetarian, teetotal, and 'loving friends to all', into meat-eaters and alcohol drinkers, who also smoked and were 'addicted to coarse language'.

Ernest Wood, though, was not critical. He saw much of Krishnamurti during this period and they remained on good terms - perhaps because Wood himself had become disillusioned with Theosophy. In fact, after a running a failed campaign to replace Annie Beasant as its leader, after she died in the early 1930s, Wood left the society and devoted himself to Yoga until he died in the 1960s.

The World Teacher scheme proved to be Theosophy's last big splash and the society slowly declined over the century. Yet it didn't become completely moribund, and some of those who joined during the early decades of the century remained loyal. Hodson, for instance, remained a member until he died in 1983, at the age of 96. The society also managed to attract a trickle of new members - such as Geoffrey Farthing, from Heaton Mersey, who signed up in the early 1950s and was elected as the leader of Theosophy in 1969.

Prior to this, Farthing had contemplated giving up religion and mysticism - but when visiting a local canon, at a church somewhere in Manchester or Stockport, he had a strange experience. After silently asking for 'a sign', and deciding that he would become an atheist if none was forthcoming, he waited for something to happen. As he sat in the church study, not listening as the canon theologized, he entertained the idea that he might be swallowed by the earth or struck dead by a thunderbolt. But he waited a while longer and nothing happened. Then his mood changed drastically:

> *I was suddenly filled with an uncontainable elation and had a great urge to get out of that study as quickly as I could. Outside the feeling of elation and happiness was amplified to a greater and greater extent. It seemed to me that although I was actually walking home, my feet were not touching the ground. It was an incredible experience. From then on, right through till the 2nd World War, I was consciously on a quest to discover TRUTH.*

His quest led him to Theosophy, and after reading some of the movement's literature he became convinced that the 'original outpouring of occult knowledge by the Masters', which occurred during the Blavatsky era, was a 'unique world event'. It was an event which, he believed, 'was not properly appreciated'. His dedication to the Masters, though, put him at odds with what he called the 'generality of members of the society', who voted him out of office in 1972. The Masters, it seems, had fallen out of fashion.

CHAPTER NINE

The Wicca Man and the Witch Queen

> Manchester was to Wicca what Liverpool was to popular music in the mid-1960s'.
>
> Ronald Hutton, *The Triumph of the Moon*

During the early 1950s, a Manchester medium called Paul Dallas channelled a spirit called 'Red Feather', who was said to be a 'full-blooded American chief'. The spirit visited every time Dallas put on an Indian headdress and imposed both its character and features on to the medium. Dallas, who had worked as a healer since he was a teenager in the 1940s, proved to be popular and was offered a slot as a supporting act for a medium called Harry Edwards. This was a good opportunity because Edwards, who claimed to heal people by channelling the spirits of Louis Pasteur and Joseph Lister, pulled in large crowds. In 1948, for instance, he performed for six thousand at Belle Vue's King's Hall - and his fans claimed many were healed at the event, including children with paralysis who 'walked down steps for the first time'.

Edwards's act had a modern flavour because it owed more to American evangelism than traditional spiritualism. Dallas's shtick, though, seemed old - like a strange relic from the last century. Red Feather evoked the darkened sitting rooms of the 1880s and resembled the 'exotic' spirits that contacted the Angelic Order of Light.

Perhaps Dallas realised this because rather than taking up Edward's offer, he hung up his headdress, reverted to his real name - Alex Sanders - and converted to Wicca. It proved to be a wise decision, for Wicca had a vigour that spiritualism could not match and Alex became nationally famous as the 'King of the Witches'.

Margaret Murray and the Coming of the King

Many Wiccans claimed their faith was an ancient pagan religion which was forced underground by Christian persecution, and which survived through the centuries by dividing into secret covens of thirteen members. The Wiccans were said to have worshipped both a Goddess and a God, known as the Moon Goddess and the Horned God; to have believed in magic and the healing properties of plants and herbs; and to have celebrated the equinoxes and solstices, as well as four main 'Sabbats', or seasonal festivals - Candlemas, May Eve, Lammas, and Halloween.

The underground nature of Wicca meant that details of its history were hard to come by, but modern practitioners claim that evidence of its traditions can be found in 'pagan survivals', such as dancing around the Maypole. Another survival, 'Beating the Bounds', which involved an annual marking of the limits of a community's territory by people of all ages, is thought to have evolved from an ancient Roman festival which honoured Terminalia, the god of boundaries. Manchester Wiccans noted that John Dee took part in such a ritual on 4th May 1597, when he took a survey of the parish and was accompanied by, as he put it: 'diverse of the town, of diverse ages'.

Most academics, though, refute the claim that Wicca survived through millennia and see the religion as a creation of the twentieth century. They argue that the term Wicca only appeared in print in 1962; that many survivals were of medieval rather than pagan origin; and that the Wiccans took their beliefs from modern books such as Charles Leland's *Gospel of the Witches* (1899), Robert Grave's *The White Goddess* (1948), Sir James Frazer's *The Golden Bough* (1922). and Margaret Murray's: *The Witch-Cult in Western Europe* (1921), and *The God of the Witches* (1933).

Margaret Murray

Murray, who most influenced the Wiccans, began her working life as an Egyptologist; and due to Manchester being a centre of Oriental studies she ended up working at the city's museum. In 1907, she caused a stir by publically unwrapping a mummy. The event, which was publicised by the *Evening Chronicle* and the *Manchester Guardian*, attracted a crowd of 500. The reporter for the latter found the unwrapping to be a 'gruesome business', and noted that 'one or two people left early'. There were also complaints in the press about the disrespectful nature of the demonstration.

Although Murray wrote influential books which dealt with

magic, she was dismissive of supernaturalism when it came to Egyptology, and dismayed by the popular belief in the 'curse of Tutankhamun'.

Arthur Weigall, who spent his childhood in Salford, was responsible for circulating tales of the curse. By the age of 25, he was the Chief Inspector of Antiquities for Upper Egypt, but after a nervous breakdown, he left the job and resurfaced in England as a film-set designer. He returned to Egypt as a journalist to cover the opening of Tutankhamun's tomb, and along with H.V. Morton, the famous travel writer who spent his early years in Ashton-under-Lyne, he stymied the attempt by Howard Carter and Lord Carnarvon's to monopolise the story for the *Times*.

On February 16th, 1922, when he observed Lord Carnarvon acting frivolously whilst preparing to enter the tomb, Weigall said to Morton: 'If he goes down in that spirit, I give him six weeks to live'. Carnarvon died on April 5th Carnarvon - probably from blood poisoning, but rumours soon spread that he was the victim of a curse. Weigall fuelled the rumours by reporting that a cobra entered Carter's house on the day the tomb was opened and killed a caged canary. The locals, he claimed, interpreted this as an omen - for cobras were symbolic of the Pharaohs.

As noted, Margaret Murray was not impressed by such tales. In fact, she claimed she wanted: 'To make a strong protest against the absurd stories of the occult practices of the Egyptian objects as well as the wild tales of curses'.

Later in her career, Murray herself was the subject of wild tales. For instance, it was said that she began to put curses on people after she became interested in witchcraft. Ronald Hutton, who might have been expected to rubbish such stories, recounted one of them in *The Triumph of the Moon:*

> *Once she carried out a ritual to blast a fellow academic whose promotion she believed to have been undeserved, by mixing up ingredients in a frying pan in the presence of two colleagues. The victim actually did become ill, and had to change jobs. This was only one among a number of such acts of malevolent magic she perpetrated, and which*

the friend who recorded them assumed (rather nervously) were pranks, with coincidental effects. [4]

If Murray *had* been in the business of cursing those who crossed her, then she may have been tempted to hurl a few at the critics, for they hated her books. They accused her of committing the sort of crimes common to pseudo-historians: such as taking quotes out of context and ignoring evidence that did not fit her argument; and she was criticised for taking literally the confessions of women who were tortured and gave their inquisitors what they wanted to hear.

Murray's central concepts, such as the existence of covens, were also questioned. Ronald Hutton, who was a later critic, wrote: 'Did cunning folk ever work together, or meet in lodges, guilds, or covens? The answer seems to be an almost complete negative, for all the vast body of eighteenth and nineteenth-century evidence shows them operating as solitary practitioners'. Hutton did, though, concede that the 'single real exception' was provided by Manchester. 'It was where', he explained, 'some wisemen gathered round a famed one called Rawlinson'.

The critics may have panned Murray's books, but the public loved them. Her tales of secret covens were far more exciting than the fodder served up in schools. They were also seductive, for she presented an ancient belief system which was ripe for revival. Those who felt the need to rebel against the church now had access to a faith which they could claim predated Christianity.

Gerald Gardner was one of those who loved Murray's work. Born in 1884, in Lancashire, his family moved to Ceylon when he was 16, where he lived next to a bungalow that had just been vacated by Aleister Crowley. After spending thirty-odd years in various countries, he returned to England and joined the Folklore Society, which Margaret Murray later presided over. By the late 1930s, he was living in the New Forest and was a member of a local Rosicrucian group. He discovered that the group had an inner sanctum of witches - and this led to him being stripped naked and initiated in the house of old Dorothy Clutterbuck, a well-heeled local lady. This coven, he believed, was a little remnant of a pre-Christian Witch-Cult. But it was probably not. It is likely to have been inspired by Murray's books and was probably formed either in the late 1920s or early 30s.

In the 1940s, Gardner enhanced his esoteric credentials by befriending Aleister Crowley, and by briefly becoming the head of the Ordo Templi Orientis after the Great Beast died. Yet Gardner was not particularly interested in the OTO and soon relinquished the leadership. He did, though, take some of Crowley's rituals and synthesise them with the practices of the New Forest Coven. The result came to be known as Gardnerian magic.

The first coven of Gardnerian witches was formed at Bricket Wood, and one of the earliest initiates was Barbara Vickers - the wife of Gilbert Vickers, who was a scion of Manchester industrialists. Gilbert was also rumoured to be in the craft.

For a time they lived at Barnfield, a large old house in Prestwich, which the witches could not afford to heat. Consequently, they closed off most of the building and mainly occupied the kitchen area. Barbara claimed that whilst looking for Gilbert in one of the seldom-used sections of the house, she opened a door and noticed a group of people dressed in archaic clothes and busy toasting crumpets over a fire. She quickly closed the door, and after reopening it she saw nothing but dust sheets covering the furniture.

Barbara left the craft sometime in the 1950s because she felt it was incompatible with her family's Catholicism. But several other women who joined Gardner in the same era, such as Doreen Valiente, Eleanor Bone, Lois Bourne and Patricia Crowther, stayed the distance and became stalwarts of the Wicca movement.

In 1961, after Alex Sanders saw Patricia Crowther on Granada television's *People and Places*, he contacted her and arranged a meeting. It didn't go well, and Crowther refused to initiate him. Another Gardnerian witch, though, who was disenchanted with Crowther's coven, agreed to take Alex through the first degree. Wicca historians disagree on the identity of this witch. Some claim she was Pat Kasprzynski, whilst others believe she was a mysterious character from Derbyshire called Medea. Maxine Sanders, Alex's wife, muddied the waters by claiming there was some truth in both versions.

Yet another version of his initiation came from Alex, who claimed he was a hereditary witch and had been initiated by his grandmother. This was said to have occurred when he was a schoolboy after he barged in on her as she was conducting a ritual at her house on Wilton Road, in Chorlton. This tale created a furore within the Wicca community, for Sanders maintained that the ceremony involved cutting his scrotum and taking his virginity. June Johns, the biographer who revealed this grizzly yarn in *King of the Witches*, claimed that 'it was strictly a ritual and Alex did not feel the slightest repugnance at losing his virginity to a woman of seventy-four'.

More tall tales followed. Sanders, for instance, claimed his grandmother took him to London when he was ten years old, to meet a man called 'Mr Alexander'. After young Alex performed an 'Egyptian ceremony' with the man, his grandmother received a seal which she mounted on a ring. Sanders boasted it had once belonged to Eliphas Levi, the French occultist, and that it was remarkable:

> *I've met many magicians and witches and not one of them has seen anything like this except in Levi's own book. I've given it to jewellers to try and have a copy made and they say that they have no idea how it was made. The silver's not been chiselled off, chased off, eaten off, nor cast.*

Many years after the meeting, Alex claimed to have seen a photograph of 'Mr Alexander' and to have realized that he was none other than Aleister Crowley.

This is almost certainly not true, but we shouldn't be too harsh on Alex - for claiming to have worked with Crowley was something of a tradition amongst witches of a certain age. The Staffordshire Wiccan, Sybil Leek, dubbed 'Britain's most famous witch' by the BBC in the 1950s, maintained that Crowley was a family friend; and Madeline Montalban, an occultist born in Blackpool in 1910, claimed that her father sent her to study with him in London. Once again, this was probably untrue, although Montalban *did* meet Crowley in later life.

Alex Sanders

Other creative tales linked Alex to Lancashire's occult history. He claimed, for instance, to have been evacuated to the 'foothills of Pendle Hill' during the war, and to have experienced visions whilst there. June Johns put it this way:

> *One autumn day Alex was taken on a picnic to the top the hill . . . Although it was sunny, he shivered as he stood on the bare hillside. Emanations of previous ages chilled him to the bone . . . One by one the long-dead witches flickered across (his) consciousness, indistinct, but with the symbols of their witch-hood clearly defined: the horns - sign of the fertility cult - the broomsticks, the raised athames.* [5]

Years later, when Alex was head of a coven based in Chorlton, he claimed to have channelled the spirit of a seventeenth-century warlock called Nick Demdike. (The Demdikes were one of the Pendle families involved in the witch trials). Nick told the coven that his old athame lay in a brook near Whalley Abbey, and the following morning they drove to the spot and retrieved the rusty relic.

To prove that Alex hid the dagger on a previous visit would have been impossible for June Johns, but a little research into Nick Demdike would have revealed he never existed. Johns could easily have discovered that Alex had claimed to channel a fictional character from William Harrison Ainsworth's *The Lancashire Witches*.

By his mid-twenties, Alex had married, fathered two children, and secured a position with a pharmaceutical company. It was after losing both his job and his marriage that he began experimenting with black magic. The chapter in *King of the Witches* that covered this period was intended to be a cautionary tale about the dangers of dabbling with the forces of darkness, but it turned out like a script for a particularly bad episode of *Tales of the Unexpected*. It began with Alex burning incense and candles, whilst sitting within a circle and 'commanding the demons' to deliver him wealth and power. Two days later, as he walked through Piccadilly Gardens, he became aware that a middle-aged couple were following him. The couple, it transpired, were grieving, and became fixated with Alex because he resembled their lost son. It also transpired that they were wealthy.

After he lived with them in Fallowfield, they bought him a house on Demesne Road, Whalley Range. It was a substantial place called Riversdale, which had been built for Lord Egerton of Tatton in 1872, and Alex claimed to have initially seen it in his crystal ball.

The house was renovated, and painted on the parquet floor of the 'ballroom' was 'a huge magic circle adorned with cabalistic symbols handed down from the ancient Hebrews'. Once Alex was ensconced, wild times followed. He held sex parties, indulged in a little sadomasochism, and had gay affairs with a magistrate and an Italian aristocrat. Through it all, he referred to the Tarot and kept dealing death. The cards, claimed Johns, foretold the suicide of a girl he had treated badly, and also the death of his younger sister. When the predictions proved to be true, Alex decided to change and gave up Riversdale and his possessions.

Although Alex and Johns embellished this period - and every other period - of his life, there is some truth in the account. He did live in Riversdale, and the Fallowfield couple did help him out. But rather than bewitching the pair, he probably used his skills as a medium to exploit them. They may have been as ripe for the taking as Charles Blackburn had been seventy years before, and Alex may have conducted séances and passed on messages from the couple's dead son. That he reverted to the name Paul Dallas during this period gives credence to the notion.

Alex claimed to have lived austerely after his Riversdale period, and to have studied the Hebrew AbraMelin system of magic, which was said to be of 'great value for purification'. This led to much ritualising, fasting and chanting, and to an understanding that he was to devote his life to Wicca.

During this period, after spending two or three years under the wing of Pat Kasprzynski's coven, Alex began his own coven. One of the early recruits to his new coven was a middle-aged lady called Sylvia, who became his High Priestess, and he also attracted a couple called Bill and Eunice. This pair, who seemed unlikely witches because they were devout Christians, claimed they joined the coven because they wanted to converse with angels.

Around this time, Alex attempted to further his occult knowledge by studying the *Key of Solomon* - a 14th or 15th-century Italian grimoire, and also by reading Sir Frances Barrett's *The Magus*.

The tale which he told June Johns about the acquisition of the *Key of Solomon* was bizarre. It involved him becoming a book-duster at John Ryland's Library, which he believed was worked on by tradesmen who were well versed in witchcraft because of the demons, green men, and dragons and imps that were carved into the walls. He claimed to have taken the job just so he could get access to the *Key of Solomon*, which he began to copy. After realising that it would take too long to reproduce the many elaborate symbols, and after deciding the volume was too large to smuggle out, he dismantled it and delivered it page by page to Bill, who photocopied them. But before the job was done, the library authorities discovered the mangled book. They also discovered that Alex was involved with witchcraft, and promptly sacked him.

It was a laborious way of obtaining the book, for it was not exceedingly rare in the early 1960s, and there were versions of MacGregor Mather's translation in circulation. Perhaps Alex wanted to get his hands on the Ryland's version because it was older; perhaps he wanted to handle the same pages that generations of adepts had pored over, or perhaps it was another tall tale.

The story of how he came to read *The Magus* was also strange. He claimed to have been instructed to find the book by the archangel Michael, who was channelled by the twelve-year-old son of Bill and Eunice during an elaborate ritual which involved four pounds of rose petals that had been picked between two and four o'clock in the morning. Alex looked in his local library for the book but was told it had been stolen. Finally, he tracked down a copy at the University and referred to it when holding a further ritual. During this session, the archangel told Bill and Eunice to forgo Wicca and devote themselves to Christianity.

The departure of the couple left Alex with a fairly threadbare coven, but he would soon be joined by a young man from Stockport called Paul King, and Maxine Morris of Blackley, who was blonde, statuesque, and perfectly suited to the role of a Wicca priestess.

Alex claimed to have foreseen Maxine's arrival during a skrying session. In reality, he knew her through her mother, who had been a nurse at a factory where he had worked.

Enter Maxine: Witch Queen and Firechild

When she was a child, Maxine fell into a fire and began astral travelling during her convalescence. 'I wandered with my mind to other places', she revealed, 'where the colours were totally different to those of this world, where beings made up of light would comfort and entertain me'.

Later, a spirit guardian helped her with mathematics at school, which displeased her teachers because Maxine simply wrote the answers and refused to show the working out.

Her father, who was also often displeased with her, told Maxine that she was 'weird'. Fortunately, her mother, Doris Morris, was more supportive. She was something of a bohemian and was attracted to the city's painters, writers, musicians, and occultists - and in the early 1960s, she became involved in a spiritual organization called Subud and dragged Maxine along to meetings.

Subud initially found a foothold in Manchester amongst a group which studied the work of George Ivanovich Gurdjieff, the Russian spiritual teacher. After travelling through the east, where he met several fakirs, yogis, and monks, Gurdjieff concluded that the systems of these wise men were not completely suited to the West. So he developed a 'fourth way', which he described in *All and Everything*.

It involved a series of challenging physical actions, or sacred dances, which were known as 'movements'; it also included group labour and the development of an awareness of self. To try and instil this, Gurdjieff suddenly shouted 'stop' when his students were going about their tasks, and they had to freeze. Such procedures were designed to extricate the individual from the 'waking sleep' - from the condition in which they drifted through life.

Gurdjieff often told his students that after he died a teacher would emerge and further their spiritual education - and Subud, it seems, took up this role. It was introduced to the devotees of Gurdjieff by John Godolphin Bennett - one of the main tutors of the Russian mystic's philosophy in England, who ran a study group at a house called Coombe Springs in Kingston. He surprised his students when he stepped down and declared that representatives of Subud would take his place.

Most of the students were not familiar with Subud, but they soon learnt that it was founded in Indonesia by Muhammad Subuh Sumohadiwidjojo, also known as Pak Subuh, after he underwent a mystical experience. In 1925, he suddenly found himself suffused with light and presumed he was having a heart attack. After lying down and accepting he would die, Subuh felt the urge to stand and perform movements similar to those of a Muslim prayer. As he did this, he felt his body was not under his control.

The experience inspired him to found a system of spiritual training known as the *Latihan*. It involved the student sitting quietly, then standing and relaxing until something which 'arose from within' took hold and caused the individual to jump, walk, laugh, cry, dance, sit, rock about, or carry out any number of actions. Once this occurred the individual was said to have been 'opened'.

Pak Subhu predicted that a non-Indonesian individual would arrive in the country, be opened, and then export Subud to the world. This character turned out to be Husein Rofe, who was born in Manchester in 1922. His grandfather was a Syrian Jew who moved to Egypt and then to Manchester, where he established a successful business. Rofe introduced Subud to J. G. Bennett, and soon most of the Gurdjieff group in Manchester were opened.

In the 1950s, Pak Subhu spent some time in the city and inspired his new followers to arrange meeting places - such as the Seven Circles Cafe. It was the venue for Maxine's first experience of Subud, but she was not keen on the place: *'Above the entrance',* she wrote,*' seven intertwined circles were pictured on a swinging sign; the cafe was seedy and most of its customers looked like beatniks and one or two, rather more dubious'.* The clientele, though, proved to be welcoming, and after a three-month probationary period, Doris and Maxine were 'opened'.

At a Subud conference in Paris, Maxine met J. G. Bennett, who deeply impressed her. 'His spiritualism', she wrote, 'was palpable to those near him'. He certainly proved to be an antidote to her father's boorishness.

Trips to Coombe Springs followed, but as Maxine explained, the place was not always tranquil:

There were a few odd characters', she claimed: *'who were permanent residents. One chap would go mad at the full moon. He would take an axe and chop at everything in front of him. I learned to avoid him. He would scream and sob until eventually Mr Bennett would come and calm him. Then there was the 'full moon nudies' who insisted on walking the grounds stark naked even in the middle of winter.* [5]

At approximately the same time as the Subud experience, Maxine was launched on another esoteric adventure. It began when

Doris met a woman called Pat in the Seven Circles cafe, who was interested in Subud and Gurdjieff and claimed to be related to Howard Carter - the archaeologist who discovered Tutankhamen's tomb.

Pat was something of a character. She liked her nails to be red and long, her eyelids to be silver, and the rest of her make-up to be green. Her wardrobe consisted of vividly coloured dresses, rich heavy cloaks, and 'flowing scarves'. Maxine, displaying a Les Dawson-esque talent for bathos, revealed that Pat was an initiate of the Egyptian mysteries, was dedicated to the Goddess Sekhmet, and was also 'the main owner of a successful business that sold all things connected with motorbikes'.

Pat regularly held forth on Gurdjieff, ancient Egypt, and astral travelling. 'She constantly tested my knowledge and senses', recalled Maxine, 'and pushed me to refine my level of attention and to retain the memory of events that occurred whilst out of my physical body'. After nine months of these sessions, Pat revealed that Maxine was being prepared for initiation into a magical Egyptian order.

Maxine never disclosed the name of this group, or the identities of its members, although she did explain its purpose:

The order studied the wisdom of the ancient Egyptian priesthoods and recreated, where possible, the ceremonies that enabled them to practise the worship of the Egyptian Gods and to work the magic of those original priesthoods.

On the day of the initiation, Maxine took a 'purifying bath that filled the house with the aromatic smells of herbs and oils', and then opened her front door to two men who 'stood there in ominous silence'. They drove her to Alderley Edge and led her to a: 'vast rocky cavern full of dancing shadows'. Maxine recalled that 'five flares were burning, giving off an eerie light', and that 'the vastness of the cave created the impression of a cathedral'.

A small group of 'richly robed priests filed into the chamber', Maxine was anointed with oils, and then a fire-walking ceremony commenced. Next, she was forced to swim along a stream that led to another 'vast cavern' which was 'suffused with brilliant light'. Waiting were a bunch of priests, each wearing a mask of a god. She answered questions about her 'past behaviour, attitude and potential right to the gift of life', and was led to a smaller cave. Here she felt her 'spirit slip away and enter the world of nightmares; the plane of being where the Lords of Opposition dwell'. After travelling 'amongst the old gods', she was revived and given a warm drink.

Maxine Sanders

The drive home with Pat was one of 'almost complete silence'. Maxine felt that: 'the depth of the experience' had left her 'with nothing to say'.

Her involvement with the order ended abruptly when she began to show an interest in Wicca and to associate with Alex Sanders. 'They made veiled detrimental references to Alex', she recalled, 'and considered him not to be the person with whom I should tread the path of the Mysteries'.

It was soon after the initiation at Alderley Edge that Maxine's mother bumped into Alex in the Seven Circles cafe and invited him to one of her 'Sunday soirees'. These events were attended not only by the city's occultists, beatniks, and bohemians, but also by a strange brew of barrow boys, villains, and police officers who Doris met during a stint as a store detective.

Initially, Maxine was disturbed by the fact that Alex was a witch. She was reassured, though, after he explained that Wicca was a 'religion which celebrated seasonal rituals with as much devotion as a Christian sect'. Later, Alex impressed her by stimulating hair growth in a woman known as 'Susan the dancer', who had inexplicably gone bald. Also impressive was the way he dealt with a neighbour's child, which suffered from epilepsy. 'The child', wrote Maxine, 'was difficult at best, but when Alex was with her she became totally relaxed, smiling and giggling with delight. He would take her on his knee, and appeared to make deliberate passes with his hands over her head. Within a few weeks of their first meeting the fits stopped'.

Maxine was attending Lorebourne College in Manchester during this period, but she began to skip lectures to visit Alex at his 'old two up two down' on Oldham Road in Newton Heath. The house shook every time a heavy lorry passed, and shunting train engines made a cacophony at the rear. Yet Maxine found the place to be calm: 'Strange and wonderful aromas filled the rooms and lingered on your clothes, reminding you of the sense of timelessness and secret sacredness practised in the strange little house'.

Maxine was particularly impressed with one part of the house:

Alex had an unusual room set apart which he used for his meditations and magical workings. On entering there was a sense of walking into a secret copse ... Images of magical animals such as the hare and stag peeped out from behind woodland plants and trees painted on walls. The Great God Pan with his mighty antlers and erect phallus gazed adoringly at the gentle Goddess Aphrodite. In the centre of the room was a log from the base of a tree trunk. This was constantly changing as Alex carved beautiful magic sigils, this he employed as an altar; it would always be adorned with wild flowers collected from hedgerows, no matter what time of year. This was the temple and as with everything magical that Alex created, it reflected his present spiritual aspirations and so was always different. The magical space was incongruous in the centre of all the noise and bustle of its surroundings . . .[6]

The house was too small for the coven, so meetings were held at 24 Egerton Road in Chorlton, and it was here that Maxine was initiated. Soon after, she embarked on what she called her 'basic training' - and learnt how to achieve a trance state, and how to 'walk the earth or astral planes in spirit'. She also acquired knowledge of rites, spells, chants, charms, incense, drugs, wine, healing herbs, poison, sacred dances, blood and breath control, and sexual power.

Spirit evocation was also on the syllabus, and the coven experimented with the kind of magic circles and triangles that Crowley and Victor Neuberg utilised in the North African desert when they conjured up Euphemia Lamb.

Before she finished her training, Maxine decided to create an elemental, which in this case was an entity formed from the power of thought and ritual. Her account of this episode, which involved conjuring up an animated creature from a popular television advertisement, is the most bizarre part of her biography, *Firechild*.

She claimed to have 'worked secretly every night in a circle performing the rituals in readiness for the creation' of the elemental. For days nothing happened and she was kept busy because she was preparing to move house. Then, as she sat in her kitchen, she noticed a movement: 'I thought I caught sight of something about eight inches high sitting on the draining board.' It was her elemental, the figure from the advert, who could not speak but walked up and down with a determined look on his face. 'He was my creation', claimed Maxine, 'and I was spellbound'. The other witches, who were helping her move house, were not spellbound and didn't notice the entity. Alex, though, did notice it and was furious as he pointed out that it was multiplying.

Other occultists have mentioned similar cases. Perhaps the most famous was recounted by Alexandra David-Neel, a Belgian who was born in 1868. She was part of the Victorian crowd which believed the east to be the home of mysticism - but whereas some of her contemporaries merely donned faux-eastern costumes and mouthed incantations, David-Neel spent years travelling through India and Tibet and became the first woman to be called a Lama.

In 1932, she published *Magic and Mystery in Tibet*, in which she referred to a 'Tulpa'. These were Tibetan versions of elementals, and David-Neel described how she created one: *'I proceeded to perform the prescribed concentration of thought and other rites. After a few months the phantom monk was formed. His form grew gradually fixed and lifelike. He became a kind of guest, living in my apartment'.*

David-Neel was followed by the monk when she went travelling, and she noticed it was slowly beginning to grow sinister and to gain independence. *'The features which I had imagined when building my phantom gradually underwent a change. The fat, chubby-cheeked fellow grew leaner; his face assumed a vaguely mocking, sly, malignant look. He became more troublesome and bold'.*

After realising that he had escaped from her control, David-Neel decided to dissolve the entity. *'I succeeded'*, she wrote, *'but only after six months of hard struggle. My mind-creature was tenacious of life'.*

Maxine also had trouble dissolving her creations: 'I worked late into the night with the stubborn little imps who proved to be most impossible to get rid of'. It took Alex's greater power, she claimed, to finally banish the entities.

Alderley Edge and Park View

Directly after her strange encounter with the elementals, Maxine moved to 9 Park View, opposite Queen's Park in Harpurhey. The three-storey Victorian house was said to be 'rather grand' in appearance but dilapidated inside. Alex, who had lived nearby at 390 Collyhurst Road, felt it was 'wonderful' and declared that 'the atmosphere is right for magical workings'. (Perhaps this atmosphere persisted in the area after the houses were demolished, for the pub at the bottom of the road was turned into a gothic-themed restaurant and bar).

Despite the vibe at Park View, the coven's most sacred site was Alderley Edge, which Maxine believed was 'ambient and magical' and home to many 'powerful forces of nature'. Those passing through the village for the first time, though, could be forgiven for thinking that the only discernable 'powerful forces' were those of capitalism and conspicuous consumption. Yet the Edge, which is a sandstone ridge, *is* atmospheric. It affords views of the Cheshire countryside and is peppered with mines, caves, and attractive landmarks such as the Druid's Circle of stones. Marriot, in *Antiquities of Lyme*, claimed the circle was ancient. It was, he wrote, 'a very perfect model of the rude yet awe-inspiring religious system of the ancients of the place'; and he speculated that sacrifices might have been committed on the 'frontispiece of the edifice'. Several others, though, claimed the circle was an eighteenth-century folly which may have been created by an ancestor of Alan Garner - who based his novels The *Weirdstone of Brisingamen* and *The Moon of Gomrath* around Alderley Edge. Yet Garner does not mention the circle in his memoirs - although he notes that his 'grandfather's grandfather' was responsible for local landmarks such as the carved face of an old man above the Wizard's Well.

The wizard in question played a part in the legend of the place - which maintained that an army slept underneath the Edge and would rise and help Britain when she needed it most. This tale was probably derived from the prophecies of Robert Nixon - whose spirit informed James Johnson of the spiritual aspects of the Peterloo Massacre.

The legend evolved in the 19th-century when the wizard became Merlin, and the sleeping men became King Arthur and his army. During the Second World War, locals joked that the time had come for the army to wake and get busy. But according to the Gardnerian witch Phillip Heselton, there may already have been occult forces working for the good of England. In a lecture that touched on the 'Cone of Power,' which was said to have been raised by the New Forest witches against Hitler, he claimed that other anti-Nazi rituals were performed by covens in 'Kent, on the Sussex Downs, and at Alderley Edge'.

This is the bones, then, of Alderley's reputation for mysticism. It was a reputation that Alex reinforced in 1962 when he performed a ritual on the Edge for the *Manchester Evening Chronicle and News*. Three media men, including the reporter David Duffy, turned up for what they described as 'a secret rendezvous' with the coven, and were 'tied up and blindfolded'. 'You will be able to listen to the rituals', Alex told them, 'but because they are secret we cannot allow you to witness them'.

The ensuing article, which was headlined: *Amazing Black Magic Rites on Cheshire Hillside*, was melodramatic. Duffy opened the piece with: '*Burning incense penetrated the midnight air and a chill wind swept the hillside at Alderley Edge*, and then he revealed that: '*Only feet from where I was sitting - the very spot where the Wizard of Alderley practiced his ancient cult centuries ago - was a magic circle surrounded by lighted candles, shielded from the wind with ferns*'. That the wizard had existed must have been a revelation for local folklorists.

Duffy went on to note the various magical implements which decorated the site, including a human thigh-bone which was said to have belonged to a Templar; then he revealed that the rituals included the ringing of bells, the summoning of gods from the four points of the compass, and incantations recited in a 'barbaric tongue'. As was customary in pieces about witchcraft, a clergyman was quoted: the Reverend C. A. Shaw of St. Ambrose Church, Pendleton, claimed that Alex's: 'midnight initiation' was the 'type of thing which might have took place in Lancashire in the 16th century'.

But Alex's ceremony was no such thing - for it was mostly improvised. It was a bespoke offering to the modern gods of publicity, and the 'barbaric' incantations were words from a Swiss Roll recipe recited backwards.

Two years later, Alex informed reporters that Alderley Edge would be the site for a naked ritual 'on the night of the next full moon'. He had not, though, told Maxine that photographers were invited to the ceremony. In *Firechild,* Maxine described the event:

> *The full moon rite is known as 'Drawing down the Moon', in which the Goddess is invoked onto the body of the priestess by the High Priest. The worship that is accorded to her is of the Goddess made flesh. On the night of the full moon, a cauldron containing wood had been lit in the cave directly under the altar stone. I was standing naked in the pentacle position on the stone slab of the altar. The flames reached up to my waist and must have made a remarkable sight. I was preparing myself for the descent of the Goddess as the priest intoned the prayer of invocation. Out of the corner of my eye I caught the sight of a bluish-white light and heard a clicking sound. I put this down to the crackling of the fire. As the metabolism speeds up in anticipation of a spiritual experience flickering lights are often experienced.* [7]

The lights were, of course, the result of flash photography rather than any spiritual phenomena. Maxine realised this two days later when she saw a photograph of herself plastered on a local newsagent's billboards. 'I was naked', she wrote, 'surrounded by fire and looking like some beautiful demon from a fairy book illustration'. Within two hours of the paper appearing, the national press began knocking at her door, and for weeks after she was pursued by reporters. Through the letterbox came abuse from Christians, propositions from sexual opportunists, and general fan mail.

Overall, the effect of the publicity was devastating for Maxine. It led to her being fired from her job and threatened with eviction. It also strained her relationship with her mother and set in motion a series of events that resulted in a policeman attempting to rape her. Alex, in contrast, was said to have been 'in his element'. He justified his glee at the publicity by claiming it was essential if the old religion was to survive. He argued that 'the thousands who sought initiation', but didn't know where to find it, would be given an opportunity to contact the coven.

Soon after, Alex and Maxine were invited to give a talk on witchcraft at a village hall. When the event was advertised on the church notice board it caused a furore - and the press took up the story, with one headline reading: 'Ban This Evil'. Inevitably, this led to greater demand for tickets and the event was moved to a larger venue.

After the talk, which was chaotic, the couple were whisked to Granada studios to make their first television appearance. Maxine hated it, but Alex revelled in the experience.

The King of the Witches

In 1965, more publicity was garnered by Alex when he claimed that an election amongst sixteen hundred Wiccans resulted in him being crowned 'King of the Witches'. This outraged the Gardnerian contingent, which protested that the ritual had no historical precedent. 'The title was', wrote Doreen Valiente, 'simply a modern invention, much favoured by the media, but previously never heard of'. Valiente also wondered where the sixteen hundred witches had appeared from - for 'Sanders was at that time only the leader of three covens in Manchester'.

Alex was uncowed by the criticism and told June Johns that he was elected because his peers considered him to be the country's foremost occultist. Years later, Maxine embellished the yarn in *Firechild*. She conjured up two 'messengers from the Council of Elders' - an 'odd-looking' ex-public schoolboy with 'an overbearing and pompous manner', and a 'smartly dressed woman' - who were said to have turned up in Chorlton to try and persuade Alex to assume the role of King of the Witches. After being cajoled, Maxine revealed, he accepted.

The coronation was said to have taken place at the Didsbury home of Joan Redcliffe, who was a painter and a member of one of the covens. Redcliffe was, claimed Maxine, 'a neurotic fidgety little being who could write, draw and paint using her toes like fingers'. Maxine viewed her as a typical struggling artist and wondered how she managed to maintain her house, which was 'rambling, old, and wonderful'. She managed, it transpired, because she was wealthy.

On the day of the ceremony, many 'robed priests and priestesses' filled the house. One elderly priestess placed a gold crown on Alex's head and said the word: 'Verbius' - his chosen witch name. And with that, the coronation was complete.

It is easy to understand why such stunts outraged the Gardnerians: for Alex was more showman than shaman; and yet during the 1950s, similar criticisms were made of their High Priest, Gerald Gardner, when he courted the press.

In later years, the press caused problems for Wiccans, but the early 50s articles about modern witchcraft were not entirely negative and exploitative. *Illustrate* magazine ran a long and informative feature: *Witchcraft in Britain*, that described the nature of fertility rituals and explored the four great Sabbats. But in 1955, the *Sunday Pictorial* - one of the era's most notorious tabloids - set the tone for the following decades when it published pieces linking witchcraft with Satanism. The paper found a woman in Birmingham who described rites involving the sacrifice of chickens and the drinking of blood, and the obligatory clergymen were wheeled out to denounce witchcraft.

The Charles Walton murder was also revisited by the tabloids. In 1945, this 74-year-old farm worker was brutally killed as he cut a hedge at Meon Hill in Warwickshire. Soon after, speculation that he may have been despatched by occultists pricked the ears of the 81-year-old Margaret Murray. After she disguised herself as a landscape painter and spent a week in the area investigating the murder, she concluded that Walton might have been murdered because the locals feared he had supernatural powers.

Despite Murray's Miss Marple-style efforts, no further evidence was uncovered and the case remained unsolved. Although during the 1950s witchcraft scare, one tabloid paper found a woman, described as 'attractive . . . but with haunted eyes', who claimed that Walton was sacrificed by occultists. Thirteen witches were said to have gathered from around the country and to have murdered Walton. 'Afterwards', she asserted, 'they danced around the body'. This was, of course, nonsense.

Gerald Gardner was particularly dismayed by this story, and soon after it appeared he met a *Sunday Pictorial* journalist and tried to present him with a more measured account of Wicca. He felt the interview went well, and so he was shocked when he was denounced in the ensuing article as a 'whitewasher of witchcraft'.

After this scenario repeated several times, members of Gardner's coven begged him to stop giving interviews. This was not unreasonable, for it was a time when, remarkably, witch hunts still occurred. Salacious tabloid headlines ensured that practising Wiccans lost their jobs, were ostracised by their families and friends and were subjected to violence. Gardner, though, could not be convinced to stay quiet, and Doreen Valiente, one of his coven's most respected witches, realised that he 'had a considerable love of the limelight and of being the centre of attention'.

The Dark Side

The media's coverage of the occult increased during the 60s, and in Alex and Maxine the tabloids found a pair of witches who were much better value than old Gerald Gardner. Alex could be relied upon for an outrageous quote, and Maxine was young, blonde, physically attractive, and not adverse to going naked in the name of her religion. Years later, Derek Jameson, the legendary Fleet Street editor, admitted: 'the Sanders' witches were a godsend when news was thin on the ground . . . (they were) good for a sales boost'. At the time, though, the tabloids certainly did not claim the Wiccans were a godsend and continued to portray them as Satanists.

The notion that Alex and Maxine worshipped the devil was, of course, ridiculous. Yet there were groups in the 1960s and 70s who represented the dark side of the occult - such as the Manchester-based Orthodox Temple of the Prince, which was led by Ray Bogart, who was prosecuted for sex crimes. A similar set-up, the Temple of the Black Pentacle, was headed by the Failsworth-based Ramon Shareth. This group gained notoriety in the mid-70s after the tabloids focused on their sexual initiations, but they were seldom mentioned afterwards - although Umberto Eco referred to them in *Foucault's Pendulum*.

Alex and Maxine were never involved in such exploitation, but theirs was a strange profession and these were strange times - so they were occasionally exposed to suspect characters and situations. For instance, they were linked, albeit peripherally, to the Moors Murders investigation, and they also met Sharon Tate, who was killed by the Manson Family.

The Sanders' coven abandoned Alderley Edge in the mid-sixties because the publicity made it difficult for them to carry out their rituals in peace. Saddleworth Moor was thought to be a good alternative, and the group found a workable site at a 'bleak circular tarn consisting of a sheer rock face', where there was a 'large flat-topped stone' which was used as an altar. When speaking of this place, Maxine recalled a photo which caught her as she 'invoked the Horned God' under a starry night sky, whilst above her a 'great horned ram peered down from the top of the crag'.

This link to Saddleworth, which was where the Moors Murderers buried their victims, and the fact that books on the occult were found amongst the murderer's possessions, prompted the police to question the coven. Maxine explained the situation: 'Attention fell on occult groups with whom Brady might have links. The question was: 'Were Hindley and Brady simply disturbed individuals or were they part of a wider cult of satanic abuse?'

The day before the police interview, Alex and Maxine were at the MGM studio in Elstree, on the set of a film about witchcraft called *Eye of the Devil*, which starred David Niven, David Hemmingway and Sharon Tate. It was a mediocre effort, and as Gary Lachman noted, it has only been remembered because: 'It has been seen as an eerie presage of (Tate's) unfortunate encounter with real life demons'.

The studio claimed the couple were employed to guarantee that the film's depiction of ritual magic was accurate, but they were really there to drum up publicity. The press were invited in, and Alex and Maxine gave them something to write about by posing in full regalia within a magic circle that was strewn with candle holders and chalices.

That these Manchester witches were hobnobbing with Hollywood stars did not please other Wiccans. Two Gardnerians - Mrs Ray Bone, and Patricia Crowther, who had refused to initiate Alex, protested the loudest. Mrs Bone claimed that Alex was not a genuine witch, and Crowther revealed he had been desperate to join her coven just five years previously. It is a sign of very different times that this spat made the news. The *Sun* reported the story under the headline: *Toil and Trouble as Witches Fall Out*.

Alex responded by stating that Crowther and Bone were the pseudo-witches because they followed the 'modern version of witchcraft', and he argued that he had more credibility because he was a hereditary witch. It was an audacious response, for the historical authenticity of their craft was a touchy point for the Gardnerians; and now here was a character, considered by them to be an upstart, who was trumping them by claiming to be from a long line of witches.

Back on the set of the film, Maxine met Sharon Tate and liked her. She did not, though, pay the actress too much attention. Often meeting outré characters on the Wiccan scene had left her a little jaded, and she felt that Sharon Tate was 'just another cookie'; just another vulnerable character with 'a need to belong'.

Tate certainly felt the need to belong to Wicca and asked Alex to initiate her, which he duly did. Maxine learnt of this later in the day when Tate whispered to her: 'I am your sister now. I am one of you'.

The initiation was, needless to say, meaningless, and the two women never met again. Maxine returned to Manchester the day after and was forced by the police to listen to a horrific recording that Brady and Hindley made when torturing a child; and Sharon Tate, after completing *Eye of the Devil*, left England for her fate at the hands of the Manson Family.

Two years after working on the film, Maxine and Alex accepted jobs as housekeepers in London. The Manchester coven, much upset and annoyed by this, declared that they would use magic to prevent the move. And things, Maxine claimed, began to go wrong: the starting dates for the jobs were repeatedly put back, and the offers of the positions were withdrawn and then reinstated. Finally, though, they left for the capital.

'The news of our move to London', wrote Maxine, 'spread like wildfire through the occult grapevine'. And several of the city's witches, who felt they might be usurped by the couple, were less than welcoming. Many others, though, were curious about Maxine and Alex and flocked to their flat. The visitors were not just occultists - the couple also pulled in hippies, European aristocrats, waifs and strays, drug addicts, and a Maltese stripper called Lil who was an associate of the Kray Twins.

They also made the acquaintance of a few characters who eschewed the colourful hippy garb for more menacing attire, and who struck Maxine as 'strange'. 'They dressed completely in black', she remembered, 'with high leather boots and hip length black coats fastened with a silver clasp'. And as they patrolled in twos, 'they walked with an arrogant stride that suggested it would be wise to move out of their way'.

This bunch belonged to the Process Church of the Final Judgement - which became infamous because of its supposed links with Charles Manson.

The Process Church was founded in the early 60s by two ex-Scientologists: Robert Moore and Mary Ann Maclean. Moore had enjoyed a fairly comfortable upbringing and trained to be an architect, but Maclean had a tough childhood in Glasgow and was rumoured to have worked as a prostitute in America. Other rumours had her either married or engaged to the boxer Sugar Ray Robinson, and also involved, in some unspecified way, in the Profumo Affair.

Initially, the Process gained popularity with a middle-class and fairly respectable crowd, but by the time Maxine encountered them they had evolved into an apocalyptic sect and had a sinister image. At their Mayfair mansion, which was purchased with the help of a member's inheritance, they produced films about 'war, degradation, violence, despair, power, lust, fear, hate, sin and horror'; and they published a magazine which contained articles on Hitler, necrophilia, brainwashing, and other disturbing subjects.

Maxine, not surprisingly, detested the Process. She claimed its members had poor personal hygiene, and one character was said to be such an 'odoriferous demon' that incense had to be burnt after he left the flat.

The incense got rid of their odour, but their aura lingered. 'The books they fingered felt besmirched', wrote Maxine, 'the glasses they had drunk water from, tarnished. It became a rule to clean and purify everything after they left'.

The Process, 'who never smiled', were so unpleasant that they drove away other visitors, and even Maxine began to make her excuses and leave. Whenever a particular 'superior member' of the movement called by, who she felt 'suffered from depression and had a bad psychic smell', she took herself to Kensington Gardens and 'meditated or read in the orangery opposite the palace'. It was, she remembered, 'a peaceful sanctuary, removed from a presence which I knew boded ill'.

Alex felt differently about the Process. He discussed magic rituals with them, and was, claimed Maxine, 'flattered by the attention of such a rich and powerful order'. Consequently, a strain was put on the couple's relationship. A particular point of contention occurred when the Process asked to borrow a Crowley manuscript so it could be sent to the United States where it would be examined by a Great Beast specialist. Maxine wanted to refuse, but Alex acquiesced.

The evening before the manuscript was returned began calmly, with Alex and Maxine and friends watching *The Mad Magician*, a 1954 shocker starring Vincent Price. Soon, claimed Maxine, the horror seemed to spill from the screen: a wine bottle rose in the air and then smashed; a table 'flung itself across the room'; the television floated whilst still on; 'large wing backed chairs were flung over'; and 'a four foot high statue of the Goddess lifted itself to the centre of the room, wavered next to the television, and then smashed against the ceiling'. On went the chaos until the witches curtailed it by chanting 'words of banishment'.

Maxine described the aftermath:

By now it was morning and the postman arrived with the usual batch of letters plus one shabby brown packet. The postmark was from California; there was no accompanying note; just the Crowley manuscript now rather tattered. Obviously, it had been well-read if not respected, certain passages had been underlined and indistinguishable notes scrawled in the margins.

Maxine noticed that 'one line of the text had been singled out for particular attention, the words 'KILL THE PIGS'. . . had been heavily underlined'. She remembered this phrase when the news of Sharon Tate's murder broke in August 1969. 'KILL THE PIGS', she noted, 'had been daubed on the walls with Sharon Tate's blood'.

Maxine described how she felt at hearing the news:

My senses reeled as I recalled the young woman who I had instructed in the ritual movements of the witchcraft circle. She had been so attentive and sincere in her attitude towards me. There had been a link, an almost casual bond between us then, and now - I could not bring myself to ponder any further.

There are some factual errors in Maxine's account of the murders. The Manson Family did not daub 'KILL THE PIGS' on the wall of Tate's house; rather, 'PIG' was daubed in blood on the front door by Susan Atkins, and 'DEATH TO PIGS' was scrawled in the house of Leno and Rosemary LaBianca, who were murdered by the Family on the following night.

The links between the Process Church and the Manson Family are disputed, but Maxine was not alone in making such a connection. Others noted that members of the Process visited Manson in jail; that Manson either lived near or with them, on Cole Street in Haight Ashbury; and that Robert DeGrimston joined in events at the Esaleau Institute new age community, which Manson visited a few days before the murder of Tate.

The most vocal of those who linked Manson and the Process was Ed Sanders, the author of *The Family*, an account of the murders published in 1972. He described them as 'an English occult society dedicated to observing and aiding the end of the world, (so that) they should survive as the chosen people', and he claimed they 'shaped the mind of Charles Manson'.

Ed Sanders, though, could not prove any of this, and so the Process took legal action. A $1.5 million lawsuit was taken out against the publisher of the book, and further action was taken against magazines which published articles by Sanders. Eventually, the matter was settled out of court and mentions of the Process were removed from the book.

Witchploitation

In the late '60s, our two witches embarked on what Maxine called 'an adventure in the world of show business'. Unfortunately, the adventure did not produce quality work: there were cheesy gigs with the rock band *Black Widow*; a disastrous Wicca show which toured nightclubs; and several appearances in exploitation films.

The directors of these films, like the tabloid hacks and editors, were not concerned with producing realistic accounts of Wicca. They were more focused on getting nudity on to the screens - so there were shots of Maxine and other young witches with little in the way of clothes on, and the promotional blurb promised viewers *'erotic prayers . . . macabre orgies . . . and sensual ecstasies'*.

The features were also marketed as if they were horror films: for this was a golden age of gore. The Hammer studios were churning out films at a shocking rate, and Dennis Wheatley, who was selling more than a million of his occult chillers per year, had never been more popular. Consequently, posters for the documentaries showed witches posing against blood-red backgrounds whilst holding human skulls, knives, swords and other implements of doom.

The worst of the Witchploitation films - or the best, depending on your taste - was *Witchcraft 70*. It was directed by an Italian called Luigi Scattari, and the American Lee Frost - who was also known as David Kayne. Had Alex and Maxine glanced at the pair's back catalogue, they would have known what was coming: for Frost was responsible for such delights as *Hollywood's World of Flesh* and *Love Camp 7*, (and would go on to make *Chain Gang Women*, *The Thing with Two Heads*, and *Black Gestapo*); whilst Scattari directed, among others, *Primitive Love*: a documentary about Jayne Mansfield's investigation into 'human sexuality'. It was also supposed to be a comedy, and so Mansfield was pursued throughout the feature by two lusty Italian bellhops.

Primitive Love was part of the *Mondo Cane* craze. These films were a series of pseudo-anthropological documentaries - 1962's *Mondo Cane* being the first - that cobbled together footage of natives doing such things as dancing and slaughtering animals. *Witchcraft 70*, which was firmly in this mould, featured citizens of Rio, who danced with 'wild abandon', and were said to have both a 'heavy regard for Christ' and a 'healthy respect for Satan'. Also present were Brazilians who offered flowers and a 'celluloid doll' to a sea god; and Voodoo practitioners from somewhere between Baton Rouge and New Orleans, who were busy 'putting a hex on somebody'.

It was not just Latin and Afro-Americans who were shown to practise suspect rituals, but also white suburban types from the United States. A police patrolman in Capitola, California, explained that the country's young people were creating a 'spiritual revolution problem' which involved black magic and the ritual slaughter of pet animals.

Also featured was Anton LaVey, a Ming the Merciless lookalike who founded the Church of Satan. This character, who had been a lion tamer, fortune teller, and hypnotist, created the church after he settled in San Francisco. It had a right-wing, libertarian philosophy and attracted figures such as Kenneth Anger and Jayne Mansfield. Susan Atkins - a member of the Manson family who joined in the attack on Sharon Tate - was also associated with La Vey, having worked for a time as a dancer in his Topless Witch Revue.

Despite this proliferation of black magic types in North and South America, England, claimed the narrator, had the best occult credentials: 'In England the practice of witchcraft seems to be widely accepted. When one discussed the black art, it's the witches of England who always seem to hold the most interest and display the highest degree of knowledge'.

The witches of England who featured in the film included Eleanor Bone, who was shown at Speaker's Corner, and then with a naked coven, working a ritual which was designed to nullify a curse. Another so-called witch, who was probably an actress, was shown invoking the god Pan at a church in Bedford. After this ceremony, revealed the narrator, the coven indulged in a 'final act of sacrilege' by having sex in the church. The director claimed that his 'good conscience' prevented him from showing the sex act - which no doubt disgusted most of the audience. They were soon pepped up, though, by the appearance of Maxine and several other naked witches.

The sequence featuring the Sander's coven was supposed to expose devil worship within wealthy English society. They were shown in a plush house in Grosvenor Square, eating at an elaborately laid table as the narrator revealed their middle-class professions. Alex was introduced as a 'real estate broker in London', which probably amused those who remembered his two-up two-down on Oldham Road.

All members of the coven were said to have 'admitted openly their love for Satan and his powers', and to have found 'financial success and happiness due to their association with witchcraft'. The 'curious thing about Alex and his friends', continued the narrator, 'was that they not only didn't mind but rather seemed to have enjoyed allowing the public knowledge of their evil activities.'

The evil activity that the film crew captured was the 'wedding of Alex and his fiancé Maxine, according to the rites of the occult'. One of the rites involved the drawing of blood from the bride with a ceremonial knife, which was said to 'link her with the devil': for she would 'primarily be linked with Satan', rather than her husband.

After also linking themselves with Dionysus - merely by drinking from a chalice - the ceremony was almost over. 'All that now remained', revealed the narrator, 'was for the bride to reveal herself as the gods created her'. Which was the cue for Maxine to slowly disrobe and step into a magic circle, 'where she will be sexually united with the devil'. This part of the ritual, though, was only symbolic.

Another documentary featuring the couple, and also directed by Scattari, was *Occult Experience*, which was released in 1970. It was essentially a rehash of *Witchcraft 70* and featured the same footage of Eleanor Bone, the midnight 'black mass' at Bedford, Anton LaVey, the Rio carnival, and the sequences with Alex and Maxine. There was, though, new footage featuring spiritualists in Belgravia, American mediums, and other occult characters. It also began with a fresh segment in which the police investigated damage to crypts in Highgate cemetery. (The cemetery would soon become the focus of much media attention as tales of the 'Highgate Vampire' began to circulate).

The script was also new. Rather than dining in Grosvenor

Square, the Sanders' coven was said to be 'somewhere off the Bayswater Road'; and rather than being Satanists they were now dedicated to the 'sacred mysteries of Orpheus and Dmitri'. Their wedding was supposed to be a celebration of both Dimika, the goddess of fertility, and Zeus, the 'master of heaven and earth'.

It is clear, then, that the couple had no control over the content of the documentaries, and that they took part mostly because of the paycheck. The desire to cash in also explains why Alex acquiesced to June John's ludicrous biography: *King of the Witches*, which was published during this period. Maxine admitted that the book, which caused a furore among the Wiccan community, and something of a stir in the media, was 'a means to an end'.

It was not, though, simply a means to make money, but also a way to massage Alex's rampant ego - for he had turned, Maxine believed, into 'a megalomaniac'. He wore dark glasses because his 'gaze was too powerful for the public to bear', and he bolstered his image by making increasingly outrageous statements. Maxine disapproved and dismissed the stunts as 'tacky shock tactics'.

Whilst he was not in the same league as Anton LaVey, Alex often insinuated that there was something of the night about him. He pulled plenty of Crowley-esque poses for shadowy photographs, and on one occasion, when asked if his magic was black or white, he replied that it was 'a dirty kind of grey'.

By 1970, Alex was notorious enough to have earned an appearance on the Simon Dee show. Dee - a scion of a wealthy Manchester family - was part of the swinging sixties zeitgeist: his was the first voice heard on Radio Caroline; he was an early presenter on Top of the Pops, and he was said to have been considered for the James Bond role. His shows, which drew audiences of up to 18 million, featured the likes of John Lennon, Sammy Davis Jnr, and Zsa Zsa Gabor; and on the night that Alex appeared, Dennis Wheatley was also a guest.

It was a hackneyed scenario, with the bestselling author cast as a campaigner against black magic, and Alex, of course, as the embodiment of evil. It was a role he played with gusto by wearing a cape, dark glasses and a crux ansata pendent. He also produced a wax effigy and began to stick needles in it - which was supposed to ensure that one of his enemies who had criticised him in the press would have a heart attack.

The enemy was Charles Pace, a self-styled 'master-Satanist'. He was also an artist who had been hired by Jimmy Page to paint occult murals on the walls of Boleskine House on the shores of Loch Ness, which Crowley had lived in. By the time of his spat with Alex, though, Pace was reduced to raising money by penning a series of sensational articles on the occult scene for the *News of the World*.

Despite Alex's diabolical work, Pace did not die. Simon Dee's career, though, definitely did. After a disastrous interview with George Lazenby - during which the actor rambled on about the conspiracy theories surrounding the Kennedy assassination - his show was cancelled. Within a few years this once ubiquitous television personality was reduced to applying for a job as a bus driver. Perhaps the effigy had resembled Dee rather than Charles Pace.

Incredibly, many took the effigy stunt seriously, and as Doreen Valiente recalled, it caused trouble for the Wicca community: 'As a direct result (of Alex's performance) Mr Gwilym Roberts, the Labour MP for South Bedfordshire, asked in the House of Commons if the Home Secretary would introduce legislation to provide penalties against individuals claiming to practise witchcraft'. Valiente claimed to have persuaded the MP that such legislation was unnecessary.

In a 1971 British television documentary, *The Power of Witchcraft*, which was directed by Michael Bakewell, Alex once more revealed his experiences of the dark side of the occult - he speculated that if he had continued with black magic then he may have evolved from carrying out 'animal sacrifices to human sacrifices'. More sensationalism followed as Bakewell covered the murder of Charles Walton. Yet the documentary was not purely a witchploitation piece, for it was evenhanded in its depiction of Wicca and featured some credible academics, such as Keith Thomas, who was the author of the influential text: *Religion and the Decline of Magic*.

Legend of the Witches was classed as a B-movie, which meant it shared a bill with a skin flick and had a naked girl on its promotion posters, yet it was the most serious of the Wicca documentaries of this period. Malcolm Leigh, the producer, managed to avoid casting comic book characters like Anton LaVey, and Alex was not required to make any shocking statements.

Whilst the historical accuracy of the piece might be questioned - for it drew upon some of Margaret Murray's ideas - *Legend* at least attempted to give an even-handed history of Wicca: fertility rites which were undertaken in the nude were said 'not to warrant the degrading description of sexual orgy'; and rather than claiming that pagans worked for Satan, it noted how the most diabolical acts in the history of the craft had been performed by witch hunters.

Like the most effective witchcraft films of the era, such as the 'folk horror' productions *Witchfinder General* and *The Wicker Man*, *Legend* made good use of the British landscape: a witch was shown foraging in a forest for hallucinogenic plants; a naked pagan priest stood on a rocky shore looking out to sea, and there were plenty of nice shots of menhirs. Stonehenge was also featured, for the documentary drew on the fascination with these sites which had been fostered by John Michell in *The View over Atlantis*, and by others in the burgeoning Earth Mysteries movement. These standing stones, informed the narrator, were 'temples and complex observatories' which had allowed the ancients to observe the progress of the gods across the heavens. (Which no doubt fascinated those who waited for the main feature - *Do You Want to stay a Virgin Forever?* - to start.)

The most effective sequence of *Legend* was shot at Alderley Edge, where the Sanders' coven was shown dancing around a fire, enacting a ritual called 'Drawing down the Moon', and initiating a young male. This novice, who was blindfold and naked, followed a female witch as she called his name and led him down a route which exposed him to water, air, earth and fire. Although it was all highly choreographed, Malcolm Leigh *did* manage to convey a sense of magic. The initiation was shown to be meaningful, and the Edge looked beautiful. The shots of rocky paths, hillocks, tall trees, caves and the Wizard's Well were atmospheric, and the closing scene, which captured the sun rising over rolling hills, made the location seem like a true wilderness rather than a place which was twenty minutes walk from the nearest greengrocers.

Breaking the Spell

In 1973, the golden age of Alexandrian magic came to an end with the divorce of Alex and Maxine. As individuals they still attracted media interest - more documentaries were made, and the tabloids still featured them - but they never again commanded the attention they had as England's foremost occult couple. The spell was broken.

Soon after the split, Maxine once more became involved with the 'Egyptian Order' that had initiated her in the early '60s in the caves under Alderley Edge. It was now, she claimed, an extremely wealthy organisation with an international scope and the members were said to be 'eminent souls who held positions of influence in the wider world'.

The order began to interfere with her life. It attempted, unsuccessfully, to persuade her to wed one of its priests, and it offered to provide her son with 'the best academic tuition the world had to offer' - on the condition that she would only be able to visit him once a year. Maxine refused the offer, noting that 'even that single visit was discouraged'.

Ultimately, the organisation dissolved after its leading figure - who Maxine looked upon as a mentor - passed away.

During the early 1980s, she sought enlightenment from the British Liberal Catholic Church, which was founded by C.W. Leadbetter - who had earned Crowley's enmity by promoting the Indian boy Krishnamurti as a new messiah. Maxine's membership caused a few eyebrows to be raised within the Wicca community. Doreen Valiente claimed that it was a 'surprise' - for although Leadbetter's group was not related to the Roman Catholic Church, and was definitely of a mystical nature, it was still a Christian organisation and therefore related to the old enemy.

Despite her adventures with these organisations, Maxine remained faithful to witchcraft. She continued to run her coven, and still visited the old sacred haunts.

> *We organised pilgrimages to power sites',* she wrote, *'such as Glastonbury and Alderley Edge . . .* (and conducted) *open meditation and guided 'path-workings' that would allow us to tune into the energies and vibrations of the location. At Glastonbury this would take place on the Tor and at Alderley Edge on the High Altar.*

One session during the 1980s saw the coven sharing the Edge with revelling punks. As the first lines of Aleister Crowley's *Hymn to Pan* were spoken, the punks 'edged their way through the trees to the perimeter of the circle and watched the rite'.

The presence of the witches offended the suburban sensibilities of some of Alderley's residents, and on a national level Wiccans were still occasionally treated negatively by the press. In 1990, a series of anti-pagan articles appeared after social workers in Rochdale erroneously reported that children were suffering from 'satanic ritual abuse'; and in the mid-nineties, *The News of the World* ran a series of articles under the banner 'Sex, Sin and Satanism', which resurrected dodgy old characters from the 70s, including Manchester's Ray Bogart.

On the whole, though, Wiccans became more acceptable as the public learnt to separate them from devil worshippers. Witches came to be viewed as mildly eccentric rather than satanic, and as harmlessly new age rather than diabolical remnants of the dark ages. Consequently, Maxine Sanders, once the wicked skyclad witch of the tabloids, became a respected elder of a movement that was accepted by many as a legitimate religion.

The Return of the King

But what of Alex? What of the King of the Witches?

He led a debauched life after the divorce. 'He indulged', wrote Maxine, 'in all manner of wickedness'. Exhausted and spiritually drained, he returned to the coven in 1979 and was purified by a rite called the 'Renewing of the King's Soul'. 'By performing this rite', Maxine recalled, 'the life of the king was guaranteed for seven years. Alex lived for just ten months over this allocated time'.

Like several of Manchester's mystics, such as Ann Lee, James Johnston and Emma Hardinge Britten, Alex was said to have made contact with the living after he died. His first appearance occurred on May 1st 1988, at the apartment of Jimahl di Fiosa in the northeast of the United States, just hours after he died in England.

Jimahl became interested in Wicca after reading a book by Stewart Farrar - a journalist who coined the term 'Alexandrian magic' after being initiated by Alex in the early 70s. Years after reading it, Jimahl joined a local coven that was run by a witch called Morven. Just two weeks into his membership, he claimed to have woke in the early hours and to have found Alex stood in his living room. The novice witch, who recognised Alex from photographs, thought he was having a lucid dream. Alex blessed Jimahl's athame and his Book of Shadows and informed him that he was destined to play a prominent role in the Alexandrian craft. Then he disappeared and the novice realised he had not been dreaming. After waiting until a decent hour he called Morven and told her of the experience. She went quiet and then revealed that Alex had just died.

Ten years later, after Jimahl had become a fully trained witch and had formed three covens, he claimed to channel the spirit of Alex. And in a sense he did, for his tales were as creative and outrageous as anything that the King of the Witches conjured up.

In *A Voice in the Forest,* Jimahl recounted contacting Alex via a Ouija board whilst celebrating Lamas with fellow Wiccans. Alex was said to have sent cryptic messages and to have asked Jimahl to deliver them to various people. Many of the recipients felt the messages were authentic. During further Ouija sessions, Alex revealed that he was to be reincarnated and even supplied the date of his rebirth and the name of his future mother.

Buoyed by this contact, Jimahl decided to take a further step and raise the spirit of Alex by a 'rite of necromancy'. The details of the rite illustrate how the age-old traditions of magic have survived - for Jimahl, along with two fellow witches, headed to a forest to create a magic circle: just as Edmund Hartley had in the 1590s when he tried to impress, or intimidate, Nicholas Starkie.

Hartley's circle led to disaster for him, but the results of Jimahl's experiments were more ambiguous. On one hand, he claimed that the rite worked and that Alex appeared in the circle; but on the other hand, Jimahl's friends scoffed at him for making such claims, and several of them warned him that he was becoming a little unhinged. There is little doubt, though, that Alex would have wholeheartedly approved of the affair.

Conclusion

> A city is a kind of pattern amplifying machine -
> Steven Johnson, *Emergence*

Why did Manchester produce so many sects, prophets, occultists, cunning-folks and mystics?

The obvious answer would be that the town was part of Lancashire - an area with strong traditions of witchcraft and superstition. It would be wrong, though, to see Lancashire as unique in its attachment to magic and superstition: for as Reginald Scott noted in 1584, every parish in England 'had a miracle worker'. Similarly, Robert Burns, in *Anatomy of Melancholy* (1621), noted how 'cunning men, wizards, and white witches as they call them, (could be found) in every village'.

But if all of England had such traditions, then why was Lancashire singled out as being a dark and superstitious corner of the land? The answer lies with the Reformation - for it was only after the break with Rome that the county was deemed to be particularly superstitious and backward, and this was not because Lancastrians were all busy casting spells - rather, it was due to so many of them remaining attached to Catholicism, which the Puritans liked to equate with witchcraft. Thus when a curate in the Bolton district of Harwood was warned against using 'predictions, divinations, sorceries, charmings or enchantment', he was targeted more for his Catholicism than witchcraft.

Not all of Lancashire, though, resisted the Reformation - and Manchester certainly didn't. In fact, many in the town believed it did not go far enough - they believed it was betrayed and watered down, and they turned Manchester into a Puritan stronghold. According to the Warden Richard Heyricke, it became a 'place of light when most places of the land have been places of darkness'.

For the authorities the fact that the town was Puritan was not ideal - Archbishop Whitgift especially found the Puritans to be irksome. But it was reasoned that it was better to have rebels who were Protestant than rebels who were Roman Catholic - and so Manchester was indulged. So indulged that the fellows of the Collegiate Church not only ignored the Archbishop of York when he tried to impose conformity on the town but felt they could hit back with a letter of protest. According to the historian Glyn Parry, preachers from other areas would have been 'hounded' if they had shown such defiance.

It was through such actions that the Puritans laid the foundations of Manchester's dissenting tradition, and soon after the town began to attract rebels and nonconformists from far and wide. By 1609 so many had made their way to the town that, as noted in Chapter Two, Edmund Hopwood complained of the: 'fanatical and schismatical' sorts who 'resort into this corner of Lancashire'. Just over fifty years later, Manchester's preachers refused to comply with the Act of Uniformity, and the town's reputation was reinforced. Once again, it attracted renegade preachers from other areas, and was said to have 'a greater dissenting population than most other towns in the kingdom'.

A century later, Manchester was so full of nonconforming characters - Boheme enthusiasts, lone mystics, apocalyptical ranters and their like - that Charles Wesley was driven to distraction. The Manchester Methodist Society, he complained, was the most 'unadvisable' of all his groups; and, as noted in Chapter Four, he feared that his followers would split into a multitude of sects if he was to leave the town.

Many of the sects fell away and became mere footnotes in the history of Manchester. Others, such as John Clowes' New Church, were more influential. By accepting Swedenborg's vision of the spirit world, and by believing that communication between the living and the dead was possible, the Swedenborgians paved the way for Victorian spiritualism and the occult revival.

Industrialisation also paved the way - for the Victorians sought to escape from the boorish materialism of the age by immersing themselves in magic and mysticism; and Mancunians had more reason than most to seek refuge because theirs was the city that had been most transformed by the factories and the mills.

Another factor which influenced Manchester's occult and spiritualist scene was the city's progressive political ethos: for many who believed in reform and social justice, such as Edward Brotherton, had a mystical bent. As the nineteenth century advanced, this ethos remained strong and manifested in such things as the Manchester Progressive Discussion Class, which was founded in the 1870s, and was dedicated to both political and occult subjects; it was evident in the *Two Worlds*, which claimed to be: 'A Journal Devoted to Spiritualism, Occult Science, Ethics, Religion and Reform'; and it was found in the strong links between the women's movement and the Theosophical Society during the early twentieth century.

So Manchester's tradition of mysticism was due to the Reformation, Puritanism, industrialisation, and progressive politics. But if that seems a little dry we can turn to the writer W. R. H. Trowbridge, who claimed in 1910 that 'the people of the north are naturally mystical'. Although he meant northern Europe in general, rather than the north of England, he did single out Manchester as proof of his theory. The city, he explained, was home to thousands of mystical Swedenborgians - a group which he referred to as 'illuminized Jerusalemites'.

The Secret History of Manchester

NOTES

Chapter One: The Labyrinth
1 - Glynn Parry, *The Arch Conjuror of England, John Dee*, Yale university Press, 2011, pg259
2 - Stephen Bow, *John Dee and the Seven in Lancashire*
3 - ibid
4 - Peter French, *John Dee: The World of an Elizabethan Magus*, Ark, 1987, pg 123

Three: The Machinations of John Byrom
1 - Joy Hancox, *The Queens Chameleon: The Life of John Byrom*, Johnathan Cape, 1994 pg199
2 - Ibid, pg 232
3 - Joy Hancox, *The Hidden Chapter*, Byrom Projects, 2011, pg 279

Four: A Mancunian Messiah
1 - Richard Francis, *Ann the Word* - Richard Francis

Five: The Occult History of the Peterloo Massacre
1 - Grevel Lindop, *The Opium Eater*, Weidenfield, 1993, pg 51
2 - ibid, pg 51
3 - Edward Green, *Prophet John Wroe*, The History Press, 2005, pg 10
4 - J Godwin, *Theosophical Enlightenment*, University NY Press, 1994, pg103

Seven: Ghosts in the Machines
1 - wiki
2 - Trevor Hall, *The Spiritualists*, Helix Press, 1963, pg139
3 - ibid, p138
4 - Marc Demerest - *Chasing Down Emma* website
5 - Ronald Hutton, *Triumph of the Moon*, Oxford University Press, 1999, pg 103
6 - Karl Bell, *The Magical Imagination*, Cambridge University Press, 2012, pg 75

Nine: Ernest Wood and Theosophy
1 - *The Mahatma Letters*, online version
2 - Alice Bailey, *The Unfinished Autobiography*, online version
3 - ibid
4 - ibid
5 - Ernest Wood, *Is this Theosophy?* Rider and Co, 1936, Chapter III, Book II online

Ten: The Wicca Man and the Witch Queen
1 - Wikipedia
2 - Mavis Smethurst - boltonspiritualistchurch.talktalknet
3 - Ronald Hutton, *Pagan Britain*
4 - Ronald Hutton, *Triumph of the Moon*, Oxford University Press, 1999, pg 200
5 - June Johns, *King of the Witches*, online version
6 - Maxine Sanders, Firechild, Mandrake, 2007, pg46
7 - ibid
8 - ibid

Printed by Amazon Italia Logistica S.r.l.
Torrazza Piemonte (TO), Italy